# THE SHADOW AND THE LIGHT

# THE SHADOW AND THE LIGHT

## A Defence of
## Daniel Dunglas Home, the Medium

by
### *Elizabeth Jenkins*

Hamish Hamilton
London

First published in Great Britain 1982 by Hamish Hamilton Ltd,
Garden House 57–59 Long Acre London WC2E 9JZ.

Jenkins, Elizabeth
   The shadow and the light: a defence of Daniel
   Dunglas Home, the medium
   1. Home, Daniel Dunglas    2. Mediums—Biography
   I. Title
   133.9'1'0924    BF1283.H/

ISBN 0–241–10892–6

Printed in Great Britain by Unwin Brothers Limited, The Gresham Press, Old Woking,
Surrey

# CONTENTS

# ILLUSTRATIONS
(between pages 150 and 151)

1. DANIEL DUNGLAS HOME
   Photo Maull & Co, London
   Mary Evans Picture Library/Society for Psychical Research

2. (a) SIR DAVID BREWSTER
   Mary Evans Picture Library
   (b) SIR WILLIAM CROOKES
   Mary Evans Picture Library/Society for Psychical Research

3. DR JAMES MANBY GULLY

4. SACHA HOME (d. 1862)
   Reproduced by courtesy of the Harry Price Library, University of London

# FOREWORD

The material for this book is taken chiefly from Home's two works: *Incidents in my Life*, Series I and II, and from the two written by his widow: *D. D. Home, His Life and Mission*, and *The Gift of D. D. Home*. In the case of Home's books, which consist largely of accounts of séances, I have been selective because in a great many, the phenomena were repetitive; also I did not think it in the reader's interest to relate the séance unless I could identify the sitters, and bring them into focus by some biographical detail, however small.

Two books on Home have appeared in recent years: *Mr. Sludge the Medium* by the late Horace Wyndham, and *Heyday of a Wizard* by Jean Burton. Both of them were widely researched, but Horace Wyndham's, on a comparison with the sources he used, shows a shocking disregard for accuracy and honesty and a maniacal hatred of Home which drove the writer in several instances to abandon even common sense; while Jean Burton's book, though more valuable in that it is much less prejudiced, speaks of Home throughout in a tone of slight contempt. A reading of both of them led me to feel that there was room for a book treating the subject in a serious and sympathetic manner.

To any impartial person who reads the very strong evidence for Home's super-normal powers: his levitation, his fire-handling, his telekinesis, his appearing in supernatural light, it appears impossible to accept that these effects were produced by fraud. Whether they proved a communication with discarnate beings, or were ascribable to some, as yet, unexplained physiological cause, I am not qualified to judge. That Home himself completely believed that he was a channel for spirit communication can hardly be doubted by anyone who reads the evidence. I have omitted all discussion of other mediums or of the spiritualist position as a whole; I have tried only to give some impression of what it was like actually to see this extraordinary being.

This book contains two features which I believe have not appeared in print elsewhere. One is a thorough following-out of the story of Robert Browning's conduct to Home; the other is the account of the behaviour, surroundings and past history of Mrs. Jane Lyon, the plaintiff in the famous case: Lyon v. Home. For the latter I am deeply indebted to the kindness of the Society for Psychical Research, who have allowed me to quote from the transcript in their archives of the affidavits taken from Home's witnesses, material most of which did not appear in the trial. I am also exceedingly grateful to Dr. John Beloff of the Department of Psychology, Edinburgh University, for his assistance generally and for his having gained me the opportunity to read the unpublished English version of Dr. George Zorab's work on Home; Dr. Zorab's wide learning and the authority of his opinions have made this permission an inestimable advantage. Dr. Eric Dingwall, pre-eminent in psychical research, is referred to by Dr. Zorab in a passage of great importance which I have quoted. I must record also my debt to Dr. Dingwall's essay on Home in his collection *Some Human Oddities* (London, 1947), which contains, inter alia, two references to the impression Home made on people who actually saw him.

The famous séance held by Home at the house of Mr. and Mrs. Rymer, at which the Brownings were present, has been described in every account which I have seen, merely as 'the séance at Ealing' with no information as to its actual whereabouts. Mrs. Barbara Goodwin discovered the site of the Rymers' now demolished house, its name and the composition of the household from the Census Return of 1851. Many readers interested in this celebrated event will be glad to have curiosity on this matter put at rest.

I must also say how grateful I am to Mr. Alan Wesencraft of the Harry Price Library of the University of London, for his kindness in showing me the treasures connected with Home in the Library, especially a letter from Home on writing paper engraved with a portrait of his first wife Sacha, the only one I have been able to discover. Home's second wife, Julie de Gloumeline, was, like his first wife, a Russian lady; she therefore spoke French as her second language, and her two books about her husband were written in French and translated by her secretary. She was generally spoken of as Madame Home and I have retained the usage. Of her books, *The Life and Mission of D. D. Home* is referred to in the references as L and M, and *The Gift of D. D. Home* as G of D. D. H.

It is perhaps useful to explain the alphabetical techniques, several times mentioned, for spirit communication. The letters of the alphabet were present, either in a book or on separate letters arranged on a table. The medium, beginning at A, pointed to the letters in turn, and when a rap was heard, the letter at which it occurred was noted and the pointing began again at A. The next rap indicated the next letter and so on, until a word or sentence had been received. The process was of course made very rapid by practice.

April 1982                                                                    E. J.

# I

## Escape into Another World

The sudden development of interest in spiritualism in the second half of the nineteenth century might, in one aspect, be seen as an instinctive reaction against materialism: that system which declares that the facts of experience are all to be explained by reference to the laws of physical or material substance, which denies the reality, of the soul and the existence of God as a supreme spirit. This system of thought was encouraged by the rapid and enormous development of industry, science and mechanical invention which had changed the conditions of daily life more thoroughly than they had been known to change in the history of mankind. Within a hundred years, England had ceased to be predominantly a granary and a sheep-fold and had become the factory of the world. Between the opening of the nineteenth century and its close, the English had become accustomed to travel in balloons, railway trains, bicycles and steamships, to communication by the lightning swiftness of telegraphy, to gas-lighting, to anaesthetics, to antiseptic surgery, to plumbing and the efficient sanitation of cities. The invention and manufacture of goods for domestic and personal use expanded on a tremendous scale. At almost the middle of the century, in 1851, the triumph of material achievement was celebrated; there was opened in Hyde Park, the Exhibition to Promote Peace and Understanding through Free Trade. Housed in a vast, arched, transparent building, described by *The Times* as 'a fairy palace with walls of iron and glass, the strongest and most fragile materials happily and splendidly combined,' the stupendous spectacle of the world's outpoured riches, from France, Italy, Greece, Germany, Austria, Switzerland, Russia, America, Canada, South Africa, India, arranged over eleven miles of stalls, gave a sensation of joy, of confidence in their age, to the six million people who visited the Exhibition during the six months of its existence. The material triumph had, it is true, been inspired by a spiritual conception. In 1849 the Prince Consort had opened Liverpool Docks and the impressive panorama of British shipping had suggested to him a vision of what commerce might achieve for humanity. This idea was reflected in *The Times'* comments on the opening of the Exhibition on 1 May. There was displayed, the paper said, 'all that is useful or beautiful in nature, art or science. Above them rose a glittering arch, far more lofty than the vaults of even our noblest cathedrals. On either side, the vista was almost boundless. It was felt to be more than what was seen, or what had been intended.' The lavish display of consumer goods: the carriages, locomotive equipment, scientific instruments, household appliances, safes, clocks, watches, musical instruments, furniture, carpets, textiles, glass, silver, china, ornaments, jewellery, statuary, to name but some of the exhibits, was exceeded in importance by the demonstration of machines for multiple and rapid production. Of all the bewildering array of objects for use and decoration, none, it has been said, was as significant as the American exhibit, the McCormick Reaper.[1] 'This machine, able to harvest grain with hitherto unimaginable speed, was gazed upon by visiting rustics who sowed by hand and reaped with a sickle.'

The admiration, wonder and delight of the visitors was increased by the enchanting appearance of the building itself. The transparent structure was so lofty that it covered two giant elm trees standing side by side in Hyde Park; at the end of the North Transept there rose a fountain, twenty seven feet high, of solid glass with the water spreading out like a flower at the summit and falling from chalice to chalice down the gleaming shaft; the fountain epitomised the transparency and brilliance of the whole glittering edifice. Queen Victoria called the scene 'indescribably glorious, really like fairyland.' The writer for *Punch*, Douglas Jerrold, coined the name by which it was to be immortalized: 'The Crystal Palace'.[2] Beautiful as it was, exciting and of absorbing interest, not everyone was gratified by the spectacle. To some it looked too much like Bunyan's description of Vanity Fair, and Cardinal Wiseman issued a pastoral letter in which he urged the people 'to lay up blessing and grace' to 'avert any evil which may result from this national display of greatness.' Some, however, did not need a warning against reckless indulgence in the pleasure of materialism. In 1849, Matthew Arnold had written to Arthur Hugh Clough: 'These are damned times, everything is against one . . . the spread of luxury, the height to which knowledge has come . . . newspapers, cities, the sickening consciousness of our difficulties.'

Matthew Arnold, a poet and a philosopher, saw many causes for disquiet, but he was not a fundamentalist and criticism of the historical accuracy of the Book of Genesis left him undismayed; but such criticism was felt by numbers of devout Christians to be a more deadly temptation than the miles of sparkling booths laid out in Vanity Fair. The idea sometimes held that the Victorian age was one of profound and imperturbable religious conviction is altogether mistaken. Though belief in the verbal inspiration of the Bible was still widespread, scepticism based on geological and anthropological evidence aroused a violent resistance which suggested panic rather than confidence. In 1859, Charles Darwin published his *The Origin of Species* in which he demonstrated that the fishes, animals and birds on the earth were not created in their present forms as the second chapter of Genesis relates, but arrived at them by a process of evolution through 'natural selection', 'the survival of the fittest'. 'We can no longer argue', he said, 'for instance, that the beautiful hinge of a bi-valve shell must have been made by an intelligent being, like the hinge of a door by man.' Since the theory of evolution left intact the teaching of the New Testament, a later age finds it strange that such overwhelming importance was attached to a rejection of the Book of Genesis; nor did all Victorian clergy subscribe to it. Charles Kingsley, the Rector of Eversley in Hampshire, took the attitude to be expected of a distinguished naturalist. He wrote: 'The years between 1854 and 1863 cover epoch-making developments.' Darwin, he said, 'was conquering everywhere and rushing in like a flood, by the mere force of truth and fact.'[3] In 1863, Kingsley himself published *The Water Babies*, one of the greatest children's books ever written, in which he reconciled the theory of evolution with that of a superior creating power. Tom the Water Baby hears Mother Carey say: 'I am not going to make things, my little dear. I sit here and make them make themselves . . . anyone can make things if they will take time and trouble enough, but it is not everyone who, like me, can make things make themselves.'

Kingsley was, however, in a minority among Christians of the age. Two cardinal points insisted on by conventional ecclesiastical opinion were, a belief in Biblical inspiration and a belief in hell. In 1860 there was published a collection entitled *Essays and Reviews*. The contributors were clergymen, one of them being Dr. Jowett of Baliol. Though all the essays were of a radical cast, two of them were of such daring that the writers were accused of heresy and summoned before the Judicial Commission of the Privy Council, which, however, found in their favour. It was said of the verdict that the Commissioners had dismissed Hell with costs and taken away from orthodox members of the Church of England their last hope of everlasting damnation.

This disturbance was confined to a relatively small sphere, but in 1862 an attack on Biblical inspiration received worldwide attention. John William Colenso, who had been inducted as Bishop of Natal in 1853, had set himself to translating for his Zulu flock, simple works of history and geography, the New Testament and some books of the Old. He said that as he sat, translating the first chapters of Genesis, he found himself, time after time, looking up from the work, and saying: *Is* all that true? In 1862 he published his *Critical Examination of the Pentateuch* — the books Genesis, Exodus, Leviticus, Numbers and Deuteronomy; of these he demonstrated that a great deal, apart from the mythological element of Genesis, was unhistorical, one of his arguments being that the ecclesiastical legislation recorded in Leviticus and Numbers was the product of an era much later than that to which it claimed to belong. This publication caused pandemonium. In December 1863, Bishop Gray of Cape Town, the metropolitan bishop of South Africa, asserted his right to depose the Bishop of Natal. The Judicial Committee of the Privy Council, again called upon to act, declared that Bishop Gray could not depose the Bishop of Natal on his own authority, and that Bishop Colenso was not deposed. But though the law supported Dr. Colenso, a force stronger than law supported Dr. Gray. The Society for the Propagation of the Gospel and the Society for the Promotion of Christian Knowledge administered very substantial funds, and had generously supported missions in the diocese of Natal. They now withdrew these grants and re-allocated them to the diocese of Cape Town.

This tempest wreaked injury on one of the most interesting and valuable clergymen of the century. When Colenso published his Natal Sermons, they proved, as was said, 'the thorough compatability of the deepest spiritual faith and trust with the most advanced and searching historical criticism.'[4] But however this might be accepted as proved in some quarters it did not save Dr. Colenso's reputation with the conventional Church party. Charlotte M. Yonge's novels — *Heartsease, The Daisy Chain, Hopes and Fears, The Clever Woman of the Family*, reflect the indignation and horror aroused by biblical criticism, while the predicament of numbers of the thinking public was expressed from the opposite point of view by Matthew Arnold in 'Dover Beach'. The sea of faith, he said, once surrounded the world but now it was ebbing, in a melancholy, long, withdrawing roar, like the retreating tide down a pebbled strand,

> And we are here, as on a darkling plain,
> Mixed with confused alarms of struggle and flight,
> Where ignorant armies clash by night.

Darwin and his colleagues in the mid-century and the textual critics of the same era, were reinforced by the attack of another assailant on the existing structure of society. In 1867, Karl Marx published the first volume of *Das Kapital*, which demanded the overturning of the economic system of the Industrial Revolution, under which the people did the work in factories which they did not own. The last great blow to the established order of thought was wielded only towards the end of the century, when Freud relieved the human race from responsibility for its actions by ascribing these, not to deliberate choice, but to involuntary mental processes. This formidable array of intellect had, it seemed, by the last years of the Victorian age, swept away the bastions of belief and faith which thousands of years had erected with a slow amassing like the formation of coral reefs. The perspective of a hundred years makes the change appear more sudden and more complete than it actually was, but the unnerving influence was, if only partly recognized, deeply felt. Uncounted numbers of men and women were eager to explore a belief which reassured them on two matters they felt to be of vital importance: spiritualism confirmed their hope that there was a life beyond death, and that the personalities of the dead whom they had loved remained unaltered and could sometimes communicate with them.

Great poets speak for every age, but Tennyson was perhaps the one who spoke most directly for his own. He was tormented by the fear of annihilation. The idea was so dreadful to him, he declared that if it were true, it would be pointless to go on living:

> 'Twere best at once to sink to peace,
> Like birds the charming serpent draws,
> To drop head-foremost in the jaws
> Of vacant darkness and to cease.
>
> (*In Memoriam*, XXXIV: 1850)

The intense yearning after the lost was felt by thousands, as he felt it, though none of them had his power of uttering it:

> Oh that it were possible
> After long grief and pain,
> To find the arms of my true love
> Round me once again . . .
> Ah, Christ, that it were possible
> For one short hour to see
> The souls we loved, that they might tell us
> What and where they be!
>
> (*Maud*: 1855)

Most poignant of all was the verse addressed to Hallam and omitted by Tennyson himself from the published version of *In Memoriam*:

> Speak to me from the stormy sky!
> The wind is loud in holt and hill,
> It is not kind to be so still.
> Speak to me, dearest, or I die!

Reassurance from the spiritualist plane had been offered, and accepted by some, though it contradicted the Protestant Church's vision of after-life, which, since Protestants did not accept the Catholic doctrine

5

of Purgatory, defined the prospect as one either of endless torment or static bliss. Emmanuel Swedenborg was an almost universal genius in scientific affairs: a military engineer, a mining engineer, a metallurgist, a physicist, an astronomer, an anatomist, a zoologist, a financier and a political economist. In strange alliance with his scientific genius, he possessed psychic powers of an extraordinary scope. He was 'a travelling clairvoyant' and he brought back to this world the most complete picture of 'the other side of life' which mankind has received. This consists, he said, of a number of different spheres, each of us going to that for which our spiritual condition fits us. In these spheres, the frame-work of the society of this life is closely reproduced: houses, palaces, temples, public halls are the scenes on which we act and we lead a life of increased spiritual and mental power. Marriage exists in a form of spiritual union; the old, infirm and diseased renew their young energies. At death celestial beings attend the newcomer to help him into his fresh state of existence. There is no eternal punishment. Those in hell can work their way out of it, those in heaven are working their way to something higher. This body of revelation was received by him over a period of twenty-seven years, but the first of his visions was astonishingly complete. On a night in April 1744, he said: 'the world of spirits, hell and heaven, were convincingly opened to me, where I found many persons of my acquaintance of all conditions. Thereafter the Lord daily opened the eyes of my spirit to see in perfect wakefulness what was going on in the other world, and to converse, broad awake, with angels and spirits.'

Swedenborg died in 1772, and his revelation, received over nearly three decades of the middle of the century, was in harmony with a movement of thought that was beginning to prevail. As E. Moir ably said, in the late eighteenth century, the conception that had so long obtained, endorsed by Newton and Locke, that God had constructed a reasonable world, and put reasonable men into it, was beginning to fail.[5] A reaction was no doubt inevitable against a system of rigid belief, and this was given force by the Lisbon earthquake of 1755, which let loose apocalyptic terrors of wind, waves and fire, a destruction as senseless as it was vast. On the surface, the world of business and politics was based on reasonable assumption, but 'more and more people were seeking to escape from this tamed world into another world, in which things deeper than reason, dream images of enormous power and strange beauty, could be recognized and explored.'[6] The study of spiritualism was a scientific one, based on the evidence of spirit communication, but it was also emotional and occult, and Moir's assessment helps to explain the mental climate whose growth in the first half of the nineteenth century fostered its development. The scene of this development was America.

## II

## Spiritualism in America

Daniel Home was born near Edinburgh in 1833. As his birthday was March 20, he was on the cusp of the Zodiacal sign Pisces; the subjects of this sign are said to be confiding and trustful, but not self-reliant, sympathetic and kind but changeable, gentle and affectionate but vain. They are imaginative and deeply moved by the beauty of nature. They are strongly drawn to spiritualism and the investigation of the unseen. The incidence of tuberculosis among them is high. It is estimated that more mediums are born among them than among the subjects of all the other signs put together. This classical description of the character of the rising sign is frequently modified by the actual moment of birth, but it reads like a map of Home's personality and constitution.

He was born to parents in a humble walk of life, and as they had six sons, twin daughters, and a third daughter, they allowed Mrs. Home's sister, Mrs. Cook, to adopt Daniel. When he was nine years old, Mrs. Cook and her husband emigrated with him to America. With what we think of as the modern developments in the rapidity and safety of travel, it comes as a surprise that the connection between America and England in the first half of the nineteenth century was so intimate, in spite of the vast ocean between them, to be covered only by steam ships still aided by sails. The possible terrors of the Atlantic crossing were evoked by Dickens in *Martin Chuzzlewit*, of 1843:– 'Darker grows the night and louder howls the wind, and more clamorous and fierce become the million voices in the sea, when the wild cry goes forth upon the storm: "A ship!" Onward she comes . . . her tall masts trembling and her timbers starting under the strain . . . and every storm-voice in the air and water cries more loudly yet, A ship!' The final laying of the Atlantic cable was not accomplished till 1866, but the exchange between English and American newspapers in the 1850s, in which news was published, answered, and answered again with supporting comment, seems, viewed in the perspective of time, to have been so rapid that the Atlantic was no barrier against the penalties of indiscretion. In both countries people knew of spiritualism, an age-old belief; it was practised, but in a private manner, not much talked about, it was not, it seemed, a topic of public interest; but in America, in 1848, an outburst of passionate curiosity, of hysterical agitation, showed that an interest hardly, till now, recognized, was there, wide-spread and very near the surface. In Hydesville, near Rochester, in New York State, a couple named Fox who had recently moved into a cottage, found that it was disturbed by inexplicable sounds, bangings and rappings and these noises not only were heard only in the presence of their two younger daughters, Margaret and Kate, aged 15 and 12, but that when the children, amused by what they supposed to be a ghost, challenged it to answer when they snapped their fingers, sounds replied. With the help of neighbours, the use of the alphabet was devised. What was believed to be a discarnate intelligence gave communication: it announced itself as a man's spirit, restless and unquiet because the man had been murdered in that house and his body buried in the cellar. An attempt at exhumation was abandoned because the cellar floor was flooded, but some time later the remains of a corpse were found bricked up in one of the cellar walls. The fatal element in the history of this extraordinary case was that the Fox family used it for commercial gain, Margaret and Kate holding séances and giving demonstrations of psychic power for money. There would naturally have been, in any case, many people who, in spite of the ghastly discovery in the cellar wall, did not accept the phenomena as supernatural, who, whatever proofs were adduced, would have been abusive and contemptuous; but the fact that the Fox sisters were making money turned their expressions of disbelief into violent rancour and vindictiveness. The whole tone of the subsequent history of the Fox sisters was morbid and disreputable. The eldest sister, Mrs. Culver, was not psychic but she gained a share of the family notoriety by publishing a supposed confession, made to her by her sisters, of their fraudulent practices, which was afterwards discovered in itself to be largely fraudulent,[1] and Margaret in later life made admissions of fraud while her mind was deranged by alcoholism, which she afterwards withdrew; but the experiences of Margaret and Kate as children, ignited, as a dropped match starts a forest fire, a vehement, infectious belief in spiritualism as a means of communication with the dead, while at the same time, there developed with astonishing rapidity, other forms of supernatural manifestation by other mediums: glossalalia or 'speaking with tongues', automatic drawing and painting, poltergeist disturbances, the imparting of hitherto unknown matters by discarnate intelligences. Instances of these phenomena were known in England and all over Europe, as related by Catherine Crow in *The Night Side of Nature*, but the concentrated blaze of their development in America was something unique in the history of the supernatural.

William Howitt, an English quaker, writing in 1863 a book which he gave that very title, *A History of the Supernatural*,[2] compared the state of spiritualism in America and England; he ascribed the force and brilliance of the American development, compared with its less spectacular English counterpart, first, to the fact that English society was blinded and hardened by materialism, compared with the more highly-strung tone of the American personality, and secondly to the physical atmospheres of America and England. 'We have', he said 'for the last two centuries, been undergoing a double process of induration. Trade, and Protestant abjuration of spiritual relations have been mutually doing the work of internal petrification and ossification upon us . . . the wonderful progress of physical science, colonial expansion, manufacturing immensity and their streams of wealth, luxury and social aspiration . . . have produced a condition of general mind and opinion more destructive to a healthy faith than any period of the world, the most pagan or corrupt, ever saw.' The Americans, on the other hand, 'are conspicuously a more nervous and excitable people than we are. They have grown up rapidly under new climatic influences, new blendings of blood and international idiosyncracies. They have shown a singular genius for mechanical inventions and an audacity approaching to rashness in inaugurating new social schemes, new religious organizations and vast plans of political dominion. Their minds, like their institutions, have shot up with a rapidity of growth resembling that of tropical jungles, and have, in consequence, greater openness and receptivity.' Howitt then adduced, though of secondary importance, the fact of 'our denser atmosphere, less electrical and magnetic in its character', our different 'telluric conditions', he said, were less favourable 'to the transmission of spiritual impressions.' Howitt's vision of the contrast between the America and England of 120 years ago, is a reminder of the wonderful visibility conferred by American light. Choking fogs were something peculiar to London; in 1856, Mr. Guppy proudly claimed the almost annihilating fog in which *Bleak House* opens, as a 'London particular'; in the country, though the English landscape may be seen to a great distance, its exquisite beauty often owes something to the mingling of sunlight and mist, so that its farthest reaches are etherealized by vapour. The American light gives a combination of far distance with complete distinctness. The prospect in Virginia from Harper's Ferry, where the Shenandoah and the Potomac rivers join, under the hanging woods on the farther shore, has an extent of flowing water and a prospect of rising trees which the English spectator would never see in such radiant clarity at home. An English painter of the first half of the nineteenth century imagined preternatural distinctness of vision over a great distance as a celestial impression. John Martin's painting, The

Plains of Heaven, of 1853, strikes the English eye as something visionary; to an American, it would have appeared much closer to a normal scene.

To this country, whose national character and whose atmosphere, Howitt said, made it exceptionally favourable to the development of spiritualist faculties, there was brought, at nine years old, the boy who was to prove the most remarkable medium the world has seen for centuries.

## III

## A Glorious Mission

Shortly after the arrival in America of Mr. and Mrs. Cook with their
nephew, the latter's parents followed them with their other children.
The two families settled near each other in Connecticut, on the Atlantic
sea-board. When his second wife wrote Home's life in 1880, she said
that the town of Greenville had been 'swallowed up in the adjoining
city of Norwich', but that in 1842, it had been a village among woods.
Mr. Carpenter, afterwards Mayor of Norwich, remembered Home
from their schooldays. He spoke of Home's unusual sensitiveness to
unkindness; he suffered from it, whether it were done to himself or
other people. Home, he said, was interested in their lessons, but his
passion was for the woods and streams, among which he spent all his
free time with one or two special friends; Wordsworth would have
asked nothing better. The happiest days of his boyhood were spent in
the Greenville woods, roaming with his friend Edwin, another boy
dreamy and bookish as himself. They were obliged to part when Mr.
and Mrs. Cook removed to Troy in the State of New York, and as the
boys had often talked about apparitions, they made a mutual promise
that whichever of them died first would try to appear to the survivor.

Home was thirteen years old when the move was made to Troy.
One night soon after his arrival, he was going to bed, lighted only by
the brilliant moonlight streaming through his uncurtained window,
when, in his own words, 'a sudden darkness pervaded the room.' The
moon, he said, was shining still, but 'on the other side of the darkness'.
A gleam of the light which in after years he recognized as a spirit
appearance, showed through the dark. Then, he said, 'my attention
was drawn to the foot of my bed, where stood my friend Edwin. He
appeared as in a cloud of brightness, illuminating his face with a
distinctness more than mortal.' Home's own descriptions of his experiences of phenomena are exceptionally interesting, none more so than
this one, the first, and undergone at such an early age. He saw the
apparition 'slowly raising his right arm and making three circles with
it in the air.' Then the hand and arm began slowly to disappear, and

finally 'the whole body melted away. The natural light of the room was again apparent. Home found that he could not move or utter a sound. When this paralysis passed, he rang the bell in his room and the family hurried in, thinking he must be ill. His first words were: 'I have seen Edwin — he died three days ago.' Two days after this, a letter arrived, confirming that Edwin had died suddenly after a very short illness.

Home's parents were living with the rest of their children a little distance away in Waterford. A stream ran before their door, crossed by a narrow bridge. Mrs. Home, crossing the bridge on her return to the house, saw, as she thought, a bundle of clothes floating in the water; a moment later she realized to her horror that it was her daughter Mary. She got down into the stream and pulled her to the bank, but the child was dead already. Some time later Home was on a visit to his family, and his mother told him privately that in four months' time she would have to depart. Mary had appeared to her and said: 'In four months time you will come to me.' Four months later Mrs. Home was away on a visit and a telegram announced to her family that she was dangerously ill. Her husband set out at once to be with her; he could not take Daniel who was in bed with a severe illness on his chest. That evening his aunt heard him calling loudly; as she came into the room he said his mother had died at twelve o'clock that day, 'because I have seen her and she told me.' It was true.

These feats of clairvoyance disturbed his aunt considerably but worse was to come. Home had lived apart from his mother since he was nine, but he had a deep affection for her, and her second-sight made a private bond of trust between them. Her loss was the shock which gave him his first serious religious impulse, and he joined the local Wesleyan body. His aunt, a member of the Kirk of Scotland, had a strong dislike of this evangelical sect. Never fanatical and wanting only the support of some Christian community, he hoped to mollify her by leaving the Wesleyans and joining the Congregationalists, whom she also disliked but not so much; but the disapproval and dislike which Mrs. Cook had felt for her nephew's manifestations and states of mind now changed to acute dismay, for Home began to develop paranormal symptoms of the most disconcerting kind. One night there were loud raps on his bed-head; he could not sleep and when he appeared, pale, at breakfast time, his aunt asked him sarcastically if he had been agitated by his prayer-meetings? A shower of raps was heard all over the breakfast table. Convinced that he had brought the devil into her house, Mrs. Cook put aside her prejudices against the local clergy and sought the aid of a Congregational minister, a Baptist and a Wesleyan. The first declined to meddle with the matter, the second relinquished it when he found that his prayers were accompanied by raps: even if these spelled encouragement he could not bear it; as for the Wesleyan, Home said: 'He was so unkind, treating me as a black sheep, that I derived no comfort from him.'

Unnerving as the raps were, they were followed by events more alarming still. The extraordinary phenomena of telekinesis; the moving of furniture and objects in the presence of a medium, but without movement or volition on the medium's part, began to occur, and drove the mistress of the house nearly to distraction. This grotesque rising into mid-air of heavy pieces of furniture, the rocking walk or wanton sliding about of tables and chairs, is very difficult to accept as harmonious with anything as solemn as communication from the dead, but it does at least prove that there was something about Home so totally abnormal that the super-natural effects produced in his presence demand some explanation other than fraud. His first experience of telekinesis, according to himself[1], was so alarming that it may well have accounted for the dislike he afterwards expressed of furniture's moving about over the floor in séances. Now nineteen years old, he was in his room brushing his hair at the glass, 'and in the glass I saw a chair that stood between me and the door, moving slowly towards me. My first feeling was one of intense fear and I looked round to see if there were no escape, but there was the chair, between me and the door, and it still moved towards me as I continued looking at it. When it was within a foot of me, it stopped, whereupon I jumped past it, rushed downstairs, seized my hat in the hall and went out to ponder on this wonderful phenomenon.'

In the scared, disorientated condition brought about by his first supernatural experiences, made more painful by the anger of his aunt, Home went for comfort to the house of another female relation, a widow living in the neighbourhood, whose kindness and heartfelt sympathy, he said 'did much to cheer and console me.' In her house, he began for the first time to interpret the sounds he heard, to ask questions of an unseen presence and to gain intelligent replies. One evening when the raps started, he began to tell over the alphabet, and when the letters which were greeted with an answering rap were written down, it was found that they composed sentences of a personal importance. The very first of these communications was from his mother; she said: 'Daniel, fear not, my child, . . . seek to do good, be truthful and truth-loving, and you will prosper . . . Yours is a glorious mission — you will convince the infidel, cure the sick and console the weeping.' Home said: 'I have never forgotten it and never can forget it, while reason and life shall last.'[2] This communication, which he regarded as one of the most important he ever received, was given to him at the very outset of his mediumistic career; it came to him during the last week he spent in Mrs. Cook's house. The position here was becoming intolerable. Word had got about of his mysterious and exciting powers, and neighbours and strangers besieged the house, hoping for a sign of them. Mrs. Cook's state of mind was pitiable. Alarmed and outraged by sounds and sights inside her own house, pestered at all hours by inquisitive intruders, her agitation may also have been increased by the recollection of those scenes of public commotion which had occurred in Rochester, when two young people had been seized with spirit powers and their parents' house had been filled with salvos of loud, percussive sounds, conveying an appalling message from the dead. She could bear it no more. All the affection which had inspired her to adopt her nephew and to bring him, frail and highly strung, through his difficult childhood, succumbed before the sweeping flames of panic. She declared that Daniel must leave her house. She wanted no more of him.

In a life of much emotional stress, without permanent security, Home possessed one great advantage; whatever calamities and disappointments he underwent, his gentle, ingenuous personality always aroused the sympathy of someone who was ready to be good to him. He proved this good fortune now. Without professional education, without a livelihood, without private means, without a home, for the next four years, he passed from family to family, the guest of people who were not only anxious to investigate his psychic powers but felt a strong personal affection for him. He was first taken in by some friends at Williemantic, a small town outside the state capital of Hartford; but here his presence caused too much commotion; the house was surrounded by people some of whom wanted to see supernatural signs, merely, and others who were longing to have a communication with their dead. The local newspapers took him up, and untried as he was at this time, the strident publicity was too much for his nerves. A family named Ely, living on a farmstead in Lebanon, New Hampshire, the beautiful country of lakes and woods, asked him to stay with them. Home had already suffered from a chest complaint. The country air, the quietness and the thoroughly sensible kindness of the Ely family were just what he needed. They took care of him and they warned him against exhausting himself by too frequent sittings. His fame was now considerable, and in a community which was eager for spiritualistic experience, he was invited from one family to another, but in September 1851 he returned to the Ely household, where he performed a striking feat of clairvoyance. Their son, Ezra, a youth of Home's own age, appeared to be slightly ailing. Home saw in a vision that within three weeks the illness would end in death. He told the parents this, and performed the more difficult task of telling Ezra himself. A fortnight later the family doctor made the same prognosis, of almost imminent death; he asked Home, as the patient's young friend, to break it to him, and Home answered that the boy knew it already. The doctor would not believe it; Ezra was so contented and serene, it was not credible that, a young man with everything to live for, he could understand the nearness of the awful prospect. Home suggested to the doctor that he should stand at the bedroom door while he himself approached the bed. In his own words: 'I told him the doctor had left some news for him. He laughingly said: "I suppose it is to tell me that I am going. Little does he imagine that I've decided who my bearers are to be!"'

Home remained with these affectionate hosts till January 1852; he then accepted an invitation from Mr. Rufus Elmer, a wealthy manufacturer of Springfield, Massachussets. The Elmers were, like the Elys, delighted to have him, but unlike that of the Ely family, their eager interest in his powers was not restrained by any idea of what was good for him. As a result of the newspaper furore of the past year, their house was surrounded by anxious enquirers, not from the neighbourhood only but from other states. People who could not get themselves indoors waited in the street. The Elmers were as excited as their visitants. Home said that 'the power', always unpredictable, was at this time 'very strong'. Frequently, he held séances six or seven times a day. This visit, in spite of the Elmers' kindness, must have been most injurious to him, but it was the scene of two very remarkable séances. The first was an exhibition of telekinesis which was the more valuable because of the detailed evidence which attested it. This was produced by an investigating committee from Harvard, which included Professor Wells and the poet William Cullen Bryant. With two colleagues they signed a statement that the table at which they were sitting 'was moved in every direction against each one of us, so powerfully as to move us from our positions — together with the chairs we occupied — in all, several feet ... Occasionally we were made conscious of the occurrence of a powerful shock, which produced a vibratory motion of the floor — it seemed like the motion occasioned by distant thunder or the firing of ordnance far away — causing the tables, chairs and other inanimate objects and all of us, to tremble in such a manner that the effects were both seen and felt.' It was not credible that any one human being could have produced these effects, but Home urged them to hold his hands and his feet. 'During these occasions', the witnesses continued, 'the room was well lighted, the lamp was frequently placed on and under the table, and every opportunity was afforded us for the closest inspection; and we admit this one emphatic declaration: we know that we were not imposed on.'

This séance which took place so early in Home's mediumistic career, established, if the signatories are to be believed, that physical effects of movement, vibration and sound took place in his presence which could not possibly be ascribed to his own action. Another, held on 28 February at the Elmers' house, signed by eight people including Mr. Rufus Elmer, had a more interesting because a spiritualist bearing. A party was collected one evening, on a merely social occasion. One of the company was a Mr. Brittan, who afterwards published his experience.[3] While the conversation was general, Home suddenly fell into trance. As soon as this was noticed, the conversation died away. Home said: 'Hannah Brittan is here.' Mr. Brittan was astounded. He had last seen this woman when he was a small child; he knew that he would never see her again and though he occasionally remembered her, he had not thought of her for months. He said in his statement: 'I mentally enquired how I might be sure of her actual presence.' In response to this unspoken appeal, the medium got up and paced about the room, showing signs of frantic distress, wringing his hands, groaning, uttering broken words of prayer; he began to describe some fearful scene that was present to his inward sight: 'Oh, how dark! What dismal clouds! What a frightful chasm! Deep down — far, far down I see the fiery flood. Save them from the pit! . . . I see no way out. There's no light! The clouds roll in upon me, the darkness deepens! My head is whirling!' As Mr. Brittan said, with Home unconscious and the rest of the party altogether ignorant of what he was talking about, their astonishment was complete. Only Brittan himself understood. Twelve years before Home was born, Brittan's relative Hannah, sensitive and highly-strung, went out of her mind, driven into insanity, it was said, by fears of eternal punishment. It would seem more likely that fears of eternal punishment obtained a terrible force over a mind whose sanity was already in the balance. At all events at his last sight of her, thirty years before, she was in the throes of hideous terror. He had mentally demanded a proof of her identity and this scene 'was re-enacted to assure me of the actual presence of the spirit.' It is open to argument that this manifestation was the result of telepathy, since in essentials it told Brittan nothing that he did not know before, but he was convinced that it was one of spirit communication, the more so as, he said, after that night the spirit of his once-unhappy kinswoman had been in touch with him and had assured him that her present existence was calm, peaceful and beautiful, and that the burning gulf and all its horrible imagery existed only in the traditions of men and 'in the fitful wanderings of her distracted brain.'

The most impressive of the supernatural experiences brought about by Home's presence, are, naturally, those which conveyed information unknown to and even unsuspected by any of the persons present. In August 1852, he was the guest of another wealthy manufacturer, Mr. Ward Cheney, a silk-merchant whose family house was in South Manchester, on the outskirts of Hartford. This visit was the origin of

16

a life-long friendship and Mr. Ward Cheney himself visited Home in England and was present at manifestations there. While staying with the Elmers Home had had a severe attack of illness. When he was ushered into the Ward Cheney drawing room, he heard the sharp rustling of a stiff silk dress, but on looking about the room, he could not see anyone in company whose clothes could have made such sounds. The host asked him why he looked so startled and perplexed. Home replied merely that he had been ill and that his nerves were still shaky; as he spoke, he saw through the open door a little old lady standing in the hall, wearing a grey silk dress. He was satisfied, and when Mr. Ward Cheney himself heard the sibilant sound and said: What can that be? Home answered at once: Only the dress of that elderly lady in the grey silk, rustling. To this, his host made no answer. At dinner, Home was surprised the old lady was not present and that nothing was said about her. It had not, up till then, occurred to him that she was anything but a member of the house-party; but as he was leaving the dining room, the dress rustled again and he heard a voice say: 'I am annoyed that a coffin should have been placed above mine'. He repeated the words to Mr. and Mrs. Cheney, who, in amazement, said that they could place the appearance and the dress that he described, but that the words were senseless and ridiculous. Home could say nothing as to this; he never defended the truth of, or even offered an opinion on, any message that was received through his extraordinary function; but an hour later, the voice said in his ear what it had said before, and added: 'What is more, Seth had no right to cut that tree down.' He repeated these words to Mr. and Mrs. Cheney, who were astounded. They admitted the previous existence of an elderly relative who wore just such a grey silk dress as Home described, and Mr. Cheney said that when his brother Seth had cut down a tree that obscured the view, it had been said in the family that the old lady, if she had been alive, would never have allowed it; but the rest of the message made no sense. It was gibberish. Home went to bed in a state of utter despondency. It was the first time he had received a message declared to be unauthentic and factually untrue. Next morning he told Mr. Cheney how disturbed his night had been. Mr. Cheney was very sorry for his young guest's distress, and that he should have suffered it while under his roof, but he said he would prove to Home that if the apparition were the spirit it appeared to be, and he was not disposed to deny this, yet the words it had uttered were completely delusive.

In the local burying-ground was a vault in which the coffins of more than one family were interred. This was the place in which space had been bought for depositing the remains of the old lady. After breakfast Mr. Cheney walked with Home to the ground and sent for the keeper of the vault. The man unlocked the door and as he did so he turned to Mr. Cheney and said, in half-apologetic tones, that as there was a little space above the old lady's coffin, he had put the coffin of a baby on top of it. 'I suppose it is all right,' he said, 'but perhaps I ought to have asked you about it first. I only did it yesterday.' Cheney turned with a look Home said he would never forget. 'It's all true, then, it's all true!' he said.[4]

The Ward Cheney household was altogether very important as the scene of Home's psychic development; it was here that the first instance took place of his most famous demonstration of psychic power: his rising into the air, balancing in it and moving through it as if it were water. The description printed by Home[5], is ascribed simply to 'a gentleman who was present'. The narrator had had two relatives drowned at sea, and a message was delivered to him which he accepted as absolute proofs of spirit communication; it was accompanied by the dread sounds of shipwreck: 'the loud sound of a prolonged, wailing, shrieking blast of wind . . . and the creaking of the timbers and masts as the vessel surged to one side or the other, was heard by all. Next came the regular, sullen shock of the waves as they struck the bows . . . and now the large table was capsized on the floor.' At the culmination of these wild and terrifying effects, Home suddenly rose into the air. 'I had hold of his hand at the time,' the narrator said, 'and I and others felt his feet — they were lifted a foot from the floor.' The medium sank to the floor again, and again rose to the level of about a foot; he sank again, and then 'he was carried to the lofty ceiling of the apartment.' Home's description of his sensations was, that on this, the first of his levitations, he was frightened, but he added that he never was again, 'though', he said, 'should I have fallen from the ceiling of some of the rooms in which I have been raised, I could not have escaped serious injury.' The company on this occasion saw that he was not astonished only, but alarmed, but they themselves gazed with a fascinated interest which left them 'calm and undisturbed.' This description as published by Home himself was unsigned, but it was in fact written by Frank L. Burr, then editor of the *Hartford Times*, who reprinted it in the *New York Sun*, 1875, as 'A Strange and Startling Story' and repeated it at the request of Madame Home for her book: *The Gift of D. D. Home*, which she published in 1888. This version gave further details about the levitation: 'He gasped as if frightened — like one strangling or drowning. At the same moment there flowed upon his head and shoulders, and also upon me (I was not so tall as he), a wave of cold air, which felt in that close, sultry August night, almost like a sudden bath of ice-water — and Home began to go up. He rose till his head struck the ceiling'. The month before Burr wrote to Madame Home, he had been visited by his brother. The latter had been present at the séance and remembered it perfectly. 'Home came down, not abruptly but easily,' he said.

Speaking of his sensations in these levitations, Home said the only abnormal one was a swollen and tingling feeling in his feet. 'I am generally lifted up perpendicularly,' he said; 'my arms often become rigid and drawn above my head as if I were grasping the unseen power which slowly raises me from the floor. At times when I reach the ceiling, my feet are brought on a level with my face and I am, as it were, in a reclining position.' Sometimes he was hanging in air for as much as four or five minutes. 'I have been lifted in the light of day on only one occasion,' he said, 'and that was in America.' But, he added: 'I have been lifted in a room in Sloane Street, London, with four gas lights brightly burning, with five gentlemen present who are willing to testify to what they saw.'[6]

During this year, 1852, Home first found that music was heard at his séances. If musical instruments: a guitar, an accordion, a bell, were provided in the room where the séance was held, unseen agencies would play on them. He himself found that music was played to him 'without any earthly instrument'. He would hear it when he was asleep and its volume would increase to such a degree that it was heard by people awake in other rooms of the house; but if he suddenly awoke, the strains would cease.

Among many distinguished professional men who felt a keen interest in him, the question was now argued as to what career he should adopt, for it was not considered at this time that his whole life should be spent merely in exercising his gifts, marvellous as they were. He had shown a great talent for natural healing, both in diagnosing the presence of disease by occult means and using an occult influence for their cure. Two doctors, Professor Bush and Dr. Hull, came independently to the idea that he should have a medical training. The plan was formed but not immediately put into action as Home was now launched on a round of visits, the outcome of his success and fame. In 1853, however, he accepted Dr. Hull's arrangement for him to begin his academic career by an intensive study of French and German. Though in the end these languages were not used for the purpose Dr. Hull intended, their acquisition was to prove extremely useful to Home. Dr. Hull had arranged that while he was studying them, he should be lodged in the Theological Institute at Newburgh. This building stood on a hill overlooking a landscape of great beauty. The city lay immediately below the hill, but beyond the city the Hudson River wound among rocks and could be traced for many miles; on the farther side of the river lay a great expanse of country, all visible in that transparent air. He often sat of an evening as twilight was diffused, watching the lights that came out in the little scattered farmsteads. On one of these evenings he had an almost annihilating experience. He asked himself whether he were awake or asleep. Then he heard his mother's voice telling him not to be afraid. Like the sensations of those about to drown, 'there came rushing with a fearful rapidity, memories of the past . . . till at length I felt as if I had fallen from the brink of a fearful precipice.' In a state of dissociated consciousness, he saw his own figure lying on the bed. Then his mother's voice said: 'Be very calm, for in a few minutes you will see us all, but do not touch us.' At these thrilling words he found himself awaking from a dream of darkness to a sense of light. 'And now I was bathed in light', and there they all stood round him, ' those for whom I had sorrowed.' He had the sensation of being carried upwards and was able to see the earth, far beneath. One of the visions he had from this height was of a cottage, in which the walls, the furniture, were as transparent as if made of solid air. Inside it, were sleepers with spirits watching over them. He felt that his spirit was approaching his body once more, and cried imploringly: Why must I come back so soon? They said: 'It is now many hours since you came to us.' He remembered that when he lost consciousness, he had been gazing at a little star. Now that he opened his eyes again, he found that he was looking at the sun; the visionary state had lasted for eleven hours. 'My limbs were so dead,' he recounted, 'half an hour elapsed before I could reach the bell-rope.' When he managed to summon help it took an hour's massage to restore his circulation enough to let him stand up.[7]

His physical sensations were strangely connected with his psychic powers. Sometimes it seemed that a physical sensation opened the door to the psychic experience. While he was staying near Lebanon, he fell into trance and was directed to go to a house three miles off, where two brothers lived with their mother. He had met the two men a week before, and no suggestion of visiting had been made. Home felt reluctant to call on people he barely knew, uninvited and without having anything to say to them. The mysterious compulsion, however, drove him on. The April evening was chilly and overcast and as he neared the house, a drop of rain fell on his bare hand. Instantly, he knew that the mother was indoors, critically ill. He rang the bell and when one of the brothers appeared, Home said: 'Your mother is ill. I have been sent to say what will do her good.' As the woman's attack had occurred less than an hour ago and the doctor who had been sent for had not had time to arrive, the young man was astonished. While he stood there, Home again fell into trance; he led the way unerringly to the woman's bedroom and finding her in acute pain he made some passes over her with his hands; this relieved her and in a few moments she fell into an exhausted sleep. He then told her son what herbal remedies she ought to take at once, and of others for continual use.

After this, as he said, he was led by unseen power into the living room, returned to his normal state and was greatly surprised when these happenings were related to him. The doctor who had been afraid that he might arrive too late, said that the attack had been so severe that if other help had not been forthcoming, it might have proved fatal.[8]

Another instance of a single physical contact being the herald of psychic experience, occurred when Home was crossing from Brooklyn to New York in the ferry boat; he was returning from a dinner party in a friend's carriage; the gate-keeper had allowed the carriage on to the slope which led down to the boat; but another man caught one of the horses by the bridle and pulled the carriage up, as the boat was already full. The chains were down and the boat was drawing away. As Home said: 'There we were, on a steep, inclined plane, with restive horses and the deep waters within a foot of them.' The lady exclaimed that she must get out and Home, jumping out of the carriage, gave her his hand to help her alight. 'As her hand touched mine,' he said, 'with the instantaneous sensation of contact . . . I saw with the most perfect distinctness, that a little sister of mine had passed from earth. I was not aware that the child had been ill, and the illness being apparently slight, my relations had not thought it necessary to write to me about her . . . There I stood in the cold night air, and heard the impatient pawing of the horses on the worn deal boards; I heard the waters as they broke against the side piles of the ferry; I felt a life-warm hand in mine, yet there, shielding her from the cold, beyond all fear, and where harm could not come, I saw my mother with one of the three children she had left me to care for on earth.' His mother was holding the child in her arms, with its hair scattered over her shoulders. Beside them was the spirit of the drowned child Mary, 'who seemed trying to reassure the bewilderment of her newly-arrived sister. The next day letters came to announce what I already knew.'[9]

The subjects of Pisces have numbered some eminent doctors among them, but many of them are unfit for the medical profession as they are so sensitive that they absorb the states of mental and bodily ill health of those with whom they are in touch. Home was sometimes made ill by the sufferings of people with whom he was brought into contact. This was not immediately understood by Dr. Bush or Dr. Hull, reasonable and sympathetic as they were; from hind-sight however it is clear that not only was Home unfit on this account, he had not the intellectual or bodily strength needed for a medical career. He was frail and excitable, and much of his remarkable make-up was a mystery to himself as well as to everyone else. He also found that a course of intensive study, which demanded work done in solitude for long hours, cut him off from ordinary human companionship, without which his child-like nature suffered a blighting chill.

The matter was taken out of his hands. The cough which had troubled him for some time grew alarmingly worse. In January 1855, a winter severe even by American standards brought on a serious increase of his illness. This was now diagnosed as tuberculosis affecting the left lung, and the doctors who examined him said he must seek a milder climate at once. Though English tubercular patients were often ordered abroad for their health, Home was told that he should go to England for his. He was most unwilling to comply. America was the home of all his relations and his many friends; it had been his own home since he was nine years old; but he was now accustomed to listening to unseen agencies. Today these elements would be called his 'controls'. He spoke of them as his spirit friends, among whom he recognized the presence of his mother; and he had got into the habit of allowing himself to be guided by the messages which seemed to come from them. Illness and the bitter cold had brought him to a depth of depression bordering on despair; he felt he would rather stay where he was and let death find him; but his spirit friends told him he must go to England and he passively accepted their decision. Frank Podmore[10] says that a group of professional men, Professor Bush among them, who were keenly interested in Home's psychic qualities, put up the money for sending him to England. They were convinced that his life depended on a change of climate, and Podmore suggests that they wanted to send this remarkable young man to England as a missionary in the cause of spiritualism. The close connection between certain areas of American and English society was shown, not only by the fact that Home's promoters were able to give him introductions to various literary and scientific men, but that a circle of the socially distinguished, warned of his arrival, were eager to meet him as a renowned medium; his fame, where it did not rest on word of mouth, had been spread by the accounts of him in American newspapers, which were read in London, as *The Times* and the *Daily Telegraph* were current in New York.

In the last few years, Home had developed the faculties of telekinesis, clairvoyance, clairaudience, spirit communication, and levitation. As he was now preparing to leave America for an indefinite time, he made a round of farewell visits, and during one of these, spirit hands were materialized.

This episode was related by Mr. F. L. Burr in his article in the *New York Sun* before referred to. Mr. Burr checked his recollection with that of his brother who had also been present. They said that the table cloth was lifted up at the side opposite to the medium, and in the full light of the lamp.[11] 'There seemed to be something under the cloth which moved about . . . It felt, through the cloth, like a hand,' but, as he held it, to look at it, 'it seemed to evaporate or dissolve and was rapidly lost.' As Mr. Burr leaned forward, he upset the lamp, which went out, 'but as a good light was reflected on all of us from a grate of glowing coals immediately in front of the party, it was decided not to break the circle to re-light the lamp.' Presently a piece of paper was taken up from the floor; a long, thin, feminine hand of deathly paleness appeared with it, and, laying it on the edge of the table, taking up a pencil began to write on it. The hand was of a very distinctive shape, with long, thin fingers, wide apart and pointed at the tips. 'The hands of each one present,' Burr said, 'were on the table in full view, so that it could not have been one of the party who was thus writing. Being the one nearest to the hand, I bent down close to it as it wrote, to see the whole of it. It extended no further than the wrist . . . I brought my face close to it . . . to see exactly what it was, and in so doing, probably destroyed the electrical or magnetic influence by which it was working, for the pencil dropped and the hand vanished. It had written its own name on the paper and the word "dear" '. Madame Home said the name was that of Mr. Burr's cousin who had died of consumption five years ago. The handwriting was recognized as hers. A daguerrotype taken shortly before her death showed the unusual shape of her hands. The Burrs gave it to Home after the séance; his widow had it before her as she wrote. Mr. Burr added a detail which seems in keeping with what has been published on the nature of ectoplasm. He had held in his the hand that 'ended at the wrist'. 'Turning this strange hand towards me, I pushed my right fore-finger entirely through the palm, till it came out, an inch or more, visibly, from the back of the hand . . . When I withdrew it, the place closed up, much as a piece of putty would close under such circumstances, leaving a visible mark or scar where the wound was, but not a hole. While I was looking at the hand . . . it was gone!'

This took place in Boston on the evening of 14 March, 1855. On 31 March, Home went on board the *Africa*, lying in Boston harbour, and bound for England. On 9 April, she docked in Liverpool.

## IV

## A Sensation in London

Home's instinct to return to the land he had not seen for the greater part of his life, had been scarcely understood by himself, but even that impulse had died away and as the ship drew near to the quay-side, he felt a sensation of blank uncertainty and desolation. His unhappiness was increased by the enthusiasm of the other passengers, their impatience to land, to meet the families and friends who were waiting for them, to experience the exhilaration of seeing the sights, the treasures of the Old World. Home had always a child-like fondness for affectionate companions and social pleasures. The contrast between this scene of the passengers' warmth and excitement and his own wounding sense of being shut out, was almost too great to bear. The only prospect before him, he thought, was a dying man's: 'A few months of suffering and then to pass from the earth'. He felt that he was cruelly excluded from liveliness and human sympathy, blighted by a strange power which he could not control, which caused him to be looked upon askance by other human beings, either as the victim of a repulsive delusion or with contempt as a criminal imposter. In utter loneliness he went down to his cabin; here he prayed 'for one ray of hope.' It was not much to ask, and the prayer was granted in overwhelming fulness. 'In a few minutes,' he said, 'I felt a sense of joy come over me, and when I rose, I was as happy as the happiest of the throng.'

The spiritualist movement in England had not reached, and never did reach, the force it had already attained in America, but people who were keenly interested in it were to be found in every walk of English life — among the uneducated and simple, in the realms of what was called 'high life', among the eccentric and among eminent professional men, doctors, lawyers, politicians, men of letters, and among members of the quiet unostentatious middle class. Before his arrival, Home had been recommended by his American connections to many people likely to be interested in him; the most immediately valuable of these introductions was to Mr. William Cox, the proprietor of Cox's Hotel of 55 Jermyn Street.

This beautiful street, still occupied by elegant, expensive shops and restaurants, lies between St. James's Street, whose vista is closed by St. James's Palace, and Lower Regent Street, which ends in Waterloo Place. This spacious scene terminates in a view of the towering column supporting a statue of the Duke of York, between two wide-apart cliffs of pale plastered buildings: on the left of what is now the Institute of Directors with its pediment and rich frieze, and on the right, Decimus Burton's masterpiece, the Athenaeum Club, over whose portico stands the great, gilded statue of Athena, helmeted, leaning on her spear. Jermyn Street was therefore in the centre of a dignified and fashionable neighbourhood. At the St. James's Street end of it, Bury Street runs into it at right angles. Opposite the mouth of Bury Street stands No. 55, now a restaurant of distinguished resort. That this is on the site of the original No. 55 is confirmed by Thackeray, who said in *Pendennis*, published in 1850, that Major Pendennis left his lodging in Bury Street to walk a few yards to Cox's Hotel.

Mr. William Cox was a famous hotelier, and a man of considerable means. Beside Cox's Hotel, he and his wife had a country place, Stockton House, in Hampshire. He was a very kind-hearted man, and known to be much interested in spiritualism. He welcomed Home on the strength of the introductions he presented, and very soon adopted a fatherly attitude to the pale, *distrait* young man. He and Mrs. Cox never gave Home a bill; his stay at their hotel was always on the footing of a family friend, and realizing at once that Home was scarcely competent to look after his own affairs, for a long time they acted as bankers for him.

Almost immediately on Home's arrival, Mr. Cox found that numerous people were anxious to see the visitor and to have some experience of his powers. One of the most famous of these was Lord Brougham, now aged seventy seven, a striking relic of the vanished past. His legal and his parliamentary career had been brilliant. As Attorney General to the Princess of Wales, he defended the preposterous and pitiable Caroline against the Prince Regent's attempt to divorce her, and had so carried the House of Lords, that the majority in favour of the Bill was too small for it to be taken to the Commons. He had been Lord Chancellor from 1830 to 1834 and instituted reforms of great importance. It was said of him that he had the greatest enthusiasm for general information, and that he combined an activity in the world's business and an interest in the world's pleasures 'with the power of a mathematical intellect.' Such a person naturally wished to find out what was going on in Cox's Hotel.

In June 1855, he asked Mr. Cox if he might be present at a séance with Mr. Home and received a cordial invitation. Two hours before the appointment he sent a message asking if he might bring Sir David

Brewster with him. He was told that Sir David Brewster also would be welcome. Home afterwards recounted that as Lord Brougham's evening engagements were so heavy the séance had been arranged for the afternoon. It was held, therefore, in the light of a June day, in a large, upstairs room with three sash windows, overlooking Jermyn Street.

Sir David Brewster, a Scotsman aged seventy four, had had a distinguished career as a scientist. His achievements were chiefly in the sphere of optics. At ten years old, he had made himself a telescope; he invented the kaleidescope; he had assisted Fox Talbot in his photographic experiments at Laycock Abbey. He held the Copley Medal and the Rumford Medal, he was a Fellow of the Royal Society. When, in Brewster's own words, Brougham asked him to come with him to Cox's Hotel, 'to find out the trick,' it seemed, on the face of it, that Brougham had chosen an assistant whose investigations would be trustworthy.

When the two men arrived at Cox's Hotel, Home, whose cough had kept him awake most of the night, was still in bed, but he got up, dressed himself and came downstairs. He invited the visitors to search the room for concealed machinery; this they declined to do and the sitting began around a card table.

Brewster was on Home's left, Cox on his right and Brougham opposite. They had been sitting half an hour, when Home felt his mouth fill with what he thought was blood. He had no handkerchief with him and ran upstairs to his bedroom where he expectorated. The discharge was not blood but matter from the tubercular lung. He came back after an absence of about three minutes, and Brewster suggested they should leave the card table and seat themselves at a large circular dining table. This they did. The enquiry as to what happened at this séance cannot be better answered than in Brewster's own words, written in a letter to his daughter the following day. He said that when they were all seated at the table, it shuddered and 'a tremulous motion ran up our arms.' Rappings were heard and the table 'actually rose from the ground, with no hand upon it.' When they moved to the dining table 'it exhibited similar movements.' An accordion, held in Brougham's hand, gave out a simple note, but . . . 'it would not play either in his hand or mine. A small hand bell was then laid down with its mouth on the carpet, and after lying for some time, it actually rang when nothing visible could have touched it. The bell was then placed on the other side, still upon the carpet and it came over to me and placed itself in my hand. It did the same to Lord Brougham. These' he ended, 'were the principal experiments. We could give no explanation of them and could not conjecture how they could be produced by any kind of mechanism. Hands are sometimes seen and felt; the

26

hand often grasps another and melts, as if were, under the grasp. But,' he concluded, 'though neither of us can explain what we saw, we do not believe that this was the work of idle spirits.' To this conclusion Brewster was of course entitled; the important part of his testimony was his declaration that he accepted the phenomena as something quite outside human agency. Mr. Cox's evidence, given subsequently, was that Sir David Brewster had exclaimed at the end of the séance, 'Sir, this upsets the philosophy of fifty years.'

Mr. Benjamin Coleman, a well-to-do stockbroker who lived at 51 Pembridge Villas, Bayswater, was one of those to whom spiritualism was not a keen interest only, but a preoccupation. Mr. Cox told him of the séance with Lord Brougham and Sir David Brewster and Coleman then called at the Athenaeum Club and had a conversation with the latter; during which Brewster, he said, 'fully admitted the facts and said he could neither attribute them to trickery nor delusions of the senses; but, he emphatically added, slapping his knee, "spirit is the last thing I will give in to." '

The Athenaeum Club was the scene of another, a more momentous, conversation about Home's powers. Edwin Richard Wyndham Quin, Earl of Dunraven, of Adare Manor in County Limerick and Dunraven Castle in Glamorganshire, had also a house in Putney Vale, called Kenry House after his third title of Baron Kenry. He spent much of his time in London and was a member of the Athenaeum. His son, Lord Adare, was a Lieutenant in the 1st Life Guards. The father and the son together were to be responsible for one of the most thrilling works extant on spiritualist phenomena: *Experiences in Spiritualism with D. D. Home* (1869). One day in this June of 1855, Lord Dunraven was standing on the steps under the pillared portico of the Athenaeum when he encountered Sir David Brewster. The latter gave him such a graphic account of the séance at Cox's Hotel, saying that the impression left on his mind by what he had seen was that the manifestations were, to him, quite inexplicable either by fraud or by any physical laws with which we were acquainted, that, as Lord Dunraven afterwards told Home, he determined that he must examine them himself.

Meantime, Brewster was, it seemed, anxious to continue the investigation. Home had been invited to stay in the family of Mr. and Mrs. Rymer of Ealing, and Brewster got himself an invitation to an evening visit.

John Snaith Rymer was a solicitor with a considerable practice; he had an office of his own at No. 5 Whitehall and he was a partner in the firm of Murray and Rymer at 59 Chancery Lane. His home address was Ealing Villa, The Green, Ealing. The latter was a quietly prosperous small suburb among trees and fields, not now inconveniently remote; it was served by horse-drawn omnibuses into London, and by 1855, the Great Western Railway ran a line to it from Paddington.

The Green was a rectangle of grass with some trees about it. The surrounding premises were those of the better sort of shop-keepers; milliners, confectioners, boot-makers; there was a lady's school and a circle of dwelling houses: some still of early nineteenth-century plainness and grace with fanlights and wrought iron balconies, some in the solid gracious early Victorian manner, with lofty, round-headed windows and massive front door steps. Mr. Rymer's household was a large one; the census of 1853 returned him as living there with his wife, four sons, three daughters, a governess, a cook and three housemaids.

The origin of Rymer's connection with Home is not recorded, but as he was a man known among his friends to be intensely interested in spiritualism, the introduction was easily made. Once it was accomplished, Rymer, like Cox, developed not only a deep respect and value for the young man's psychic powers, but a strong affection for him. It appears that Home had already visited Ealing Villa in May. On 2 June, Mr. Rymer sent him a present with a letter saying: 'Accept this accompanying trifle as a very slight acknowledgement of the love I have for you.' He went on to say that he would always be happy to have Home with him as one of his family: 'do, ever,' he said, 'consider my house your home.' The letter and the packet were despatched from Rymer's office at 5 Whitehall.

But the affection and admiration which Rymer felt for his young guest were not the only sources of the pleasure of having him under his roof. Mr. and Mrs. Rymer were now able to make Ealing Villa the scene of distinguished gatherings. As it happened in Connecticut, so it happened at Ealing. Visitors were soon coming in a steady flow and Mr. and Mrs. Rymer enjoyed the occasions more than had been the case with their American predecessor.

Psychic phenomena have two distinct aspects; the production of sound and movement which impress the mind with a sense of an unseen power but which, however arresting, have no bearing on the question of the survival of personality after death; the other, of supreme importance to the people who accept it, is the demonstration of this survival by contact with a personality, discarnate but recognizable. This, as Home said, is spiritualism. Detailed accounts of many séances at which he accomplished this, have been lost; Madame Home said, he kept few records and those who could have borne witness were often inhibited by an unwillingness to expose what was private, and from the shrinking fear of public ridicule. At least one episode, however, among the séances at Ealing Villa appears to be proof of spirit communication and to be very well substantiated. Mr. Thomas Barlee and his wife, who lived at Ealing, came to a séance at Ealing

Villa on 8 May, 1855; his description of it shows that Home had at least visited the Rymers in May, before he came to stay with them in June. Mr. Barlee sent an account of the experiences to the *Yorkshire Spiritual Telegraph* in the following October; they printed it on October 23, when testimony to Home's integrity had become important.

Mr. Barlee said that fourteen people sat round 'a heavy mahogany dining table, large enough for twenty.' The hands of the company, including Home's, were laid on the table before them. The table was lengthened by leaves fastened in with brass fittings. Raps were heard and these rattled violently. Looking under the table, Barlee found that two of them had fallen on to the floor. The raps were recognized by Mr. Rymer as those made by his son, Watt, who had died at the age of thirteen, two or three years before, showing that he had already had communication with the child without Home's aid. He now said 'Dear little Watty knows Papa is always delighted to hear his merry little raps, and does Watty think he could write something for Papa, who would so like to have some of dear Watty's writing?' The raps answered 'yes.' Mr. Rymer put an unused sheet of writing paper and a pencil on the tablecloth and presently Mr. Barlee saw 'this shadow of a finger' on the part of the paper nearest to him. At that moment an accordion, lying on the table, began to play of itself. Home said, as the spirits seemed willing to give them some music, should they not listen to that first? Meantime, the paper and the pencil were put on the table under the cloth and the accordion, 'without any visible handling' played 'Home sweet home.' This song, an unsurpassed success in Trans-Atlantic alliance, the words by the American play-wright, James Howard Payne, the music by the English composer, Henry Bishop, was the perfect accompaniment to such a scene. When the pensive, emotional strains had died away, Mr. Rymer said: 'Now let us see whether little Watty has written anything for Papa.' Five raps were heard, the signal calling for the alphabet. When this was recited, the raps spelt out: 'Dear Papa, I have done my very best.' Mr. Rymer took the paper from under the cloth. On it was written: 'Dear Papa, dear Mama.' When Mr. Rymer brought out one of the last letters the child had written before he died, the sitters saw that the spirit writing, especially in the formation of the capital letters, corresponded exactly with it. Mr. Rymer produced in 1857 a small book, *Spirit Manifestations* (H. Ballière, 219 Regent Street, London). In this he said that one evening, coming back from his office he paused in the room in which a company of sitters was already assembled. Raps were heard which, to him, announced his boy's presence. Standing at the corner of the table, he asked him if he remembered how pleased he used to be, when his Papa came home to set a chair for him? An empty chair moved itself round the corner of the table and stationed itself behind him. The father sat on it.

It is at first surprising that as the boy's age at his death was thirteen, Rymer should have spoken to him as if he were a great deal younger; the explanation lies, perhaps, in the fact that the Rymer family used an affectionate and caressing idiom in which, as it was afterwards noted, they included Home, and that parents who have lost a child sometimes speak of it fondly as 'little so and so,' even if it died when it was grown up. That Watt Rymer was felt still to be an inmate of his parents' home was shown by one of Home's séances held there for a visitor of brilliant contemporary fame. Edward Bulwer Lytton combined a parliamentary career with that of a highly successful novelist and playwright. His best known novels, *The Last Days of Pompeii* and *The Last of the Barons*, were already published by 1855, but in 1842, he had produced *Zanoni*, a hectic romance on the theme of everlasting life granted to the hero on condition of his never giving way to love. After lurid adventures, Zanoni forfeits this gift by an unselfish passion for a victim of the French Revolution. Lytton was fiery eyed, of a sensational imagination and his strong interest in the occult was not, or not chiefly, concerned with the religious aims of spiritualism but with its exciting and melodramatic aspects. Madame Home when working on *The Gift of D. D. Home*, found letters from Lytton proving that he had a complete belief in the genuine nature of Home's phenomena, but he never admitted in public that he thought these were the result of communication with the dead. As Madame Home firmly believed that Lytton did think they were, she was scornful of his silence, which she attributed to a craven dread of ridicule. The phenomena he described in his story for *Blackwood's Magazine*, 'The Haunters and the Haunted,' 'the luminous form collapsing into a vivid globule, the loud, measured knocks at the bed-head, the vibrations of the floor, the grasp of an unseen hand, the hand emerging from under the table to grasp the letters lying on it, the multitude of fiery sparks that flitted through the darkness,' all these, she said, read like a transcript of Lytton's private séances with Home at Knebworth House and in Park Lane, and she greatly resented these incidental experiences of genuine séances being used as trappings to sensational and fantastic tales.[1]

It was, however, inevitable that Home's reputation and Lytton's morbid passion for the occult should bring them together and Ealing Villa was the scene of their first meeting in June 1855.[2] Lytton came, accompanied by his son. Home said that when the rappings began, they were unusually loud and firm. They must have sounded like a peremptory call for Lytton's attention. The latter demanded 'What spirit is present?' and the message was traced out: 'I am the spirit who influenced you to write *Zanoni*.' Lytton asked for some tangible proof of the spirit's presence. 'Will you take my hand?' he was asked, 'Yes' Lytton said, and put his hand under the table. In Home's words, 'it was immediately seized by a powerful grasp which made him start to his feet.' Lytton obviously suspected a trick, but seeing that everyone else was sitting with hands resting on the table, he apologized and sat down again. The message was spelt out: 'We wish you to believe in the——' the letters stopped. 'In what am I to believe?' 'In the medium?' 'No,' was the answer. 'In the manifestation?' 'No.' At that moment he felt a touch on his knee. He put his hand under the table and there was put into it a decorated cardboard cross. This had been made shortly before his death by Watt Rymer when he and his brothers and sisters had been making cardboard ornaments and his mother had kept it lying on a table ever since. Lytton asked her if he might keep it; Mrs. Rymer told him that its only value to her was that her boy had made it. He was welcome to keep it, if, she added gently, he would remember the injunction?

Another episode of the Ealing Villa sittings concerned the movement of a wreath by unseen hands, one which was repeated a little later at a séance of much greater celebrity. On this evening, the Rymer children had been picking flowers in the garden. Some of them they had twisted into a wreath and one of the children put it on Home's head. 'A séance was proposed,' said Home. It was a calm summer evening with the full moon just rising. A large circular table was selected in the drawing room, which was on a level with the garden lawns, the french windows extending to the ground and the moonlight-twilight showed through them sufficiently to make everything in the room visible. The party, which included Benjamin Coleman, sat in a semi-circle round the table, the unoccupied part being opposite the garden window. Presently the table 'rose slowly from the ground and ascended till it was out of reach of everyone except Coleman, who could just touch its rim. It then descended steadily and settled on the floor with no more sound than if it had been a feather's weight.' All the circle had hold of each other's hands, and Coleman had asked to hold both of Home's. While the latter's hands were locked in his, there rose on the far side of the table, a woman's hand and arm enveloped in a gauzy sleeve. It picked up a hand bell which had been put on the table and rang it, then carried it, ringing, beneath the table. While Home's hands were still held by Coleman, the wreath of flowers was lifted from his head. Home said:[3] 'No hand was visible. The wreath then descended to within an inch of the surface of the table. It then slowly traversed round the circle and back again to Mr. Coleman who took it.' Benjamin Coleman took the wreath home with him and kept it till the flowers died.

# V

## Sir David Brewster Changes his Tune

The flow of visitors to Ealing Villa included many who were famous. Two of these, who came in June 1855, were Frances Trollope and her son Adolphus. The battered and time-worn but still high-spirited Mrs. Trollope had, while her family was young, supported them by a career of energetic writing. Her best known work, *Domestic Manners of the Americans*, which she had published in 1832, had caused considerable offence in America and got her the name there of 'Old Madam Vinegar' but the American residents in Florence were friendly and kind to her. She had lived there long since, with her son whose literary reputation was at that time higher than that of his brother Anthony, who afterwards so entirely eclipsed him. The link between America and Europe was such, that the Trollopes, both of them interested in spiritualism, had been recommended to go over to England and experience the wonders of Home's phenomena. This advice was given them by the American sculptor, Hiram Powers, who had been working in Florence since 1837. In 1843 he had produced the work which became world-famous, the 'Greek Slave', the white marble statue of a naked girl with bowed head and manacled hands, representing a Greek made captive by the Turks. It had been shown at the Great Exhibition, posed in an alcove against crimson velvet. The admiring crowd who thronged round it at the Crystal Palace had been able also to see, exhibited by a Birmingham firm, a collection of 'shackles, chains, manacles, pinions, handcuffs and fetters,' for export to America's slave-owning states. Powers not only knew from American correspondents of Home's psychic powers, he knew whereabouts in London he was to be found, and at his earnest suggestion Mrs. Trollope, who longed for some irresistible assurance of life after death, had got into touch with the Rymers and received their kind invitation for herself and her son to Ealing Villa.

Thomas Adolphus Trollope in his autobiography, *What I Remember*, 1887[1] describes what occurred here at the séances, at the Rymers' house. Home, he said, was a young American: a natural mistake as

Home had come from America and must have had, by this time, something of an American accent. He was nineteen or twenty, Trollope thought, 'rather tall with a loosely put-together figure and red hair and large and clear but not bright blue eyes, a sensual mouth, lanky cheeks and that sort of complexion which is often seen in tubercular subjects.' Trollope's description of Home's attitude to his own powers is consistent with every other account of it. 'He was ready enough to speak of those curious phenomena . . . but altogether unable or unwilling to . . . enter into a discussion on anything respecting them.' 'He claimed,' Trollope said, '*not* to have the power (as was currently claimed at the time) but to be occasionally and involuntarily the means of producing visitations from the denizens of the spirit world.'

Sir David Brewster, after the séance at Cox's Hotel, had shown himself eager for another sitting, and had readily obtained an invitation to Ealing Villa. His visit was made a few days after the séance at Cox's Hotel and when he came out to Ealing Villa, Mrs. Trollope and her son were already there. It was a summer evening and Home said[2] that outside the French windows 'the moonlight-twilight' was enough to make visible everything in the room. Before the séance began Home was out in the garden with the youngest members of Mr. Rymer's family, carrying on with one of the pretty girls in a way which showed that he was a petted inmate, and it looked as though he would have preferred staying in the garden to coming indoors, 'to attend to the matters of another world.' However he did come in. The company seated themselves round a very heavy mahogany dining table, and after preliminary cracking sounds the table was raised from the ground. Trollope and Brewster dropped on their knees and crawled under it. Trollope said it was seen for some moments hovering in the air, some four or five inches from the floor, without its being possible to detect any means by which it might have been moved. While he and Brewster had their heads together under the table, Trollope said: 'Does it not seem that this table is raised by some means wholly inexplicable?' Brewster replied: 'Indeed it would seem so.' But, Trollope noted, 'he wrote a letter to *The Times* the next day or a day or two after, in which he gave an account of his visit to Ealing, but ended by denying that he had seen anything remarkable. But it is a fact, that he did do and say what I have related.'

Brewster, it seemed, could now hardly wait to unsay what he had already said. At the end of the séance, he declared that he would have liked it better if they had all been *standing* when the the table rose. Trollope commented on this: 'Though an ordinary person might have lifted one end of the table while the other remained on the ground, I am persuaded that no man could have raised it "bodily" unless perhaps by placing his shoulders under the centre of it.' That no one had done this, he and Brewster had seen for themselves. This was the séance at the end of which Home, in trance, uttered the words which, as Trollope said, were 'much quoted': 'When Daniel recovers, give him some bottled porter.' The words have indeed been widely repeated, usually with the aim of raising a horse-laugh. Porter, a dark bitter beer brewed from burnt malt, was accordingly administered to Home. In accounts hostile to the medium, Trollope's concluding words are always omitted: 'It may be observed, however, that he did appear to be much exhausted.'

The next part of the evening was described by Benjamin Coleman in a letter[3] which forms a link in a chain of events leading to a crisis. He said that after the séance, Sir David Brewster walked about the Rymers' garden, 'talking this subject over with Mr. Trollope and that he left the party with the conviction on their minds that if he were not bold enough to recant errors, he at least would never venture to abuse spiritualism again.' Home was elated by the success of the sittings at Cox's and at Ealing Villa, and Coleman says, he wrote to some of his friends in America saying that Sir David Brewster and Sir Edward Bulwer Lytton were 'converted.' The result of this, the letter of an enthusiastic and childish young man, was only too predictable. Sent to a country where his gifts as a medium were of great public interest, an extract from the letter found its way to an American spiritualist newspaper and, as again might have been foreseen, was published with the addition by another hand of episodes which had never taken place. The whole was picked up and published at the beginning of October, by the London newspaper the *Morning Advertizer*. This paper was both respected and popular and the passage mentioning him met the eye of Sir David Brewster. He had already, according to Trollope, written to *The Times* to deny that he had seen at Ealing what he had at first admitted that he saw. He now wrote to the *Morning Advertizer* 'condemning,' Coleman said, 'the whole exhibition at Ealing Villa as a farce,' and adding that he 'was restrained from saying all that he desired in deference to the feelings of the talented lady who was present.' As Mrs. Trollope had been deeply affected by Home's powers, after her visit she wrote to Mrs. Rymer saying that the séances had given 'a pillow to my old age which I little dreamed of[4],' Brewster, it seemed, was reluctant to expose and abuse the proceedings as much as he now felt that he might have done. What he did, however, with results that were ultimately very damaging to his reputation, was to deny that he had seen anything phenomenal at Cox's Hotel.

This was too much for the patience of Cox himself, who had presided over the séance and of Coleman who had had Brewster's original opinion of it in conversation with him at the Athenaeum. On both these occasions, Brewster, while not admitting that the phenomena had a spiritualist origin, had declared that in his opinion and Lord Brougham's, they were not produced by fraud. Brewster's letter to the *Morning Advertizer* was published on 4 October, 1855. He wrote:

'I saw at Cox's Hotel, in company with Lord Brougham . . . several mechanical effects which I was unable to explain . . . but . . . I saw enough to satisfy myself that they could all be produced by human hands and feet, and to prove to others that some of them, at least, had such an origin.'

This letter brought an answer from Cox himself. He called on Brewster to say candidly whether it were possible, even if Brewster believed that Cox and Home were in a conspiracy, that the various phenomena could have been produced by the hands and feet of anyone present? He recalled the astonishment of Brougham and Brewster and the latter's exclamation: 'Sirs, this upsets the philosophy of fifty years!' 'I think,' Cox continued, 'I am justified in asking whether you have had any opportunity since of further investigation, and if not how you can reconcile the tenor of your letter with the facts I have stated?' Coleman seconded this with a letter to the *Morning Advertizer*, relating his conversation with Brewster at the Athenaeum and quoting the latter's comment: 'I do not know, but spirit is the last thing I will give in to.' Brewster now responded with a letter to the *Morning Advertizer* which is of exceptional importance in a study of the hostile reaction to spiritualism by people considered to be of normal honesty and high reputation. He said that he and Lord Brougham had been invited by Mr. Home to see if there were any machinery concealed about him, 'an examination which, however, we declined to make.' There were 'rappings in abundance, the table actually rose, as appeared to me, from the ground. This result I do not pretend to explain, but rather than believe that spirits made the noise, I will conjecture the raps were produced by Mr. Home's toes which, as will be seen, were active on another occasion.' This was Brewster's reference to Home's having been obliged to be absent for three minutes to expectorate the tubercular discharge which had filled his mouth. 'Some time after this experiment, Mr. Home left the room and returned, probably to equip himself for the feats which were to be performed by the spirits beneath a large round table covered with a copious drapery beneath which no one was allowed to look.' Brewster had written in his first account that 'the hand bell rang when nothing could have touched it.' In the *Morning Advertizer* he said: 'How these effects were produced neither I nor Lord Brougham could say, but I conjecture that they may be produced by machinery attached to the lower extremities of Mr. Home.'

That this suggestion, absurd in itself, was in direct contradiction to what Brewster had originally said to Cox, to Coleman and in his own letter to his daughter, is almost nothing: 'A change of mind' would cover it; the truly shocking element is the flat lie, that no one was allowed to look under the tablecloth. It was replied to by Cox in the *Morning Advertizer*: 'I assert that no hindrance existed to Sir David's looking under the drapery of the table; on the contrary, he was so frequently invited to do so by Mr. Home, that I felt annoyed at Mr. Home's supposing he or I could be suspected of any imposition.'

It must have been clear to any impartial reader of the *Morning Advertizer* that Brewster's conduct had been at least open to question, but in this year, 1855, when it was, in the last resort, his word against that of Home, Cox and Coleman, some people would prefer to take his; but in 1869 Brewster's daughter, Mrs. Gordon, produced the biography of her late father; as it must be supposed, without fully realizing what she was doing, she made a complete exposé of her father's shameless disingenuousness. She published the letter he had written to her in June 1855, the day after the séance, in which he gave his actual impressions of the phenomena. Mrs. Gordon feeling, it must seem, that some sort of explanation of her father's conduct in general was called for, said: 'Brewster's character was peculiarly liable to misconstruction from its distinctly *dual* nature; it was made up of opposites, and his particularly impulsive temperament and expressions laid him open to the charge of inconsistency, although,' she added, 'he never recognized it in himself, conscious that he spoke what was consistent with the point of view whence he took his observations at the time.' Brewster had said he was certain that Lord Brougham would support him in the account he had published of the séance, but Brougham maintained a discreet silence. Home, for his part, had naturally hoped that Brougham would give evidence as to their original views of the phenomena, but there, too, Brougham was silent. From a man of such experience, it was to be expected. It was the way of the world.

But Home, publishing in 1863 his first volume of autobiography: *Incidents in my Life*, Vol I, printed in an appendix the correspondence of Brewster, Cox and Coleman, and *The Spectator* reviewing this work, said that though in their view 'the controversy was not of any great importance one way or the other, still, justice to this celebrated medium obliges us to admit that, on the face of published correspondence, the hero of science does not acquit himself as we could wish or expect.' This mild and gentlemanly reproof for Brewster's mis-statements, to call them by no harsher name, is in strong contrast to the ferocity with which Home himself, never convicted of fraud, was frequently attacked.

The case of Brewster, however, would be of ephemeral interest only, if it had not been repeated on a more public stage by an actor of much greater celebrity.

# VI

## Browning on the Offensive

Tennyson's brother, Frederick, writing to him in 1854, had said: 'The Yankees bring over the most marvellous accounts of spiritual phenomena. I met a Mr. Jarvis the other night. He read us a letter just received from his mother, sensibly written,' he added, to forestall the obvious comment, 'and stating among other things, the elevation by invisible power of a table from the floor to the roof of a room.' Frederick Tennyson said he agreed with Hiram Powers, 'as far as to believe (in) these spiritual revelations ... but I confess I cannot accompany him in his belief in their beneficent intentions.' He put his finger on the difficulty that confronts those who believe that supernatural effects are a communication from the spirit world: that these effects should often be undignified or even comical. 'God speaks to the heart of man,' he said, 'by his Spirit, not through table-legs.'[1] Frederick Tennyson became afterwards a deeply convinced spiritualist, but in 1854 he was prepared only to vouch for the phenomena's being supernatural. Mr. and Mrs. Jarvis of Boston were devoted friends of Home; he had stayed with them on the eve of his departure for England in March 1855.

In the Anglo-American colony of Florence, of which Hiram Powers had been a member for twenty years or more, the most celebrated couple were Robert and Elizabeth Browning. They had lived there since 1846 when Browning bore her off from the dark and morbid scenes of her father's house to Italy and their blissfully happy married life. Mrs. Browning, a poetess of high talent, gained a reputation which time has somewhat dimmed; Browning's recognition was long delayed even after he had published in 1855 the two volumes of poems: *Men and Women*. Two of the poems in this collection may perhaps be regarded as some explanation of his otherwise inexplicable conduct to Home. In 'By the Fireside' he celebrates an occasion of complete mental and spiritual integration with his wife:-

We knew that a bar was broken between
Life and Life: we were mixed at last.

And in 'Two in the Campagna' he laments one when the union was, at that moment, missed:—

Infinite passion, and the pain
Of finite hearts that yearn.

Wordsworth said the poet had the feelings of the ordinary man but he had them to an extraordinary degree. The passionate desire for complete union with the lover is universal, but Browning was possessed by it to a degree that made the only occasions on which his wife entertained a feeling he could not share excruciating to him. One of these was her enthusiasm for Napoleon III, which he found trying enough; the other was a source of keener suffering as it invaded a more intimate region of her mind; this was her intense interest in spiritualism.

She was living in a community in which, as Frederick Tennyson implied, spiritualism was a topic of general and consuming interest. Writing to her sister, Arabel, in 1853 she said that Robert scolded her for her credulity but 'half his nature was taking my part, therefore he had to strive against himself and me, which vexed him all the more.' Browning though not entirely repudiating the subject, did not want to pursue it, but could not withstand his wife's eagerness; she had said: 'I shall never have rest till I know what is to be known.' Her burning desire and Home's fame which had spread from America to Florence had ignited her determination to come to England and see him. The beautiful and serious Mrs. Jameson who had published a work on Shakespeare's heroines, was a friend of the Brownings. She knew the Rymers and was able to arrange an introduction. Mrs. Browning's sister, Henrietta, who had married Captain Surtees Cook (and had therefore, like Elizabeth, been excommunicated by Mr. Barrett) was living with her husband in Taunton. Mrs. Browning wrote to her on 13 July, 1855[2]: 'As to Home, we shall see *him* and I will tell you. He is the most interesting person to me in England, out of Somersetshire and 50 Wimpole Street.'

Since she was banished from her father's house, Browning took rooms for them at 13 Dorset Street, off Baker Street. An invitation to Ealing Villa had been received, and they drove out to Ealing on the evening of 23 July, 1855. Nathaniel Hawthorne who knew them in Florence, said that Browning was a 'most vivid and quick-thoughted person, logical and common-sensible.' Mrs. Browning, he said, was so small and slight as to seem scarcely embodied; her pale face was the paler for her dark ringlets, her eyes were dark and bright. In spite of her uncannily aerial appearance, 'she was a kind and good fairy, sweetly disposed towards the human race though only remotely akin to it.' Such was the couple who were set down at the gate of Ealing Villa on the evening of 23 July.

The first hand accounts of the séance exist in four versions: in Home's version, in Mrs. Browning's version, in the version Browning wrote within forty eight hours of the event, and in the version he wrote a month later. The first three versions bear each other out, the fourth contradicts them.

Browning not unnaturally took a strong personal dislike to Home. His robust, explosive nature abhorred Home's gentle, effeminate bearing, though it is only fair to remember that Home was a young man who had been sent to England because his lungs were in such a condition it was thought he would not survive another American winter. However, his manners could not be altogether ascribed to his state of health and Browning loathed the childishly caressing behaviour with which Home treated the Rymers. His first account of the occasion — the fullest of the four — was written to his friend Mrs. Kinney on 25 July, 1855. Mrs. Kinney's husband was United States representative at the Court of Turin. This letter, now in the library of Yale University, was first published in its entirety in the *Yale Review*, Autumn, 1933 by Mr. William Lyon Phelps in his article: 'Browning on Spiritualism.' The reader owes Mr. Phelps a debt of gratitude for the publication, but it is impossible not to notice the attitude of mind in which, speaking of the séance at the Rymers' house, he says: 'The Brownings were "persuaded" to attend it.' Mrs. Browning's eagerness for the invitation and the good offices of Mrs. Jameson in procuring it, do not seem to have come under Mr. Phelps' notice. The letter printed in the *Yale Review* was the subject of an article, with extensive quotations and acute comment, by Betty Miller, 'The Séance at Ealing.'[3]

Browning gave Mrs. Kinney a moderately favourable description of Home, who 'says he is twenty but very properly adds that he looks older; he affects,' Browning said, 'the manner and endearments and the peculiarities of a very little child ... speaking of Mr. and Mrs. Rymer as his papa and mama, and kissing the family abundantly.' His face was 'rather handsome and prepossessing and indicative of intelligence', and Browning noticed nothing offensive about him, 'beyond the unmanlinesses I mentioned, which were in the worst taste.' The séance, he said, began with vibrations, movements of the table and raps — which were identified with the presence of little Wat Rymer. The circle was a large one, and Home asked that it should be reduced by five sitters; this left Home himself, Mr. and Mrs. Rymer, their daughter, Miss Rymer, their son Wilkie Rymer, the Brownings and two women friends of the family.

When the circle was reconstituted, Browning said, they experienced the same vibration, and the sudden up-rearing of the table, though the table-cloth, ornaments and a heavy lamp upon it, all remained in their places. 'All hands were visible', said Browning and added: 'I don't at all know how the thing was done.' Then, it seemed, that the spirit of Watt Rymer touched his parents, 'and next', Browning said, 'my wife, whose dress, near the waist, I saw slightly but distinctly uplifted in a manner I cannot account for.' The spirit then said, by raps, that it would play on the accordion and show Browning its hand. The latter promise was not fulfilled but a sufficiently surprising demonstration followed. 'The lamp was then extinguished and all the light permitted came from the two windows through their muslin curtains — you could just distinguish any substance held up directly against them — not against the wall which divided them — but nothing of what was done at the table, the night being cloudy.' The accordion is an instrument which it needs two hands to play. 'Mr. Home', Browning said, 'took the accordion with one hand, held it under the table and sounds were produced and several tunes played on it — but how, it is difficult to imagine.' Browning took the accordion in one of his hands and the spirit attempted to supply the force which his other hand would have used. But in his case, since he was not a highly powered medium and was, apparently, in any case in a state of resistance, all that could be felt were some ineffective pushes; that these were felt at all, was surely a remarkable piece of evidence, whether music were made or not.

The most striking event of the séance was the now famous one, the placing of the wreath of clematis on Mrs. Browning's head. Of this, Browning wrote that he was not able to understand the mechanism 'whereby a hand appeared from the edge of the table opposite to my wife and myself, was withdrawn, reappeared and moved about, rose and sank; — it was clothed in white, loose folds like muslin down to the table's edge, from which it was never separated — then another hand, larger, appeared, pushed a wreath, or pulled it, off the table, picked it from the ground, brought it to my wife . . . and put it on her head.'

Home, it appears, then went into trance and uttered religious messages which Browning felt were inept and futile. The medium then asked everyone except Mr. Rymer to leave the room. Home explained in his account that this was because the spirits had a message for Mr. Rymer of a private nature. Mrs. Rymer took the party into another room, and told Home afterwards that Mr. Browning had seemed disappointed and annoyed at being excluded; he said he had not known that spirits had secrets. Presently, the company were sent for again, the spirits having said that Browning might see the table lifted. Browning wrote:— 'Light was in the room — I looked under the table and saw that it was lifted from the ground, say a foot high, more than once, Mr. Home's hands being plainly above it.'

Another phenomenon was experienced: that of the table's tilting without the objects on it being made to slide. The heavy lamp and the ornaments which Browning had spoken of, in the earlier part of his letter, remained motionless, but a silver pen rolled down the sloping surface. Browning said to Rymer: 'Will the spirits now prevent the rolling of this?' Miss Rymer, who also was now in trance, said: 'Do not put that question. Have you not seen enough?' Browning in his letter did not think it worth while to say whether the pen's rolling was checked or not, but the ornaments and the heavy lamp kept their positions. The young man Wilkie Rymer was riveted by the super-natural occurrences; he must have been peering at them, spell-bound. Home, says Browning, asked him 'not to look so closely'. This, of course, is ammunition for people who wish to explain that the manifestations were fraudulent, but those who think they were genuine can believe that the medium, in the midst of an occult process not understood even by himself, was moved to tell the boy to keep quiet.

Browning had already said in this letter that he could not explain how the table was lifted, how the tilted objects retained their balance, how his wife's dress was agitated, how the accordion was played with one hand, or how hands had picked up the wreath and placed it on his wife's head; he had stated that there was light in the room when he had looked under the table; that the phenomena were inexplicable; but by the end of the letter to Mrs. Kinney he was saying: 'I daresay my wife will give you her own notion, which differs from mine in all respects', and goes on: 'on the whole, I think the performance most clumsy and unworthy of anybody setting up for a medium.' The dichotomy already apparent within the limits of a single letter, between his account of the phenomena, which he said repeatedly that he could not explain, and his final verdict that the performance was a clumsy fraud, is already so striking that it prepares the reader for the burst of self-contradiction, venom and sheer untruthfulness for which it paved the way.

Mrs. Browning's account of the séance, written, as she had promised, to her sister Henrietta, is extremely valuable as a testimony to Home's power, because, having met him, she did not like him. She did not share Browning's violent abhorrence of him, but all her after-references to him as vain, vulgar and weak, show, at least, that there can be no idea of her having been influenced by him, except by the mere demonstration of psychic power.

The Brownings' séance was apparently held two days after that arranged for Bulwer Lytton and his son. Mrs. Browning told her sister: 'We did not see quite as much as Mr. Lytton did, but we were touched by the invisible hands, heard the music and raps, saw the table moved and had sight of the hands.' She went on: 'At the request of the medium, the spirit hands took from the table a garland which lay there and placed it upon my head.' She said: 'The particular hand which did this was of the largest human size, as white as snow and very beautiful. It was as near to me as this hand I write with and I saw it distinctly . . . The hands that appeared at a distance from me I put up my glass to look at — proving that it was not a mere mental impression and that they are subject to the usual laws of mental vision. These hands seemed to Robert and me to come from under the table,'[4] 'but Mr. Lytton saw them rise out of *the wood* of the table.' She and Robert, she said, did not touch the hands. 'Mr. Lytton and Sir Edward both did. The feel was warm and human — rather warmer, in fact, than is common in a man's hand.' Mrs. Browning was convinced that the apparitions of hands were genuine spirit phenomena, but she did not feel that any spirits were present connected with people belonging to her. She thus achieved only half of what a spiritualist would hope to compass at a séance, but what she did experience was of a very high order of phenomena.

Home's own account of the séance[5] says that before the arrival of the company he and some of the Rymer children, as often, in the summer evenings, were out in the garden, and 'Miss Rymer and I had made a wreath of clematis. This wreath was lying on a table at a little distance from that at which we were sitting.' Home went on to say that during the séance, 'this wreath was raised from the table by supernatural power in the presence of us all and whilst we were watching it.' Mrs. Browning, as Browning had told Mrs. Kinney, had left her seat beside him and seated herself by Home at the latter's invitation, and when the wreath began to move through the air, Browning left his place and came and stood behind his wife, towards whom the wreath was being slowly borne, 'and upon whose head it was placed in full sight of us all and while he was standing behind her.' The suggestion was made afterwards by the Rymer family among themselves, that Browning had altered his position so that the wreath might reach his own head, and that he was disappointed that his wife should be crowned with it instead of himself. The Rymers' treatment at Browning's hands was harsh and rude and an uncharitable imputation was not surprising, but this one showed how little they knew him. Browning would have been much more delighted by an honour paid to his wife than to himself; as he saw the wreath moving through the air towards her head, his action would seem to be one of instinctive protection. 'Shortly after this', Home goes on, the message was received that something private was to be said to Mr. Rymer only. The party were conducted by Mrs. Rymer to another room, Browning was much annoyed at this exclusion, and when they came back, Home could see that he was in a very bad temper; but Home was so much charmed by Mrs. Browning and her courteous, kind behaviour to him, that he paid no attention to her husband's disagreeableness. Browning had said in his letter to Mrs. Kinney that Mr. Rymer had asked that no questions should be put or demands made during the séance and that he had acquiesced. 'I treated the spirits', he said, 'with the courtesies observed by the others, and in no respect impeded the development by expressing the least symptom of disbelief.'

Podmore[6] laid it down, with a view to discrediting some of the more remarkable testimony given from memory, that the longer the time between the occurrence and the account of it, the less reliable the account must be; conversely, the nearer to the occurrence the evidence was given, the more reliable it was. Less than forty eight hours after the séance at Ealing, Browning wrote to Mrs. Kinney that he did not express 'the least symptom of disbelief'. Nine years later the poet William Allingham called on Browning when the latter, a widower, was living in Warwick Crescent, overlooking the canal known as Little Venice. Allingham recorded in his diary for 1864, that 'having witnessed a séance of Home in a house of a friend of Browning's, Browning was openly called upon to give his frank opinion of what had passed, in the presence of Home and the company, upon which he declared with emphasis, that so impudent a piece of imposture he never saw before in all his life and so took his leave.' It might be argued that this explosion of unbelief, taking place after the séance, ('what had passed') does not contradict Browning's assertion that he did not impede the demonstration of psychic power while the séance was actually taking place; but this is incompatible with the fact that Browning sought another séance from the Rymers two days after the first one. Allingham continued in his account: 'Next day', which would have been 29 July, 1855, nine years before, 'Browning's servant came into his room with a visitor's card and close behind him followed the visitor himself — none other than Mr. Home who advanced with a cordial smile and right hand outstretched in amity. He bore no ill-will — not he! Browning looked sternly at him (as he is very capable of doing), and pointing to the open door, said: If you are not out of the door in half a minute I'll fling you down the stairs . . . the Medium disappeared with as much grace as he could manage. And now comes the best of all, said Browning. What do you suppose he says of me? . . . He says to everybody: How Browning hates me and how I love him!' Allingham added: 'He further explains Browning's animosity as arising out of a séance at Florence (sic) where a spirit wreath was put on Mrs. Browning's head and none on her husband's.'

The blunder of saying Florence for Ealing was no doubt due to Allingham's faulty memory. He had become confused on a matter of detail, as listeners to vehement and loquacious outpourings are apt to do; but the story of Home's calling on Browning must be compared with Home's own version. This was quoted in an article in *The Spiritual Magazine* for July 1864; both versions, therefore, are given, (with a month's difference) nine years after the event; but Home had a witness, in Mrs. Rymer; there had been present another witness also, but Mrs. Browning could be no check upon her husband's evidence; she had died in the summer of 1861. The only point the two versions have in common is the description, by Home and by Browning himself, of the latter's savage ill-temper.

Home said that two days after the séance at Ealing, Mr. Browning wrote to Mrs. Rymer, asking to be allowed to attend another séance and to bring with him his friend the actress Miss Helen Faucit. This lady was, in private life, the wife of Theodore Martin, who was chosen some years later by Queen Victoria, to write the life of the Prince Consort. Helen Faucit was the leading woman in Macready's company, and had played the chief female rôle in three of Browning's verse plays: *Strafford, The Blot on the Scutcheon* and *Colombe's Birthday*, though she and Macready between them had not been able to lift the plays beyond a *succès d'estime*, to the point of popular success. This beautiful and interesting creature would have been a suitable companion on a visit to Ealing Villa, but Mrs. Rymer, according to Home[7], replied that she could not receive them. Home, she said, was now very unwell; the family were about to take him with themselves, down to Sandgate, and with all her engagements and preparations for going away, it was not possible to arrange another séance before they left town. However, a few days later, she and her eldest son, bringing Home with them, came in to London to pay some calls, *pour prendre congé* and one of these was on the Brownings in Dorset Street. Home makes the point: 'I have never seen Mr. Browning but twice.' Once was at Ealing Villa on the evening of 23 July, the second at the call in Dorset Street, therefore Browning's account given to Allingham and Home's in *The Spiritual Magazine*, must both refer to the same occasion.

'We were first shown into the drawing-room', Home says, 'and he, advancing to meet us, shook hands with Mrs. Rymer, then, passing by me, shook hands with her son. As he was re-passing me, I held out my hand, when, with a tragic air, he threw his hand on his left shoulder and stalked away. My attention', Home said, 'was now drawn to Mrs. Browning, who was standing nearly in the centre of the room and looked very pale and agitated. I approached her and she placed both her hands in mine and said in a voice of emotion, "Oh dear Mr. Home, do not blame me — I am so sorry, but I am not to blame!" I was wonderstruck, not knowing in the least what the curious scene meant, (Browning having given no indication at Ealing that he cherished any such feeling as he now showed). It would', Home said,

'have been comical, but for the sight of Mrs. Browning's suffering.'
For the moment, all was confusion, but at last they got themselves
seated. Then Browning said 'in an excited manner', 'Mrs. Rymer, I
beg to inform you that I was exceedingly dissatisfied with everything
I saw at your house the other night, and I should like to know why
you refused to receive me again with my friend.' Home intervened.
He said, 'Mr. Browning, that was the time and place for you to have
made objections regarding this manifestation, and not now. I gave you
every possible opportunity, and you availed yourself of it and expressed
yourself satisfied.' This was unanswerable. Browning could only reply:
'I am not addressing myself to you, sir.' 'No', said Home, 'but it is of
me that you are speaking and it would be only fair and gentlemanly
to allow me to reply.' Mrs. Rymer then said: 'Mr. Home is quite
right, and as regards not being able to receive you and your friend, we
could not do so, on account of our engagements.' Home says: 'Mr.
Browning's face was pallid with rage and his movements as he swayed
backwards and forwards in his chair were like those of a maniac. At
this moment I rose to leave the room and passing him, shook hands
with Mrs. Browning, who was nearly ready to faint. As she shook
hands with me, she said: Dear Mr. Home, I am not to blame. Oh
dear, oh dear!' Mrs. Browning's celebrity was great; her eager and
earnest receptiveness at the séance had made Home sympathetic
towards her, and though she had not liked him, he had found her
fascinating and attractive. Since Browning had asked Mrs. Rymer if
he might attend another séance with Home at Ealing Villa, it was
natural that the latter should include the Brownings in their farewell
calls. Needless to say, they would not have done so if there had been
a word of truth in Browning's statement to Allingham that at the end
of the séance at Ealing: 'in the presence of Home and the company
. . . he declared with emphasis that so impudent a piece of imposture
he never saw before in all his life.' As Home said: 'Browning had
given no indication at Ealing that he cherished any such feeling as he
now showed,' which is borne out by Browning's own letter to Mrs.
Kinney.

This letter had been written on 25 July; Home said the request for
another séance had been sent to Mrs. Rymer 'two days afterwards';
this therefore would have been despatched, like the letter, also on 25
July. Perhaps the half-favourable account he had sent Mrs. Kinney
had rankled in his memory and the attempt to arrange another séance
was made, to try to explode the impressions he had received and prove
to himself that they were fraudulent. He was infuriated at being
baulked, and when he saw Mrs. Rymer and Home in Dorset Street,
he was goaded, not only into disgraceful rudeness in front of Mrs.
Rymer, but into a most unusual disregard of the feelings of his wife,

who was in acute distress at his behaviour, and looked, Home said, as if she were going to faint. In fact, said Home, he behaved like a maniac; but even so, it is not credible that in the presence of his wife and of Mrs. Rymer, both of whom were entirely in sympathy with the medium, he would have threatened to fling Home down the stairs if he were not out of the room in half a minute, as he assured Allingham had been his words.

For the rest of his life, Browning pursued this course of insane vindictiveness and though it reached its climax a decade later, it was in full cry within a few weeks. He had written his letter to Mrs. Kinney, admitting that he had seen effects which he could not explain, on 25 July; by August 30 he had declared the whole manifestation to be an impudent fraud. Miss De Gaudrion, a lady engaged to Mr. Frederick Merrifield, a barrister, had come with her fiancé to a séance at Ealing; they were neither of them convinced of the genuineness of the spirit hands they had seen, and Miss De Gaudrion, using a mutual friendship with Mary Russell Mitford as an introduction, wrote to Mrs. Browning, asking for her opinion of Home's powers. Mrs. Browning wrote to her in reply, enclosing a letter from her husband. She said her own impression of the séance and her husband's were entirely different. She said she felt that the practice of seeking spirit-communication for theological teaching would be 'absolutely disastrous', and that trying to reach the spirit of a departed person would very probably end in 'disappointment or delusion'. The means of communication were as yet so undeveloped, 'the manifestations are apt to be so slow and our apprehensions so unsteady, that we could hope to see our faces as well in a shivered looking glass, as catch a clear view of a desired truth or a lost friend by these means . . . What we do see is a shadow on the window . . . the proof of a beginning of access from a spiritual world.' There were numerous instances of imposture, but, she said: 'if you ask me, as you do, whether I rank the phenomena witnessed at Ealing among the counterfeits . . . for my own part, and in my own conscience I find no reason for considering the Medium in question responsible for anything seen or heard on that occasion.' The letter from Browning said 'Mr. Browning . . . is hardly able to account for the fact that there can be another opinion than his own on the matter — that being, that the whole display of 'hands', 'spirit utterances etc. were a cheat and imposture.' He believed, he said, in the sincerity and good faith of the Rymer family and was only sorry that their good qualities, being without a grain of worldly wisdom, should lead to their being imposed on.' Browning then once more makes the statement which proves that he was completely inaccurate in what he afterwards said to William Allingham. 'Mr. Browning had some difficulty in keeping from an offensive expression of his feelings at Mr. Rymer's.' He was to tell Allingham that 'he declared with emphasis that so impudent a piece of imposture he never saw before in all his life, and so took his leave.' Nine years earlier than his conversation with Allingham, he was still speaking with a reasonable regard for truth. He added, in his letter to Miss De Gaudrion: 'he has since seen Mr. Home and relieved himself.' This is at least a recognizable version of the shocking scene with which he had repaid Mrs. Rymer's hospitality.

Forty seven years later the echoes of this affair were sounding still. In a letter to the *Times Literary Supplement* of 28 November, 1902, Mr. Merrifield wrote: 'In July 1855, my wife, to whom I was not then married, spent an evening with me at the house where Home was then staying . . . As a result, I had not the smallest doubt that the "spirit hands" which we saw were material and a fraud. My wife formed a similar opinion, but knowing that others thought differently, and that Mrs. Browning had lately been there, she wrote to her . . . and received an answer, a copy of which, and of the spontaneous expression of his opinion from Mr. Browning, I subjoin.' This was the first occasion of these letters from the Brownings being printed; but Merrifield wrote on the matter in the *Journal of the Society for Psychical Research*.[8] In these writings he described fully the sitting, which had been held in two parts. He described what was clearly the Rymers' drawing-room: 'We took our seats, about fourteen in number, round a circular table, in a room, the floor of which was on a level with the lawn and communicated with it by two windows opening to the ground.' The usual manifestations occurred: the heaving up of the table, the pulling about of dresses and patting of knees. It is clear that the whole of the first part of the séance took place in a lighted room, because Merrifield says that the lights were removed for the second part. This second session took place as he and Miss De Gaudrion were on the point of leaving. Home unexpectedly suggested a further séance. The visitors sat down again; Home and Rymer sat at opposite sides of the table, Merrifield sat between them, facing the window. The segment of the table's rim nearest the window was unoccupied. 'The lights were removed', Merrifield wrote, 'and very soon the operations began. It was about eleven o'clock; the moon had set but the night was starlight and we could well see the outline of the windows and distinguish, though not with accuracy of outline, the form of any large object intervening before them.' Merrifield now described what had given rise to his certainty that Home was cheating. 'The medium', he said, 'sat as low as possible in his low seat. His arms and hands were under the table. He talked freely, encouraging conversation, and seeming uneasy when that flagged. After a few preliminary raps, somebody exclaimed that 'the spirit hand' had appeared, and the next moment an object resembling a child's hand, with a long white sleeve attached to it, appeared before the light. This occurred several times. The object appeared mainly at one or other of two separate distances from the medium. One of these distances was just that of his foot, the other that of his outstretched hand, and when the object receded or approached, I noticed that the medium's body or shoulder sank and rose accordingly. This was pretty conclusive to myself and the friend who accompanied me; but afterwards, on the invitation of one of the dupes present, this 'spirit hand' rose so high that we saw the whole connection between the medium's shoulder and arm and the 'spirit hand' dressed out on the end of his own.' This appearance which, in 1855, seemed to Merrifield to be consistent only with fraud, is, as Zorab indicates, now capable, in the present stage of psychical research, of another explanation. 'In those days, when there was, as yet, practically no knowledge of the paranormal, it was believed that so-called spiritualist manifestations were either fraudulent or that they proceeded from supernatural power and had nothing to do with the medium's body or physiology;' but, he says, it has now been ascertained that 'the medium's phenomena are intimately con-nected with body and mind, going forth from that unity and returning to it.' The existence of ectoplasm is sometimes denied by people who have not seen it, but the fact that the substance has been counterfeited by fraudulent mediums, expelling soaked butter-muslin from the various orifices of their bodies, shows that its existence is accepted and its appearance sufficiently recognized to make an imitation intelligible. Conan Doyle[9] says: 'There comes from the body of the medium a material at first semi-fluid which possesses some of the properties of a living substance, notably that of the power of change of movement and of the assumption of definite forms. A specimen obtained from a medium's body was subjected to chemical analysis, and Schrenk Notzing reported that when it was burned to ash, it gave off a smell like hartshorn, and that common salt and phosphate of calcium were among its constituents.' Conan Doyle[10] quotes the evidence of Dr. Alfred Russell Wallace and Judge Dailey, as to seeing ectoplasm emerge from the side of Dr. Monck and form itself into human shapes. The fact that Monck was afterwards exposed in fraudulent practices did not invalidate the evidence of the appearance of this particular phenomenon, which could not have been counterfeited in the circum-stances under which it was examined: a brightly-lit room and attentive watchers, under whose eyes a patch of opalescent light on Monck's side developed into a thickening whitish substance which gradually assumed the form of human head and limbs. In all the reported cases of Monck and the now famous Eusapia Palladino, when the manifes-tation was fully formed, some tenuous, vestigial strand still connected the ectoplasmic shape with the medium's body. In the case of Home, "discontinuity" was the usual thing, but Merrifield had seen "the whole connection between the medium's shoulder and arm and the "spirit hand" on the end of his own.'

Though Merrifield had, not unnaturally, no hesitation in deciding that the apparition of the hand was a fraud, Zorab points out that, judging by Merrifield's own account of the proceedings, he had, apparently, no distrust of the phenomena of the levitation of a table large enough to seat fourteen persons, or of the accordion's playing under the table, both of which must have occurred in a lighted room, because, he says, the lights were quenched for the second part of the séance. Nor does he say or suggest that Home left the room before this second part, so that any machinery he might have used must have been on his person all the while. The charge of fraud rests on the apparition of the hand, between which and the medium's arm he saw a connecting strang. Dr. Zorab whose investigations are based on a purely physiological, non-spiritualist theory, says that Mr. Merrifield and Miss De Gaudrion were as far from the truth as the sitters who saw in these phenomena evidence of spirit contact.

# VII

## 'There's a Heart in my Chair'

One of the most interesting and reliable witnesses to Home's powers was Dr. James John Garth Wilkinson, a vigorous and genial man, very successful as a general practitioner. William Scott met him when the doctor was attending Dante Gabriel Rossetti's wife, the red-gold haired, consumptive Elizabeth Siddal; he said Garth Wilkinson was a man 'as tall and as straight as a spear.' He was one of the nineteenth-century Englishmen who had an instinctive sympathy with the growth and development of America. The American people, he said, were free to show 'how rapid an architect freedom is, in a new world all his own'. He was London correspondent for Greeley's *Tribune*, and he had other interests outside medicine; he had made a popular translation of Swedenborg's work and he was keenly interested in spiritualism.

He had a scientific approach to the subject, but he could not be said to enter on it with scientific unconcern; he longed to find reassurance in it. In his son's words,[1] he could, as a child, find 'nothing that reconciled death with nature ... the horror instilled into him by servants reigned supreme. Beyond the coffin and the vault, no tale reached home to his heart.' The sight of raw and bloody hides hung up outside a shop filled him with an indescribable, sickening terror and dismay. In adult life, the nightmare quality of these impressions faded off, but he was left with the longing desire to replace them with light and peace. When he heard of the arrival of the medium of whom American professional men thought so highly, he put himself into touch with him. The Rymers were his old friends; he had every confidence in their integrity, and this made him eager to investigate the young man's powers.

When the newspaper correspondence over Sir David Brewster's experience was at its height, Dr. Garth Wilkinson, signing himself Verax, wrote an article for the *Morning Advertizer*; it appeared at the end of July 1855, under the title of 'Evenings with Mr. Home and the Spirits', and though the phenomena it recorded were common to most of Home's reported séances, Garth Wilkinson's reports are unusually graphic and convincing. He described three séances, the first held at Cox's Hotel, the second at his own house at St. John's Wood, the third at Ealing Villa. He went to Cox's Hotel accompanied by his wife and three friends whom he judged to be honest and clear headed, and there he met for the first time 'a modest, intelligent youth of about twenty,' who told him that he was consumptive: — information which the doctor did not need, as 'he bore the marks of consumption legible upon his frame'. When the company was seated, the table began the familiar rocking movement and the sitters were frightened that the lamp on it would slide off, but Home assured them there was no fear of that. While everyone's hands were on the table-top, a bell placed on the table's pedestal began to ring, and Garth Wilkinson felt that a hand, holding it, was being put into his own, 'a soft, warm, fleshy, substantial hand', but he had no sooner grasped it than it melted away, 'leaving my hand void, with the bell only in it.' An accordion was put by invisible means into Home's hand; he held it in one hand only and it played exquisitely. Each sitter was presented with it and in each person's hand it played a few notes.

When it came to Garth Wilkinson he was astonished at the force being exerted against his hand by the unseen player. Rappings were heard all over the room, on the floor and on the ceiling. They became so loud that Home asked the spirits to bear in mind that he was but one of several lodgers in Cox's Hotel and not to disturb the rest. The séance included messages to two of the party from, they believed, the spirits of ones they had lost. Garth Wilkinson said in conclusion that to have produced by mechanical means the sounds and the tactile sensations he described, would have required apparatus, assistants, screens, all of which were patently lacking to a slight young man, with nothing about him that swelled his pockets, operating, unsupported, in a barely furnished room.

The very marked phenomenon of the materialized hand makes it interesting to hear Home's explanation to Garth Wilkinson as to why the materialization took place under the table. The medium said: 'In accustomed circles, the results were easily obtained above board, visible to all, but that at a first sitting it was not so. That scepticism was almost universal in men's intellects and marred the forces at work; that the spirits do what they do, through our life-sphere, or atmosphere, which was permeated by our wills, and if the will was contrary, the sphere was unfit for being acted upon.'

A fortnight later the second séance took place. Dr. Garth Wilkinson practised at 76 Wimpole Street, but his private house, Sussex Lodge stood, in its garden, on what is now the Finchley Road. Friends brought Home there in their carriage and Dr. Garth Wilkinson,

51

watching him in the summer evening, walk up the path to the front door, satisfied himself that the young man could have no apparatus concealed about him. The sitting was held in one half of the double drawing room, around a large and heavy circular table. The doctor, like Mr. Rymer, had no reluctance to allowing his young children to take part in these doings; the party consisted of himself and his wife, their four children and two maids. When they were seated, he said, 'The chairs thrilled under us so vividly that my youngest daughter jumped up from hers, exclaiming: "Oh Papa, there's a heart in my chair." ' Cracking sounds were heard and the table rocked on its base; then it 'suddenly rose bodily eight inches into the air and floated, wavering, in the atmosphere, maintaining its position above the ground for half a minute, or while we slowly counted twenty nine.' Its oscillations meantime were beautiful, like those of a wooden disc floating on waves. Then, 'it descended, so gently that it landed with no noise and as if it would scarcely have broken an egg.' This phenomenon was repeated three times. During these intervals the medium was 'in a state of the completest muscular repose.' Among other manifestations, a very small hand appeared, lying between Mrs. Wilkinson's hands which were resting on the table, and a large one came beside it. The maids and two of the children, as well as their parents, saw the hands. Home passed into a trance state, and spoke to each person present of ones who watched over them in spirit life. The episode, out of all those in the evening, which impressed Garth Wilkinson most, was that when Home came to Mrs. Wilkinson, he cried out in ecstacy that a spirit was with him, very tiny but most beautiful. He said it was a little sister of hers who had gone away a long time ago. Mrs. Wilkinson exclaimed that she had never had such a sister . 'Yes, you had,' Home answered, 'though she had no name on earth.' Dr. Garth Wilkinson said that enquiries were made in his wife's family, and these confirmed the birth and death of the forgotten infant.

The third séance was held at Ealing Villa during Home's stay. In the third week in July, a party of ten sat round the Rymers' table 'in the dusk of a fine evening.' The first effect Garth Wilkinson noticed was 'a gently tremulous flash of light through the room,' how caused he could not say. In a few moments he felt the grasp of a large man's hand on his right knee. He asked Home whose hand it was. Home replied: how should *he* know? and told Garth Wilkinson to enquire of the spirits. How was he to do this, the latter demanded. Home told him to think of some person. Impulse made Garth Wilkinson think of his friend who had died in the previous month, the rumbustious James Silk Buckingham, traveller, journalist, pamphleteer, formerly MP for Sheffield, contender in many causes, once turned out of India for abusing the government but finally awarded a pension. Garth Wilkinson asked if this were he? The hand which had remained motionless on his knee, delivered 'hearty affirmative slaps.' Garth Wilkinson asked, had the spirit any message for his widow, whom he was going to see in a day or two. Five touches, the number recognized as a demand for the alphabet, were received, and on Home's turning the letters over, raps spelt out the words: 'The immortal loves.' Garth Wilkinson thought this message 'somewhat thin,' but when, a few days later, he repeated it to Mrs. Silk Buckingham and her son, the son said: — 'That is very characteristic of my father; it was a favourite subject of speculation with him, whether or not the affections survive the body.' He had never, it seemed, doubted the immortality of the soul, but he wanted to be reassured as to the survival of human love. 'The words show,' his son said, 'that he has settled the problem of his life.' Garth Wilkinson who, at the time of receiving them, had no idea of the words' meaning anything, had then said: 'Will you shake hands with me?' He put his hand under the table and when it was clasped by 'the same soft, capacious hand,' he exclaimed: 'This hand is a portrait! I know it from five years' constant intercourse.'

Apparitions of feminine hands rose above the table, on the far side of it which was not occupied by sitters, showing themselves against the bright moonlight which was now streaming down on it. One of them touched Garth Wilkinson's forehead. 'It was warm and human,' he said, 'and made of no material but softest flesh.' 'Bending over as I did, to the vacant rim of the table, I saw how the arm terminated, apparently in a graceful cascade of drapery . . . on leaving my forehead the arm at once disappeared and I watched it go. It was drawn into the same drapery but so naturally, I can only liken it to a fountain, falling down again and ceasing, into the bosom of the water from which it rose, and I also saw the drapery itself vanish apparently by the same dissipative process.'

The conclusion of the article reproached Brewster for prejudice and lack of candour. 'It is not the easiest way out of a difficulty, to call this youth a cheat.' Garth Wilkinson made the point in Home's favour that at some séances with distinguished and influential sitters, almost nothing in the way of psychic phenomena occurred. 'Were the phenomena a trick,' as he said, 'they might always be produced to order without variation.' When he compared the situations of Brewster and Home, the one of 'position, wealth, worldly repute, a name no-one dare assail', while Home had 'neither riches, health nor station', he added a further disadvantage; with a doctor's judgment he spoke of Home's 'ruinous peculiarity of gift.'

When Mr. Clement Wilkinson wrote his father's life, he made no mention at all of Home, and of his father's interest in spiritualism he said merely that the latter 'refused to discuss his own experiences or the general subject, in conversation; saying only that he had gone into the subject extensively and wished to say nothing about it.' This was another instance of the satiety which sometimes descends on people whose experiences in spiritualism have been vivid and full. One of Home's most famous investigators, Lord Adare, was a further example.

Mr. John Jones lived at Peckham. In 1861 he published a book of his experiences[2] in which he described his first meeting with Home, an account that gives some light on what the Rymers and Home himself had to suffer from the persistence of enquirers. Jones wrote to Mr. Rymer at Ealing, as the latter lived 'in that village,' begging to be allowed to be present at a séance. Mr. Rymer replied that: 'worn out with the excitement from the numerous visitors to me and the manifestations of spirit as produced at our own house, we are now at Sandgate, Kent, and shall be for a few weeks. On our return we shall be glad to see you.' This appeal from an exhausted man fell on deaf ears. In Mr. Jones' own words: — 'I again wrote: Let me come to Sandgate to hear what you have witnessed.' Mr. Rymer's resistance was overborne; on 25 August 1855, Mr. Jones appeared at the Rymer's sea-side lodgings, and his pertinacity, cruelly hard as it was on the Rymers and Home himself, has preserved an exceptionally interesting sight of Home.

The family sitting room overlooked the beach. It was four o'clock of a fine August afternoon; a loo table stood in the window, Mrs. Rymer sat at one side of the table, Jones at the side facing the window. While they were talking, Home came into the room with a book in his hand and threw himself full length on the sofa, one arm round his head, the other, holding the book, resting on his knee. Jones could see that he was almost prostrate with fatigue. The conversation went on; then, despite his exhaustion, the psychic communication had begun. Home suddenly turned his head. 'Did you hear that?' he exclaimed. Knocks and raps were sounding around the sofa. 'The medium', Jones said, 'let fall the book and stretched his hand out so as to rest his fingers on the table, the other arm still over his head.' The knocks became louder and Home and Mrs. Rymer recognized that the communicating spirit was one who had not come to them before. This aroused Home's interest. 'He threw his feet off the sofa, placed himself in a sitting position with his . . . fingers' ends on the table. The sounds then became very loud, all over the table and upon the floor.' Mrs. Rymer asked a question, and the rappings, on the under side of the table, sounded brisk, lively, joyous; but at that moment some one came into the room and communication was broken off. Jones added: — 'to *me*, this whole was interesting and convincing, because the position of the medium prevented even the suspicion of trickery.'

That evening, 'a beautiful summer evening about sunset' there was a scene typical of countless family sea-side holidays; outside the window, the westering sun spreading a path of liquid gold on the sea, 'as happy faces, old and young, were clustering into the room,' a party of thirteen in all, but this family was engaged in an unusual pastime. They ranged themselves round the large loo table 'placed a few feet from the window.' The father of the family had come back after a visit to London on legal business, and sat down among them with a small daughter on his knee. The sitting began with the company's repeating the Lord's Prayer. After messages conveyed through raps indicating letters in the alphabet, the accordion, held in one only of Home's hands, played 'Home, Sweet Home' which the party understood as a welcome to Mr. Rymer on his return. Some of the group asked to see the table lifted. A vibration was felt under their hands; the table raised itself about eight inches in the air, then gently came down again; then hands were felt, touching the sitters' knees, and Mrs. Rymer who wore a watch and chain, felt the chain being moved. 'Do you want my chain?' she asked. Three raps answered: Yes. Mrs. Rymer took off her chain and passed it, with the watch, to Mr. Jones who sat next her. Jones laid the watch in the palm of his hand and rested the hand on his knee. The chain was then conveyed to Home, who sat on Mrs. Rymer's other side. 'You had better take it, Mrs. Rymer,' Home said. Jones felt the weight and tension of the chain, one end of it in Mrs. Rymer's hand, the other attached to the watch still in his own. The watch was moved up and down, as if by the ring at its winder. He then felt it slide out of his hand and the next instant it was in Mrs. Rymer's. The child sitting on Mr. Rymer's knee felt her shoe and stocking gently taken off. The shoe was placed on the knee of the small brother who sat opposite her; the stocking was found on the floor under the table after the sitting broke up.

So far the manifestations had been remarkable in themselves rather than signs of contact with a discarnate intelligence; but Home now went into trance and said that Watt Rymer was there. Turning to Mr. Rymer, the medium said: 'Pa, I was with you yesterday, and it was I who suggested to you that (here he gave a name) had the book.' The name, as in so many of Home's records, was omitted, but Mr. Rymer accepted the words as explaining his own impulse to ask from a certain person for a book he needed in a case on which he was engaged.

When Adolphus Trollope and his mother left the Rymers' house the previous month, they had invited Home to their villa in Florence. This invitation Home was now taking up, and it was fortunately timed for the winter of 1855 in England was to prove one of fearful severity. He was in fact due to sail from Dover the following day. Mr. Rymer had arranged for one of his sons to go to Italy at the same time for a course of study in the studio of a painter. He was paying the travelling expenses of both young men. The next day some of the family went from Sandgate to Dover to see the voyagers embark. Mr. Jones said that Mr. Rymer had told him afterwards that while they were all in a hotel at Dover, before the travellers went on board, 'the windows and doors of the room they were in, were violently shaken, and then followed some extraordinary phenomena of a spiritualistic character.'[3]

## Theodosia Trollope has Doubts

In Florence Home and young Rymer separated. Home went to the villa of old Mrs. Trollope where she lived with her son and his wife Theodosia. Rymer had other accommodation in the city, but he expected, naturally, to continue on terms of intimacy with his family's late guest.

Florence was then, perhaps, the most enchanting city in the world; with the river Arno, gleaming green under gold-coloured bridges, the vast cupola of the Duomo tiled in cornelian, sepia and sea green, the cypresses, the marble churches and marble villas, all, as now, steeped in the indescribable light which gives a new visual experience to the visitor who sees it for the first time. By the mid-nineteenth century it had attracted a large Anglo-American colony. Adolphus Trollope said he had never had so many friends and acquaintances as he had in Florence. The close connection of American and English society meant that Home's coming to the city was at once widely known. The Brownings however were not in their apartment, the Casa Guidi, they were spending the autumn in Paris, and Mrs. Browning who would so much have enjoyed the excitement of Home's arrival, was obliged to hear of it from correspondents only and to relay it at second hand to her sister Henrietta. Though Browning's first recorded account of the séance at Ealing, which was markedly inimical to Home, had been addressed to Mrs. Kinney, she and her husband were among the first people reported to Mrs. Browning as completely convinced of the genuineness of Home's manifestations. The scene was the house of Mr. and Mrs. Hiram Powers, which the sculptor's then world wide fame had made one of the most distinguished in Florence. Mrs. Browning had written a sonnet, 'Hiram Powers' Greek Slave', in which she made the point that the marble statue of the fettered girl was a mute appeal against slavery in America as well as Greece:—

> strike and shame the strong
> By thunders of white silence overthrown;

and the statue's fame was to receive the even wider tribute of American comic verse. In 1857, William Allen Butler published his poem: 'Nothing to Wear', in which he described Miss Flora M'Flimsy of Madison Square in this condition; not, he said, that she was 'in a state of absolute nudity, Like Powers' Greek Slave', but that out of the immense wardrobe she had collected in 'three separate journeys to Paris', there wasn't a single frock that she wanted to put on. Home naturally, and with his American background, wanted to meet Powers, and his hosts told the sculptor, who wrote to Mrs. Trollope:— 'We are right glad to hear that you are returned, all well, and that Mr. Home is now here . . . Pray thank Mr. Home for his desire to know me; it cannot equal mine to know him.'[1] The meeting was arranged and developed into a séance. Mrs. Browning wrote to Henrietta that she had just had a letter from Mrs. Kinney, 'to confess that she has been wrong, and that after having witnessed and examined for herself, again and again, she and her husband had come to the conclusion that all trickery, as a solution, was utterly impossible.'[2] Three years later, in 1858, Nathaniel Hawthorne was in Florence with his wife, and Power recreated for them numerous extraordinary experiences brought about by the presence of the medium. 'I certainly saw', he said, 'under circumstances where fraud, or collusion, or prearrangement of machinery was impossible, in my own house, and among friends incapable of lending themselves to imposture — very curious things.' He spoke of the apparition of a floating hand. 'There was nothing but moonlight in the room, it was true, and there is every presumption against such phenomena in such circumstances. But what you see, you see, and must believe, however difficult to account for it.'

A couple in Florentine society who were deeply interested in the spiritualist experiences were the Count and Countess Cotterell. Henry Cotterell had been Chamberlain at the court of Charles Louis, Duke of Lucca, afterwards Duke of Parma, and the Duke had made him a Count of the Austrian Empire. He and his wife were friends of the Brownings and the Powers. Hiram Powers told Hawthorne that 'while all our fourteen hands were on the table', there appeared the apparition of a frail, womanish hand, the forearm beneath it ending at the elbow in a white mist. 'It made efforts to reach a fan lying on the table'. The fan was pushed towards it and the Countess Cotterell, recognizing the hand of her dead aunt, exclaimed: 'Fan yourself as you were used to do, dear aunt!' The hand picked up the fan and wielded it with a particular, well-known gesture.

Powers also confirmed the sensations of other sitters, that when a spirit hand was seized, the human hand first felt it as soft but firm, and then felt it dissolve. On one occasion he felt what he was told was the hand of his dead child patting his cheek and arm. 'I took hold of it; it was warm and evidently a child's hand. I did not loosen my hold but it seemed to melt out of my clutch.'

The Countess Cotterell received a harrowing experience. Mrs. Browning wrote,[3] on 18 November, 1856; 'Sophia Cotterell had her dead baby on her knee for quarter of an hour.' This child had died in 1849, and Mrs. Browning had written of her:—

> She looked such kinship to the flowers,
> Was but a little taller.

The mother said: 'Darling, won't you give your hand to Papa? On which her husband swears he felt and held a baby's hand in his and drew his fingers down every separated finger. If you knew Count Cotterell, what a matter of fact man he is!' Not only was the Count matter-of-fact: he disliked Home; at a party given by Lady Normanby, the wife of the British Minister at Florence, he turned his back on the medium; but he admitted to Mrs. Browning that he thought the manifestations genuine.

Hawthorne recorded many instances of Home's powers; he did so with complete conviction, though he said that when he heard Browning speak about the wreath placed on Mrs. Browning's head, 'the marvellousness of the fact, as I have read of it and heard it from other eye-witnesses, melted strangely away in his hearty grip and at the touch of his sharp logic.' This statement is characteristic of so much that meets the reader who tries to establish evidence. The 'other eye-witnesses' to the Ealing séance whom Hawthorne could have encountered in Florence were Mrs. Browning, Home himself and young Rymer. He may have meant these but he does not say so, and when he says that 'the marvellousness of the fact ... melted away at the touch of Browning's sharp logic,' he leaves an abysmal gap by not producing any of the logic; his comment as it stands is a tribute to Browning's over-bearing and over-powering personality rather than to his reliability as a witness. But Hawthorne evinced also a frame of mind familiar to many people truly interested in the occult:— a conviction bringing in its train a sense of satiety. It is so, and what then? He wrote: 'These soberly attested incredibilities are so numerous, that I forget nine tenths of them ... they are absolutely proved to be sober facts, by evidence that would satisfy us of any other alleged realities, and yet I cannot force my mind to interest itself in them.'

Of what Powers had told him of the hand recognized by the Countess Cotterell, Hawthorne said: 'During this apparition, Mr. Home sat at the table, but not in such a position or within such a distance that he could have put out, or managed, the spectral hands; and of this Mr. Powers satisfied himself by taking precisely the same position after the party had retired.' Adolphus Trollope who had not applied the same test, was not altogether convinced of the genuineness of this phenomenon. He said that Home had offered to produce spirit hands for them. The room was darkened for the purpose and on the opposite side of the table from which the party was sitting, 'certain forms of hands became faintly visible.' Trollope said: 'To me, they appeared like kid gloves stuffed with some substance,' though he added: 'I am far from asserting that they were such.'

Trollope and his mother as Home's host and hostess in Florence naturally availed themselves freely of his powers. Trollope said:[4] 'Our Florentine friends and acquaintances were eager to have an opportunity of passing an evening with the celebrated medium. We generally limited our number to about eight persons, but pretty regularly had as many as that every evening. The performance generally began by crackings and oscillations of the round table at which we sat. Then would come more distinct raps; then the declaration that a visitor from the spirit world was present, then the demand for whom this said visit was intended, to which a reply was 'knocked out' by raps, indicating the letters required to form the desired name as the letters of the alphabet, always on the table, were rapidly run over.'

Several instances occurred when, the subjects declared, matters were brought out, of which the medium could have no possible knowledge. A very interesting one was related by Trollope of his wife Theodosia. Young Mrs. Trollope disliked Home personally and had had one experience, she thought, of failure on his part. One of Trollope's brothers had died of tuberculosis at Ostend, and Trollope had last seen him when they said good-bye to each other on the Ostend steamer in the Thames. Home's tubercular condition was being talked of, and from an association of ideas, Theodosia Trollope asked him if he could say where Adolphus had last seen his brother. 'At Ostend,' the medium answered. This she put down as an instance of feeble guess-work; but any one with experience of sitting with mediums would recognize that though the reply was factually incorrect, it was, from the point of view of psychic communication, very interesting, since the brothers had said good-bye on the Ostend steamer. Mrs. Trollope herself, however, received a demonstration of Home's powers which she could not fault. Trollope said that a highly-valued old female servant of his wife's, who had lived in the family since the latter's birth, had come with her to her married home and had recently died there. This woman had had a pet name for Theodosia in the nursery. 'I myself', said Trollope, 'had never heard it, or of it. My wife herself had never heard it for many, many years. She and the old servant had never, for years and years, referred to it. But one evening this name was spelled out. My wife declared that she at the same time felt a sort of pressure at her side as she sat in the circle, as if some person or thing had been endeavouring to find a place by her side.' But, said Trollope, 'for all that, my wife, though utterly mystified and incapable of suggesting any theory on the subject, was a strong disbeliever in all Mr. Home's pretensions. She strongly disliked the man.' Theodosia Trollope was entitled to her own views as to the origin of the phenomenon, so long as she did not accuse Home of producing it by fraud, and her admission that she was utterly mystified and incapable of finding an explanation, was the more valuable for being given against the grain.

Trollope's own impressions were contradictory, the result of a conscious effort to be just. 'I have witnessed in very numerous cases', he said, 'communications made by the medium to individuals who have declared it to have been absolutely impossible that Mr. Home should, by any ordinary means, have known the facts communicated. And it has appeared to me, knowing all the circumstances, to have been as nearly impossible as can well be conceived without being absolutely so.' 'On the whole',[5] he said, 'the impression left on my mind by my month's long intercourse with Mr. Home was a disagreeable one of doubt and perplexity. I was not left with the conviction that he was an altogether trustworthy and sincere man, nor was I persuaded of the reverse.' The abnormal condition under which Home habitually lived, continually invaded by forces, whose rights to his being he acknowledged, but whose immanent presence sometimes prostrated him to the point of exhaustion, would explain the fact that he did not present an unself-conscious, unimpressionable, balanced state of mind to a calm and careful examiner like Trollope; but there always had been, there were now, people who felt for him an entire, sympathetic affection. Among the French, Italian, Polish and Russian members of Florentine society, who came eagerly to his séances, the Countess Antoinette Orsini, the late Count Orloff's daughter was one. She was an excellent sitter, not receptive only but remarkably self-controlled. Once, in Home's presence, she was playing the piano, an Erard, when the instrument rose above the ground and balanced itself in the air; this was at a height where the keyboard remained within reach of her fingers and she continued to play. She and her husband were in Home's apartment one evening, where an album belonging to him lay on one of the tables. Feeling that a spirit was near her, the Countess said: 'If this is really the spirit of my dear father, convince me, I know you can. Write your name on this page.' She opened the album and laid it on her knee, holding a lead pencil. A moment later the pencil was taken out of her hand and her father's name was written. The writing did not entirely satisfy her. She said:— 'There is a slight resemblance to your hand, but I would wish it to be more distinct.' She reopened the book on her lap, and again Count Orloff's name was written, followed this time by the words:— 'My dear daughter.' This writing was unmistakably in her father's hand. Home says:[6] 'She cut the writing from the page; the first, imperfect example she left in my album, where it still is.' On going home, she showed the paper to a family friend, saying:— 'Do you know whose writing that is?' 'Of course', he said, 'It is your father's'. When she told him it had been written that evening and her husband confirmed it, the friend thought they had lost their senses 'and was much alarmed for them both.'

Another of the intense believers in Home's mediumship was, though famous, now so eccentric that his adherence to the doctrine of spiritualism was likely, not so much to further it, as to bring it into disrepute. This was the celebrated Baron Seymour Kirkup who, living in his house on the shore of the Arno, had become the prey of designing young women who counterfeited mediumistic gifts. Kirkup was old, deaf and easily deceived, but his past entitled him to some respect. He had begun his career as a student at the Royal Academy, he had known Blake, he had been present at Keats' funeral in 1821, and in 1822, at the burial of Shelley's ashes. He had discovered in the chapel of the Palazzo de Podesta a portrait of the poet, said to be by Giotto. His discovery was seized upon by others, and submitted to a process of restoration which destroyed its authenticity; but before this damage could be wreaked, Kirkup had made a drawing of the original, which is now accepted as the only likeness of Dante in existence. This prompt action by a man who could draw, saving something valuable for the world, makes it very interesting to read that when attending one of Home's séances at which a spirit hand and arm were materialized, he made drawings of them.[7]

The success and éclat of Home's introduction to Florentine society was so brilliant, a reaction to it was only to be expected. Several causes contributed to this, one of which appeared to be at first a measure of the success itself. A prominent member of the closely-knit social circle was the Lady Katherine Fleming, an elderly lady, married but living apart from her husband. Mr. John Fleming of Stonham Park and Chilworth Manor, remained in England, while the wife whom he had married some fifteen years before, settled herself in Florence. Lady Katherine's father, the tenth Earl of Dundonald, had been a distinguished admiral, and Lady Katherine herself had some of the bluffness associated with the quarter-deck. On Home's arrival in Florence she expressed a vehement wish to see him, and as this was not immediately brought about, she wrote to Hiram Powers:— 'Patience is a virtue! I have but a small quantity at any time and it is now all gone. I think of nothing but Mr. Home, and I have decided on writing to ask him to call on me. Do you think he will come! All day and night I have no other idea; as he is an extraordinary man, he will, I hope, not be astonished at my request.' Madame Home has said that Lady Katherine 'soon became greatly attached to her young acquaintance and one of the most enthusiastic of the Florentine believers in his mission.'[8] The sequel to this situation which had an unfortunate social consequence for Home, is related by Conan Doyle who had it from descendants of the Rymer family, then living in Australia. Conan Doyle says[9] that Home's health was failing, and that while he was confined to bed in his hotel, 'he seems to have been fairly kidnapped by a strong-minded society lady of title, an Englishwoman living apart from her husband. For weeks he lived at her villa, though the state of his health would suggest that it was rather as a patient than a lover.' Having regard to both the parties, mere common sense would now suggest this explanation, and there were probably many people who accepted it in 1856; but in the mid-nineteenth century, a mere rumour of impropriety could be totally destructive to reputation. Home said,[10] that one of his troubles in this star-crossed time was that this rumour alienated some of his friends to such a degree, that in severing their connection with him they refused even to send him some of his own money which was in their hands. Almost unbelievable as it must appear, the accusation seems as if it could refer only to Mr. and Mrs. Cox, since Mrs. Cox, in an affidavit ten years later, declared that Home never had any bankers except her husband and herself. At all events, if Home's statement did refer to them, the estrangement was brief and followed by a return of their complete confidence and affection.

The serious accusation against Home was, that in the height of his social success, he treated young Rymer with brusque ingratitude. Home was deeply indebted to the latter's parents for their hospitality and generosity. It was natural that even in the coruscating social success which he was enjoying, welcomed and courted by aristocrats of Russia, Poland, Italy and France and given the entrée to the intelligentsia of Florentine society, young Rymer should have expected that he would still have time to spend with the friend to whose family he owed so much. Conan Doyle met Mr. Bendigo Rymer, who showed him letters written by the latter's father dating from 'about 1857', showing that though they had been 'as close as brothers', when they reached Florence and Home became a personage in society there, he drifted away from Rymer, 'and showed no sense of gratitude for all that the family had done for him.' Young Rymer's letters to his family impressed Conan Doyle and he was 'chilled and disappointed' by those Home had written. His assessment of Home's character was that 'as an artist as well as a medium, the most unstable combination possible', Home was highly emotional, 'flying quickly to extremes, capable of heroisms and self-denials, but also of vanities and ill humours.' Home's letters to Rymer which were seen by Conan Doyle are the only positive evidence of his ill behaviour in this period, but there is a general impression of his having incurred disapproval. Since this has come down only through gossip retailed by Mrs. Browning, who was herself in Paris, it scarcely adds up to hard evidence, and what seems to have been the worst of it, though not defined, but sounding as though it might have had some reference to homosexuality, is withdrawn by Mrs. Browning herself. On 4 March, 1856, she tells her sister[11] that Lord Normanby's brother, Mr. Phipps, called on her and Robert on his way from Florence back to London. 'He told us the mystery about Home — the mystery of iniquity which everybody raved about and nobody distinctly specified; and there turns out to be, just as I supposed, an enormous amount of exaggeration.' Home's behaviour, she said, had been vulgar and weak, but there was in it 'nothing at all of the criminal character which we all supposed here.' Mr. Phipps added that there never had been. Lord Normanby, thinking Home might wish to leave Florence and not have the money to do it, offered to pay his expenses back to England, but Home refused the offer, saying that he was not a pauper. Whatever had given rise to disapproval in his personal behaviour, it did not extend to his conduct as a medium. Mrs. Browning told her sister,[12] 'persons who agree in nothing else except in disliking Home (for the foolish young man has succeeded in making himself universally disagreeable), all agree in considering the phenomena above nature ... They hate him and believe in the facts.'

Whatever might be some people's view of Home's personal conduct, Mrs. Browning was right in saying that his powers were unchallenged by anyone who had experience of them. The most unfavourable opinions were of the kind expressed by Adolphus and Theodosia Trollope; they did not believe the effects were produced by spirit agency but they could not imagine how they were produced. No one had a firmer belief in Home's supernatural powers than the Italian peasants, who were terrified by what they heard of them. They attributed to him the powers of a necromancer, and the Catholic Church had always forbidden necromancy. In their ignorance they confounded this practice with spiritualism — the deliberate calling up of the spirits of the dead with the passive attitude of the medium who allowed himself to be used by discarnate spirits who wanted to speak to living people. Home said[13] that his enemies had been playing on the peasants' credulity, telling them it was his practice to administer the Seven Sacraments to toads, in order, by spells and incantations, to raise the dead. This had so much excited and enraged them that they had determined to take his life.

Home had many friends in Florence, some merely names to the reader, some without a name. One of these had a guest staying with him, a woman who was a gifted clairvoyant. She urged her host to warn Home not to go out that evening. His friend at once sent the message to Home's apartment. This was the morning of 5 December, 1855. Home either did not credit the warning or else he forgot it; at all events he disregarded it and went out to keep an evening engagement. He was coming home, late at night, through the deserted streets, when, as he approached his front door, he saw a man step out of the doorway of an adjoining house. Home stopped on his own doorstep and looked up at a window to see if a light would show him that his servant was still up. At that moment he felt a violent blow on his left side which threw him, breathless, into a corner of the doorway. Another blow followed, in the stomach, and then another on the same spot. The man ran off, shouting: Dio Mio! Dio Mio! and Home saw the gleam of a blade in his hand. Breathless, he groped his way along the wall to the door of a neighbour who let him in. He was in a state of shock and did not know what injury he might have received, but this, as it happened, was not serious. The first blow had been parried by the door-key he carried in his breast-pocket, the second was foiled by the four-fold thickness of his fur coat, each side of which was doubled into two, and the two sides brought one above the other; the third blow, aimed at the same spot, had penetrated the fur and his evening clothes and made a slight wound on his stomach, which bled but not very much.

In the weaving of slander and abuse about Home, formed of scraps of information taken out of context, this episode is significant for the emphasis it lays on his wearing a fur coat. Several years later it was put about in the American press that Home had ordered a fur coat, priced at £50 (a sum that would today be equal to something over £1,000) and left Mr. Rymer to pay for it. The ingredients of the story were identifiable. Home possessed a fur coat and the sum of £50 was involved in dealings between Mr. Rymer and himself, but the truth of the matter was exposed by Madame Home.[14] She said that a few years after the séance at Ealing, Mr. Rymer met with such reverses in his profession that his considerable fortune was lost and he decided to begin life again in Australia. He departed, leaving his wife to follow him, but when she wanted to take ship, money could not be found for her passage. At this pass, she wrote to Home, appealing for help, and he sent her £50. Her letter of thanks, dated 1 November, 1859, was found by Madame Home among her husband's papers, of which she quoted this part:— My dear Dan, I cannot in words express my thanks for your affectionate liberality which enables me to follow my beloved husband to the new country ... Most heartily, most sincerely do I thank you for what you have given; also, Dan, for your prayers and good wishes. Believe, with affectionate greetings, how truly I am always, dear Dan, in this or a far off country, your sincere and grateful friend, Emma Rymer.

As Home had at this time no fixed income and it was generally known that he never took fees for his work as a medium, his means of support have always been something of an enigma. His family could not make him any allowance; when he had the money it was he who gave it to them; and though the American professional men who provided him with the means to go to England, may have continued their financial support, there is no evidence that they did. Ten years later in a famous court case, he explained some of his financial position: he had had some fortune with his first marriage, he had made money in America by public readings, a patron had for some time paid him £250 a year; his travelling exprenses were usually paid and many presents were made to him, often anonymously; but all of this did not add up to a comfortable income and none of it was available in 1859. It seems that he lived on successive spells of hospitality, one of the remarkable features of his existence being that one benefactor was always replaced by the next; but however his affairs were arranged, his ready money must at this time have been scanty, and the gift of £50 in money of the day, thoroughly deserved by Mrs. Rymer as it was, impressed her as generous.

# IX

## At the Villa Colombaia

In Home's state of uncertainty and unhappiness he had, none the less, the stimulus, the consolation, of performing what he felt was his life's work, with brilliant success. He existed to act as a conductor from the spiritual world to this. While he was in Florence, he said, 'the manifestations were very strong'.[1]

Hawthorne, in *Passages from the French* and *Italian Note Books*, related the first part of a very important series of manifestations, afterwards impressively completed by someone else.

The Villa Colombaia, a dwelling built round a courtyard, had once been a monastery. Its present occupant was Major Charles Gregorie, formerly of the 13th regiment of Light Dragoons, a Waterloo veteran, who lived there with his widowed sister Mrs. Crossman and her daughters Miss Crossman and Mrs. Baker.

Mrs. Baker suffered severely from the conditions in her bedchamber, which opened on to a staircase leading down to what had been the monastery's chapel. She was assailed by feelings of agonizing cold which she could not dispel, but when she sat up at night, reading and writing, alone, the worst of her sensations was the conviction that she was not alone. A séance with Home was arranged to take place in the bedroom, at which he sat with Mrs. Baker and Mrs. Crossman. It was eleven o'clock at night. They were warmly wrapped up and a bright fire was blazing, but still the intense cold 'penetrated to their very bones.' Before the sitting began, Home went down the staircase into the chapel. All was quiet there, but as he came upstairs again, he heard a sound from the chapel like the tolling of a muffled bell. As they seated themselves at a round table, a heavy chair moved itself forward, as if someone else were joining the party. They heard sounds like the sweeping of heavy garments and a scraping noise like nails on wood. 'We then distinctly saw,' Mrs. Baker said, 'the cloth on the side of the table next to me move up, as though a hand raised it from beneath.' Mrs. Baker did not describe the method of communication used between Home and the spirit, but it afterwards emerged that this must have been the usual one. On this evening, the spirit's presence was announced but Mrs. Baker and Miss Crossman felt they could endure no more for the time being. They begged the spirit to leave them and to come back next evening and tell them why it so tormented them. This it promised to do.

The next evening, the party was augmented by Major Gregorie and a friend of his, 'a gentleman,' said Mrs. Baker, 'known to Mr. Home, who was investigating the phenomena; both of them men of strong nerve and dispassionate judgment.' Their places taken, the symptoms at once began to show themselves. Intense cold came upon the sitters, a little stiletto Mrs. Baker used as a penknife was pulled out of its sheath and flung about, the table was lifted from the ground and violently pushed across the room; it stopped at the head of the staircase leading to the chapel, they followed it and sat down at it again. Mrs. Baker's elbow was powerfully grasped by a hand; she saw the fingers of it; they were long, yellow and skinny. She spoke gently to the spirit, from whom the reply was drawn that he was most unhappy and that perhaps she could help him. A promise was made to hold another séance the following evening, and the sitting broke up.

As the next evening drew on, a strong wind was rising. Mrs. Baker recorded: 'A hand raised the cloth of the table on which I was leaning and touched my arm as if to remind me of my engagement on this occasion.' The party collected as before, except that it was without Miss Crossman. She had been so badly frightened at the previous séance, she could not bring herself to face another one. This sitting developed a conversation with the haunter. Mrs. Baker said that she spoke to it in Italian only, and the replies transmitted through the alphabet by Home were not only in Italian but some of the words were spelt in what she recognized as sixteenth century spelling. Madame Home who relates this episode in *The Gift of D. D. Home*,[2] makes the point that though Home could speak French, he had known no Italian when he arrived in Florence less than a month before. Whatever degree of the language he might have picked up, he could hardly have understood Mrs. Baker's questions in it, still less invented replies to them in archaic Italian spelling.

In reply to the questions, the spirit said that he was desperately unhappy and had wandered about the house for many, many years. He had been a monk named Giannina, he had committed murders and had died in that room. When he was asked if he wanted masses said for him he said no, but he asked Mrs. Baker to pray for him. He then promised never to come back and, she said, 'since that evening, those painful sensations and strange noises of which I have spoken so much have left me and have never returned.' When Home had finished his extraordinary work, the troubles and horrors disappeared, but the room would seem to have been, for an unknown reason, suitable for psychic communication, for Mrs. Baker said that after Home's having purged it of the sensations of misery and fright, loving spirits had chosen it as their milieu for giving her family comforting messages. Unhappily, as she wrote four years later to Home, 'the noises at the Villa are worse than ever, and the new proprietor is dreadfully disturbed by them. The house has been exorcised but without effect. My own rooms are the most disturbed.'

Mrs. Baker's memorandum of the sittings had been read by Hawthorne, and Mrs. Baker had made it available to Home himself who used it in *Incidents of my Life*,[3] but in this work he had followed his invariable practice of omitting the names of all persons from whom he had not had direct permission to use them. He knew that the fate of people whose spiritualist experiences were published was to be savaged by the press, to be made the victims of ridicule and abuse, and that women, unaccustomed to any sort of publicity, would find this particularly painful. His consideration cost him a heavy price. The press did not hesitate to declare that anecdotes of the marvellous in which those concerned were referred to without their names, or by an initial and a dash, were blatantly untrustworthy. Madame Home admired her husband's magnanimity, but in her concern for his reputation, she was put almost beside herself by his quixotic treatment of people, many of whom, she felt, showed a cowardice, a treachery even, towards a man of whose powers they eagerly availed themselves, of whose genuineness they were convinced, but who would not allow their names to be used as a testimonial to his honesty. 'All the facts I can give, I shall give,' she said.[4] 'If the publication of names gives pain, I can only say I am sorry, but that the timid portion of his friends must be content with having sacrificed him during his life time to their anxiety not to compromise themselves in the eyes of the world. *I* cannot imitate Mr. Home's generosity.'

In the case of the Villa Colombaia, Home had mentioned no names, merely saying that these phenomena had occurred in the house of 'an English resident in Florence,' with the result, as Madame Home observed, 'that the narrative shared the fate of much other anonymous testimony, in being treated as fiction.' However, identifying the material used by Home with the statement made by Hawthorne who had supplied the clue to the Villa Colombaia, she wrote to the Powers family. Hiram Powers had died in 1871, but his son Preston Powers gave her the names of the Villa's inmates in 1856: these were Major Gregorie, Mrs. Crossman, Miss Crossman and Mrs. Baker.

It so happens that the trustworthiness of Home's account of the séances is confirmed by an observer who described a series of happenings at the Villa Colombaia shortly afterwards in February 1856. In

1953, Dr. E. J. Dingwall dealt with a letter discovered in the library of the Earl of Crawford and Balcarres.[5] This was written by Lord Lindsay afterwards 25th Earl of Crawford, to his sister-in-law. It describes three sittings at the Villa Colombaia: the details of the first two were recounted to him by his brother Robert Lindsay almost immediately after they occurred; of the third he was himself an eyewitness. Dr. Dingwall has described Lord Lindsay's account as that of 'a remarkably careful and accurate observer.' The sittings, Lindsay said, were held in full light; 'our ghosts have all appeared in broad lamplight and around the tea-table.' The sittings were held in the drawing room of the Villa. A brilliant light was given by a Carcel lamp, a French invention, in which oil was pumped to the wick by clockwork. This stood on a round table at which seven people sat and which was covered with a cloth which hung down about three inches over the table's edge. The levitation of a table was a usual feature of Home's sittings, but this was the first time Lord Lindsay had seen it. He wrote: 'After the party had sat down to the table and placed their hands on it, tappings were heard immediately, on the table and on all the tables in the room — very violent — the table then began to tremble — swayed backwards and forwards — then suddenly and violently rose from the ground to the height of five feet, higher than the heads of the persons sitting at it, and as violently descended — but was re-deposited on the floor like a feather.' There was nothing under the table, for Robert Lindsay stooped down and crawled under it. At the end of the sitting the large lamp was moved from the table and tea brought in; but while the party were talking by the fire, suddenly 'a marble table' — a table whose top was an unattached slab of marble — 'violently rose up to the height of three feet and re-descended in the same manner, and also tilted over, while the loose marble slab and a pencil and paper which lay upon it, remained stationary.' It bent almost to the ground, and when Robert Lindsay asked it questions, it answered by three plunges for yes and one for no. Robert tried with his utmost strength to force it back into its natural position and had the greatest difficulty in doing so.

The third sitting was the one at which Lord Lindsay was present himself. To ensure that his judgment was objective he decided that he would sit apart from the circle. The others took their places at the table, Home sitting between Miss Crossman and Mrs. Baker. 'Taps began on the under-side of the table, then the table began to vibrate, then the chairs, and then the floor, and then the whole room trembled and shook, while the china rattled on the table at the further end of the room.' Lord Lindsay looked under the table and saw nothing but the sitters' feet, but immediately afterwards: 'the table rose suddenly straight up to the height of four feet and remained suspended in the

70

air for about half a minute, swaying about in different directions — I again looked under the table while it was moving about, but there was nothing visible — and then came down again gently.'

Dr. Dingwall did not transcribe the whole of Lord Lindsay's letter as he was concerned with the phenomenon of psychokinesis, but in reply to a question of Dr. Zorab, he said that the letter stated that spirit hands appeared at this séance, that they were seen and touched. The transcription did not include anything to say that the spirits were identified, and if so, what questions were asked and what replies given; this was always the most important part of a séance to Home himself, however extraordinary the physical phenomena might be; but coming so soon after the sitting in which the manifestations were so terrifying, and the wretched spirit of Giannina was quieted, Lord Lindsay's account is valuable not only in itself but as evidence of the reliability of Mrs. Baker's statement.

The latter sittings took place in February 1856, and on the night of 10 February, Home received a spirit communication, warning him that his mediumistic powers were now going to be suspended for one year. The prophecy was fulfilled to the letter. He was cut off from the use of his powers for one year; they were restored to him on the night of February 10, 1857.

# X

## Séances with Napoleon III

Home left no description as to how the message had been conveyed to him, whether it were by an inner voice, or a soundless realization. This, the first experience of the kind he had encountered, startled and dismayed him, and it seemed that it might have unfortunate consequences of a practical nature. One of the throng of foreign aristocrats who had settled in Italy was Count Branicka, a Polish nobleman who had a Russian background; his mother had been the niece of Potemkin, the formidable minister of the still more formidable Catherine the Great. Branicka was proposing to travel with his family, via Naples, to Rome, and much impressed by what he had seen of Home, had invited him to join the party. Home assumed that the invitation was given because of his mediumistic powers, and on the eve of departure he felt obliged to explain that for the time being, these had deserted him. Branicka's reply was gratifying and charming. His interest in Home, he said, was not only as a medium but as a person, and he looked forward to Home's joining the family party.

The suspension of Home's powers was a mystery to himself as much as to anybody else; it was not only unexpected but sudden. As the warning was given to him on the evening of 10 February, 1856, it came almost immediately after he had given the sittings, in great force, at the Villa Colombaia; the withdrawal therefore was not a gradual failing of powers but a sudden extinction of them.

The Branickas' party remained in Naples for six weeks, in scenes of exquisite natural beauty, architectural grandeur and a condition of filth unsurpassed, in the opinion of English travellers, even by that of Rome. During this stay, Home under the Count's auspices, made two interesting acquaintances. The American minister at the Court of Naples was Robert Dale Owen, the American-born son of an English father, the eccentric genius Robert Owen, who had made his fortune in the Industrial Revolution as a cotton-spinner and then become famous as an economist, educator and political thinker of advanced socialist views. The fame of his doings in England had gained him an audience in America, where he had founded the New Harmony Settlement. This project had been a failure and Owen had ultimately returned to England. Becoming in his old age extremely interested in spiritualism, he was unfortunately one of those devotees who, in public estimation, do a cause more harm than good. However, living, at the age of 84 in Cox's Hotel, it was he who had advised Lord Brougham, as the latter was interested in spiritualism, to seek a sitting with Home. Owen's son, Robert Dale Owen, lived entirely as an American. He had some of his father's advanced attitude of mind and some of the ability his father had originally possessed. A philanthropist, an educational pioneer, a free-thinker, as a member of Congress he urged property-rights for married women and a more liberal attitude towards divorce. He was American Chargé d'Affaires at Naples in 1853, and had been Minister since 1855. Home was introduced to him and said afterwards[1] that he was surprised to find that though his own psychic powers were in abeyance, his presence had the effect of bringing out those which had been till that time dormant in other people. Robert Dale Owen, when Home was there, felt that he possessed these powers himself; in 1861, he published a sympathetic but practical examination of psychic phenomena[2]; he recognized Home as a medium of exceptional gifts, and dated his own interest in spiritualism from the time when he had met him. At these meetings, Home said, one of the Princes of the Royal House of Naples was also present, who was already a medium. This was Prince Luigi, the King of Naples' brother; this prince gave Home the first to be described of his collection of magnificent jewels for which he was afterwards famous. The reporters who abused and traduced him throughout his career, made great play with the fact that he wore jewelled rings on his long white fingers and no doubt he enjoyed showing off these gems which were exceptionally beautiful and brilliant, but his affection for them — he never sold one of them, even when in financial distress — was not, it may be suggested, the outcome only of a childish pleasure in display, but was also subtly connected with the relation of jewels to the visionary experience. Aldous Huxley[3] demonstrates that appearances on the mystical level of consciousness are described in terms of jewels, as in Ezekiel 28, v. 13, 14: — who calls them 'the stones of fire', 'in Eden, the Garden of God', 'the topaz, the diamond, the beryl and the jasper, the sapphire, the emerald and the carbuncle.' These mystical elements 'are self-luminous, exhibit preternatural brilliance of colour and possess a preternatural significance. The material objects which most nearly resemble the sources of visionary illumination are gem stones.' The ring which Prince Luigi gave Home had a symbolical as well as an aesthetic and an intrinsic value. The Prince had one exactly like it made for himself and wore it always from that time. Each ring was mounted with a large ruby cut in the shape of a horse-shoe. The ruby is a brittle stone, and it is difficult to cut it without breaking it; before the pair of rings were completed, seven rubies had been broken.[4]

Count Branicka's party went on to Rome, and here Home, from the sequence of events in the immediate past, felt an understandable longing to be received into the Catholic Church. He said[5]: 'I read with intense eagerness all the books I could find relating to the doctrines of the Romish Church, and finding them expressive of so many facts which I had found coincident in my own experience, I thought that all contending and contradictory beliefs would be for ever set at rest, could I but be received as a member of that body. My experience of life and its falsity had already left so indelible a mark on my soul from my recent experience of it in Florence, that I wished to shun everything which pertained to this world and I determined to enter a monastery.' But when actually faced with this prospect, he shrank from it. He realized that it was a way of life absolutely at variance with his own needs. As a student, he had wilted and withered under the effects of solitary study and before he had taken any decisive step that would lead him towards the retirement and isolation of a monastery, he withdrew from the idea of such a future. This however did not interfere with his eager wish to enter the Catholic Church. After a deliberation of three weeks by the religious authorities, it was decided that he should be received, and he was confirmed on Easter Sunday, 1856, in the Chapel of the English College of Rome with Count Branicka standing as his god-father and Princess Orsini as his god-mother. His fame was already such that he was received in audience by the Pope. Pius IX questioned him intently as to his past life and his pyschic experiences. The head of the Catholic Church did not deny the authentic nature of these, but he disapproved of pyschic phenomena's being received except under the Church's authority. At the close of the audience, he pointed to a crucifix that stood beside him. 'My child,' he said, 'it is upon what is on that table, that we place our faith.' Home in his account of the audience[6] contradicted the report which had been current, that he had promised the Pope not to receive any further communications from the spirit world. He could not have given any such undertaking, since these communications came to him without the exercise of his own will and without any warning. He could not have given such a promise, nor, he said, had the Pope asked for it.

Home told His Holiness that he meant to go to Paris, to perfect his knowledge of the French language, and the Pope advised him to take as his confessor Père Xavier de Ravignan. This priest of high mental calibre, strong personality and great capacity for affection, made a deep impression on Home, who spoke of him always with gratitude and respect, but the underlying difference could never be resolved:

Père de Ravignan thought that communication with spirits was entertained voluntarily, and that in Home's case it was inspired by the forces of evil, while Home maintained that it was altogether involuntary, and that while the gift had been in his possession, to exercise it had been the strongest moral impulse of his existence. Père de Ravignan assured him decisively that now he was a member of the Catholic Church, the mediumistic powers would not return to him. With the unselfconsciousness that was characteristic of his attitude to his own powers, Home said[7]: 'For myself, I had no opinion on the subject, as I was quite without data, except his assurance on the point.'

Home had said that during the interregnum of his gift, he meant to go to Paris to study French. He left Rome for Paris, arriving there in June 1856, but how he maintained himself for the next six or seven months is not explained. His life, in his own two volumes, and in the two works by his widow, is related with irregular emphasis; the psychic elements are naturally dwelt on at length, while passages of mere biography are often omitted or briefly dismissed. Those works on Home which are unsympathetic to him fill in the gaps with assumptions to his discredit. Home says that in Paris he became very ill with his tubercular condition, and the doctor, finding his left lung in a serious state, advised him to remove to a milder climate; but this, he says, 'could not be accomplished, and for some time I was confined to my bed.' It has been said[8], in Jean Burton's *Heyday of a Wizard*, that the Branickas 'had got tired of Home and moved on elsewhere, leaving him stranded and quite penniless.' Miss Burton has produced no evidence for either of these assertions. Count Branicka had not engaged Home for a life-long companionship, and after the visit had extended to Naples and Rome there was no ostensible reason why it should not have come to a normal conclusion. So far, it would seem, from parting from him in disgust, Count Branicka introduced Home to two of his friends, the Polish count Alexander de Komar and his brother Waldemar. The friendship that began between Home and the brothers de Komar was affectionate and life-long, as Madame Home proved from their letters to him, preserved in the enormous collection on which she worked when writing *The Life and Mission of D. D. Home*. Count Alexander had a house in Paris, the Hôtel de Vouillement, where Home afterwards became a guest. In the meantime Mrs. Browning, who in writing to her sister, had expressed herself as horrified at Home's arrival in Paris in case his presence should set Browning off again, had only this to say:— 'the last news of Home is that he is dead or dying of congestion of the lungs.' She did not say that he was destitute, a fact she would hardly have omitted to mention, if she had heard of it. Even before Home became a guest in the Hôtel de Vouillement, the little that is known of his circumstances does not, to say the least, suggest a scene like the attic in *La Bohème*. The physician who attended him was Dr. Louis, among the most famous of French specialists in disease of the lungs, and Père de Ravignan's affectionate anxiety was shown in a letter of 28 January 1857[9]: 'Mon bien-cher Enfant, Etes-vous malade? Faites-moi le savoir. J'irai près de vous, car il y a de trop longtemps que je ne vous ai vu . . . Vous savez que je vous aime tendrement en Notre Sauveur.' Home indeed appears to have been an object of care and concern to several people. Above all, his situation was the subject of eager curiosity to the Emperor and Empress of the French.

Louis Napoleon, the nephew of Napoleon Bonaparte, had been the first President of the French Republic in 1848, and four years later, by a *coup d'état*, had proclaimed himself Emperor as Napoleon III. His reign had a visual character in keeping with its social and political scene. The classical elegance of the previous era had foundered and disappeared, and been replaced by the ornate gilding, the marble, the elaborate girandoles heavy with crystal drops, the garish colours, the crimsons and bright cerulean blues, of the Second Empire. The fascinating Eugénie was of a piece with her surroundings; admirably portrayed by Winterhalter, wreathed and jewelled, with spreading, glassy satin skirts, with the effectiveness of beauty but without the unselfconsciousness dignity that comes from royal birth. When the Emperor was in Paris, his court was held in the palace of the Tuileries, adjoining the Louvre, and here Napoleon III was waiting to hear if Home's mediumistic powers had been restored to him. The Emperor knew, not only that they had been suspended, but that their return had been promised at the end of a year, a year from 10 February 1856. On the morning of 11 February 1857, he sent his Lord Chamberlain, the Marquis de Belmont, to Home's apartment, to ask if the medium were now in power again. The answer was yes. At midnight of the 10th, lying awake in his bed, still feeling the effects of illness, Home had heard the familiar rapping sounds. He had felt a hand on his forehead and heard a voice say: 'Be of good cheer, Daniel, you will soon be well,' and within minutes he had sunk into a deep restoring sleep.

Next morning he sent word to Père de Ravignan that the mysterious power had returned. The priest came to his room that afternoon and as he was speaking, rappings were heard on the ceiling and the floor. As he was about to give his benediction before leaving the patient, loud raps were heard on the head of the bedstead. Disappointed, alarmed and angry, Père de Ravignan left the room without making any comment.

Next day, Home was well enough to take a drive; on the day after that, 13 February, he was presented to their Majesties at the Tuileries.

Madame Home[10] speaking of the grotesque misrepresentations current of Home's séances at the Palace, says: 'Here is the true description of the first séance.' Her account is borne out by the Empress's own descriptions in her letters to her sister, the Duchess of Alba. 'Well, I saw him,' she says, 'and there is nothing in the whole world that can give you an idea of what we experienced. He is thin, pale, twenty-one years old (sic) in very poor health with something strange in his look. He is a Scot, he talks very little, and when asked what we shall be seeing, he answers:— I don't know anything about it. I am only an instrument.'[11]

At Home's first appearance in the Palace, the room was very full; besides several gentlemen in attendance on the Emperor, the Empress was present with her suite. Home asked the Emperor that the numbers should be reduced and Napoleon ordered that the room should be cleared. Eugénie was offended at the exclusion of her suite and left the apartment with them, saying she would not remain without her attendants. One of the gentlemen who was allowed to stay was Prince Murat, the son of the King of Naples, Joachim Murat, to whom Napoleon Bonaparte had married his sister Caroline. The manifestations began almost at once. The table rose into the air and as it did so, Prince Murat dropped on his knees and grasped the medium's feet. Napoleon III was observant and sceptical, but as the séance went on, he became deeply impressed. He told Home that he would very much like the Empress to see what was going forward, and went himself to fetch her. Eugénie returned with him, still in displeasure and told Home haughtily that on another occasion, she would not be present unless she were accompanied by her suite. Then the manifestations showed themselves again, and by the end of the sitting, Eugénie, appalled and ecstatic, was assuring Home that, whatever conditions he imposed should be willingly complied with. The table, she told her sister, had shivered like a frightened dog. Home, she said, 'sits with one hand on the table top. He sits alongside the table. As you can well imagine, we had first assured ourselves that he had nothing to do with what was happening.' She asked questions in her mind without uttering them and was given replies through the rappings. At one point she cried out, feeling some unseen one pull at her dress. Home asked her to put her hand under the table, saying:— 'If a hand takes that of your Majesty, I am confident that the touch will cause you no alarm.' 'The Emperor and the other sitters looked on Home's hands resting on the table.' The Empress put her hand underneath it, and a look of intense joy came into her face, while her eyes filled with tears. The Emperor asked her the cause; she said: 'I felt my father's hand in mine!' 'How could you tell it was his?' asked her husband, incredulously. 'There was a defect in one of the fingers,' she said, 'just as there was in life.' The Emperor put his hand under the table; he felt the hand and the defect in it of which she had spoken.

At the next séance the Emperor and Empress chose four other sitters:— The Duchesse de Bassano, the Duchesse de Montebello, and the two Chamberlains, Count Tascher de la Pagerie and the Marquis de Belmont; this, with Home, made seven sitters, and he always preferred the number not to exceed eight. The massive table rose several feet into the air, and astounded them still further by returning to the floor as lightly as a feather falling. An unseen force shook the apartment, till the crystal pendants of the chandelier tinkled loudly against each other. A bell that had been placed on the table was lifted by invisible hands, the Empress's handkerchief was taken gently from her hand and rose, floating in the air. While the hands of all the sitters rested on the table, other hands appeared. The small hand of a child moved towards the Duchesse de Montebello; she shrank back, terrified, but the Empress, exclaiming 'Moi, je n'ai pas peur!', caught the little hand in hers, and felt it gradually melt back into air.

The third séance produced what was perhaps the most remarkable effect. It was held in the Salon Louis Quinze. On the table round which the party sat, a sheet of paper and a pencil were laid, so that any messages which were received might be written down; but someone other than the sitters first made use of them. A man's hand, small and beautifully shaped as the great Emperor's had been, took the pencil and wrote the single word 'Napoleon'. The writing was recognized as Napoleon's autograph. In intense emotion, Eugénie asked to kiss the hand. It was raised to her lips and then to her husband's. The hand was distinctly seen by all the sitters, this séance, like all the others in the Tuileries, being held in a room full of light.

The acceptance, the enthusiasm, Home aroused in the royal circle, led to his giving séances at the Palace almost every night. One of the most poignant concerned Madame de Lourmel, the widow of a general killed in the Crimean War. She exclaimed how much she longed to feel her husband's hand in hers. At her words, a heavy, gilded armchair moved away from the wall and approached the sitters 'in a curiously oscillating manner, rocking up and down till it was held up by a seam in the carpet.' It raised itself to surmount this obstacle and travelled to the séance table where it continued to rock itself. Madame de Lourmel exclaimed that her husband had never been able to sit in a chair without rocking it. Home had never seen the General but he said that he saw him now; he described his appearance; he had one wound in his head, another in his chest; both were smeared with blood. At this dreadful moment, the widow felt a hand press hers. Aghast as she was, she was thankful for this token of her husband's survival, and his presence.[12]

78

The fame of the manifestations, as well as caricatured accounts of them, resounded all over Paris; it would not have been possible to conceal them from Père de Ravignan, even if Home had wished to be anything but candid. As it was, he had an interview with the priest which ended their connection. Père de Ravignan commanded him to forswear all communication with spirits. Home said, all over again, that the communications came upon him and he could not prevent them. The priest said that, this being so, it was Home's duty to shut himself up in his room and not listen to any rappings or pay the slightest attention to whatever phenomena might occur in his presence. Not, it was implied, to demonstrate them before an excited audience in the Salon Louis Quinze.

Home declared that the strain of such solitary confinement would be more than his nerves could endure, and how could he help paying attention to the phenomena? 'If I were to strike on this table with my hand, could you avoid hearing?' 'Yes,' replied Père de Ravignan without hesitation. 'I only hear when I wish to hear and see when I wish to see.'[13] As statements of mental condition, the medium's passive state and and the priest's one of conscious self-control, are each as remarkable as the other; they were of course totally irreconcilable.

Home's success in the Imperial circle was a cause of serious offence to Père de Ravignan as it absolutely prevented his obeying the priest's commands; the success continued a brilliant course, with constant séances held in the Palace and Home's developing a warm relationship with the Emperor and Empress. Within a month of his being presented at the Tuileries, Eugénie had become so familiar with his family circumstances and so much his friend that she offered to send for his young sister Christine and to have her educated at the exclusive Convent of the Sacred Heart in the Rue de Varennes where she had received her own education. The offer was accepted gratefully and Home prepared to depart on 20 March, to bring his sister from America to France.

The fact of his being about to leave Paris abruptly at such a height of success, caused rumours that he had offended the Emperor and been dismissed in disgrace. Although the truth was the opposite of this, an element in the situation seemed to support the fabrication. The fame of Home's proceedings had aroused a groundless but, on the face of it, a not unnatural fear. The Empress, emotional and easily swayed, had at this time a considerable influence over her husband. She was at the height of her remarkable beauty and she had borne the Emperor his heir, the Prince Imperial who was now a little over a year old. The possibility was entertained that Home might be the spy of a foreign government. With the Emperor himself convinced of the genuineness of Home's powers, and the Empress completely *détraquée* about him, might not a dangerous situation be immanent? Very strong protests were made to the Emperor about the frequency of Home's séances at the Palace, and the Minister of Foreign Affairs, Count Alexander Walewski, Napoleon Bonaparte's son by Maria Walewska, threatened to resign if his advice were not attended to, and Home dismissed from the Court. Napoleon III did not take the Minister's advice, but it was true that when Home returned from America, though it was to another era of court favour as brilliant as the last, he did not hold sittings at the Tuileries Palace, the official seat of the French court. The Emperor and Empress sent for him to the Palaces at Fontainebleau, at Compiègne, and at the Villa Eugénie at Biarritz. It was said, but clearly without foundation, seeing Home's steady maintenance of the Imperial favour, that he had given great offence by a prophecy. Home's powers were habitually shown through telekinesis, levitation, materialization, clairvoyance; he very rarely prophesied; but on one occasion he foretold that the baby Prince Imperial would never ascend the French throne. That he should have made to the child's parents a prophecy than which almost nothing could displease them more, is astonishing until it is remembered that in most of his séances Home spoke in trance and had no recollection afterwards of what he had said. It is more than probable that he himself did not remember having made this augury. Twenty-two years later other people remembered it, when the Prince Imperial was killed in the Zulu War.

The rumours that Home had been dismissed from the court were fostered by his sudden departure on 20 March. Before he went, he achieved, unselfconsciously and without volition, a wonderful instance of healing.

He had had a letter from a Madame de Cardonne, saying that for the last four years her son had been completely deaf after an attack of typhoid fever. Treatments and operations had been useless, but she had now had a dream in which she had seen her mother and also one whom she knew to be Home's mother, and the latter had urged her to seek out Home at once so that her son Emile might be cured.

Home was so busy in preparing for his voyage and had had so many calls and letters and applications, that he had been obliged to ignore Madame de Cardonne's letter. The next morning the lady, bringing her son with her, came to Home's room in the Champs Elysées. The urgency imparted by the dream was explained by the fact that Home was departing that very afternoon. Her desperation carried Madame de Cardonne through this situation. She sat on a chair near the sofa on which Home was sitting. Home beckoned to the boy to come and sit beside him. Emile de Cardonne was fourteen years old, 'with,' Home said, 'large, dreamy blue eyes which looked as if they would supply the place of hearing, with their deep, thoughtful, enquiring gaze.' Madame de Cardonne began a passionate account of the boy's fever, the resulting deafness, the surgical operations, that had been of no avail. Home had been carried away by his sympathetic listening; he had drawn the boy to his side, so that Emile's head was resting on his shoulder. When the mother described the acutely painful operations he had undergone, Home pityingly stroked the child's head. As he did so, Emile de Cardonne lifted his head, exclaiming excitedly: 'Maman! je t'entends!' 'Emile!' cried his mother. 'Quoi?' he said. The realization that he had heard his name and replied to it, was too much for Madame de Cardonne. She fainted. Fortunately there were, in the room, the de Komars' sister, Princess de Beauveau, and Miss Ellice, an English lady. Home said: 'On her recovery the scene was a most thrilling one; the poor mother asking continually questions for the mere pleasure of hearing her child's reply.' Writing in 1863[14] Home said: 'The boy was able to resume his studies and has continued to hear perfectly up to the present time.'

It was typical of Home's attitude, said Madame Home, that after this extraordinary feat, he left for America that afternoon, without troubling himself in the least to make public the particulars of this wonderful cure to obtain the attestations of the mother and the two witnesses; but in the great hoard of letters left by her husband, she found some which Madame de Cardonne had sent him on his return from America. One, of 30 May, 1857, said: 'Let me add myself to the number of those who love you and who welcome your return.' She asks leave to introduce to him Victorien Sardou, already celebrated as a dramatist, though the height of his fame was not reached till thirty years later when he wrote plays for Sarah Bernhardt. Madame Home found a letter of Sardou's of nearly the same date, asking permission to call. This she mentions as in 1888, the date of the publication of her book; Sardou could have been called on to testify that the story of Emile de Cardonne's restored hearing was not a groundless myth. Though Home had left the apartment in the Rue Champs Elysées immediately, without taking any steps to publicize this act of healing, Princess de Beauveau, Miss Ellice and Madame de Cardonne herself had spoken of it so freely that though the apartment was now empty of its tenant, numbers of people called there, asking to see the room where the cure had taken place.


Home was often the victim of violent and vindictive abuse; it was the natural counterpart of his great success. What was markedly extraordinary was his being the object, not of exaggerations or mistakes but of sheer, invented slanders, in which the lies about him were told with such circumstance as would lead people who knew nothing of the matter to assume that they must be true.

His departure from Paris, by arrangement with the Empress, to fetch his sister, immediately gave rise to rumours of his having been expelled from the court, or from the country, even, for a variety of grave misdemeanours. The *New York Herald* stated that he had stolen £30,000 and was 'banished for ever from France,' when, as Home said: 'I had at that very moment my return ticket in my pocket, and knew that an Imperial Prince, then on a visit to the Emperor, was awaiting my return.' The *Indépendence Belge* declared that the Emperor had banished Home because His Majesty feared the effects of further diabolical scenes on the Empress's reason[15]. The most striking instance of invention was produced by the English magazine, the *Court Journal,* which published an article about him that sounds as if it had been derived from a French source. This said that in one of the great houses in Paris, which it did not name, there had been an illustrious gathering to witness Home's phenomena; those present had included the Maréchal Baraguay d'Hilliers, Guinot the journalist and Nadaud, a composer celebrated for the words and music of satirical songs. The introductory sentence would have warned any reader familiar with Home's mediumship that the article was an impudent 'cod'. 'The wizard,' it said, 'had promised that night to evoke the' spirits and render them visible to the sight.' It was known to everyone who had sat with him that Home invariably disclaimed any power of raising spirits. He acted, he said, as a conductor merely, and until his powers were actually made use of by spirits wanting to communicate, he had no idea whether any would come or not. The article continued, all lights were extinguished 'except a solitary taper on the mantelpiece behind the figure of the practitioner, which cast its long, gigantic shadow on the walls and ceiling of the room.' Complete silence reigned, in which the wizard's voice demanded, whose spirit should be summoned? At the end of the room, a faint whisper was uttered: 'Let it be Socrates!' The wizard solemnly bade the spirit of Socrates appear and stand before him. A figure entered the dim room, enveloped in floating drapery; the bald head, beard and crushed nose proclaimed it to be Socrates, 'evoked from his slumber of centuries to furnish sport for a Paris salon.' It disappeared, and the operator. 'shaken to his very finger-ends,' declared himself astonished at the success of his summons. The whispering voice which had asked for Socrates, now asked for the evocation of Frederick the Great. The wizard again stretched out his hand towards the door, 'although doubtful if his electric current would be strong enough to accomplish two evocations so rapidly, one after the other, and called aloud for Frederick the Great, King of Prussia.' There was a moment's pause that was truly awful. Then there appeared, gliding through the doorway, a short figure, also wrapped in draperies which it held together at the waist, but with the head surmounted by the unmistakeable little cocked hat. The figure advanced to within a few paces of the magician. Great drops of sweat were seen to roll from the latter's forehead. 'Enough!' he cried, and charged the apparition to disappear, but it held its ground. 'I have been made the dupe of some mystification!' the wizard exclaimed. A loud and uncontrollable laugh burst from the apparition's lips. 'What, don't you know me?' it cried. 'I am Nadaud and here is my friend Socrates, otherwise le Maréchal Baraguay d'Hilliers, ready to appear again whenever you choose, and close at hand, my comrade Eugène Guinot, in life, and Alcibiades in death, waiting to be summoned after me, as he would most assuredly have been, had I been able to follow up the joke.' Mr. Home, the article said, was struck powerless and dumb, but pleaded that he had discovered the impostures; he 'asserted that the spirits summoned would have appeared, for that he does possess the faculty of raising them.' Home not only never claimed this faculty, he always denied that he had it. The article continued: 'in a few moments he disappeared, and next day we heard, without astonishment, of his departure from Paris.'

It was said that Home sometimes asked a certain number of sitters to withdraw, if there were too many present. He had done this at Mr. Rymer's house and at the first séance at the Tuileries. It was also recorded that he occasionally objected to the presence, not of those who were sceptical, but of people whom he immediately saw to be offensive and disrupting. The article with a certain tinge of verisimilitude, explained that the three 'mauvais plaisants' had been angered by their exclusion from a séance and were determined to revenge themselves.

It is hardly necessary to repeat Home's assertion with which he introduced the passage[16], 'I can only say that the whole of the following statements, names, dates, circumstances and persons, are false from beginning to end.' The significant aspect of the affair is the extent of deliberate lying to which someone in the world of journalism had committed himself. However wild the inaccuracy of press statements may be, it can usually be explained by rapid writing, the too hasty acceptance of a sensational story, or the alterations that inevitably modify an anecdote as it passes from mouth to mouth, but none of these explanations can account for the article in the *Court Journal*. The story is thoroughly thought-out and the details carefully added. It was of course possible to publish it in England only, where numerous papers copied it, since Guinot, d'Hilliers and Nadaud were too well-known in Paris for a French journalist to use their names. Nadaud as the writer of satirical songs was a plausible choice for one of the protagonists, and the writer credited the *mauvais plaisants*, and also their supposititious audience with knowing that the handsome, arrogant and dissolute Alcibiades was a friend of Socrates, and that if Socrates were brought on, it was appropriate to introduce Alcibiades as well: a degreee of knowledge which such jokers would hardly be expected to possess today. Home said[17] that he had taken no steps to put the slander down, because: 'If I had begun to contradict all the falsehoods told about me, my time would have been fully occupied in vain attempts to stop a torrent which seems as if it would never cease to flow.' He quotes several instances of lies about him published in newspapers, but this one is particularly interesting; it gives a long, detailed and entirely groundless narration to which Home's name is attached; this is exactly the method which, seven years later, was adopted by Robert Browning.

# XI

## The Empress's Confidence

In May 1857, Home returned from Philadelphia, bringing his sister Christine, whom the Empress took into her care and placed in the Convent of the Sacred Heart where she had been educated herself. So far from being deprived of the Imperial favour and forbidden to show his face at court, he at once re-entered the charmed and brilliant circle which had looked forward to his return. But Home had received introductions to influential persons in Constantinople and he had not long resumed his life in Paris before he determined to make a voyage to Turkey. He was an excellent traveller, intrepid in making long journeys and eagerly, good-naturedly, identifying himself with a foreign scene. This time, however, his plan was frustrated. On many occasions he had been conscious of supernatural encouragement and also of supernatural warnings; now, when all his plans were made, his boxes packed and his papers in order, he sensed a piece of ominous advice. He went to pay a call on his friend Princess Marie-Amélie, a cousin of the Emperor and daughter of the Grand Duke of Baden. This lady had married an expatriate Scots nobleman, the eleventh Duke of Hamilton, and the couple lived in Paris at the Hôtel d'Abbé. As Home was sitting in the Duchess's drawing-room, raps sounded all about, and he received the message that he must abandon the idea of a visit to Turkey, as forthcoming political troubles would make the country dangerous to a traveller. Home was in one of the recurring states of ill health to which sufferers from tuberculosis are liable, and as the Duchess was present when his scheme of a visit to Turkey was forbidden, it seems likely that it was she who suggested, instead, one to the famous health resort of Baden-Baden, which was in her father's duchy. Home stayed there, at the Hôtel d'Angleterre, during August and September 1857. Here, no doubt through the Duchess of Hamilton's introduction, he was presented to the King of Wurtemberg, the Prince of Nassau and Frederick William the Prince Regent of Prussia. All three were deeply impressed by the evidence of his supernatural powers. The Prince Regent recalled this thirteen years later. During the Franco-Prussian War, Home was acting as foreign correspondent for an American newspaper and he and Frederick William met in Paris, when the latter was King of Prussia.

While he was at Baden-Baden, Home received a supernatural warning of a more urgent nature than the one delivered to him in the Duchess of Hamilton's drawing-room. He said:[1] 'My guardian spirits continually told me at that time that there was trouble in store for me, but that from the darkness light would come, and that whatever might seem a loss, would in the end prove a gain, and in all this they were correct.' This makes particularly interesting the glimpse of Home gained by Sir Horace Rumbold[2]; the latter describes an August evening in the park, where the crowd, in closely packed seats before the kiosk, were listening to the playing of the Austrian military band; 'the moon stole above the ruins of the Alte Schloss, tipping the tall trees with silver and marking their shadows on the quiet lawn and walks beyond.' Among the concourse of German Royalty, French arts and literature, Parisian fashion and frailty (these latter all extremely charming), Rumbold distinguished many well-known figures: he said, 'a face in the throng not to be forgotten for its weird, haunted look;' — that of 'Home the spiritualist, whose startling impostures are just beginning to attract public notice.' Anyone interested in Home is willing to ignore Rumbold's phrase: — 'startling impostures', for the sake of the eye-witness view of him, in the summer moonlight and the lamps of the bandstand, among the crowd, like a French Impressionist's picture of the park.

He continued to feel oppressed, and left Baden-Baden, returning to the French coast and settling at Bayonne, as the guest of a Polish family, who may have been the brothers de Komar and their two sisters. Here he was near the summer retreat of the Imperial Court, the Villa Eugénie at Biarritz. This luxurious modern palace stood low on the shore, glittering in the heat and light and the salty air, just above the pounding breakers of the Atlantic. When the Empress heard of his arrival at Bayonne, she sent him an urgent invitation to attend the court. The Polish family came to Biarritz with him and established themselves there so that Home continued to be their guest. He said:[3] 'Here I was told that the first darkening of the cloud would come, and that those who might have understood me better would be led to think ill of me by those about them, who, to serve a purpose, would fabricate a statement, the very absurdity of which ought to have been its refutation.' At the Villa Eugénie, there was in attendance Dr. Barthez, who had been appointed physician to the little Prince Imperial. He had not seen Home before, but from what he had heard of him, he feared the medium's influence over the Empress. In letters which he wrote to his wife during the Imperial holiday at Biarritz, he said how much he admired the Empress's beauty, her charm, her graciousness, but he thought that her emotional nature made her vulnerable to such dangers as Home was likely to expose her to. He said:[4] 'She is a child, giving herself to every impression of the moment and allowing it to appear in every feature and every movement of her person.' He had seen her playing games with the Emperor himself and her ladies, 'Like an escaped school-girl, running, shrieking, gesticulating.' Seeing that she was of so volatile a temperament, the Doctor was uneasy when Home's arrival at Bayonne was the signal for him to be summoned to the Villa Eugénie. As Barthez told his wife: 'I understood at once . . . all the advantages their Majesties' enemies might derive . . . by spreading the report that they consult spirits upon the direction of the affairs of the Empire.' He expected to be unfavourably impressed by Home, nor was he disappointed. 'As soon as he entered I disliked him intensely. His simple, timid, half-awkward air seemed to me to conceal a very able *savoir faire*.' The Empress had said that the presence of sceptical persons was likely to interfere with the success of a sitting; Barthez took this as a hint and withdrew. Some evenings later at dinner he was sitting next but two to Home. 'I am convinced,' he wrote 'that his half simple air hides a real duplicity. However,' he added, 'this second impression was not so disagreeable as the first.' After dinner the company seated themselves for a séance and this time Dr. Barthez was of the circle. The date must have been 4 September 1857, because he wrote to his wife on 5 September, saying the sitting had taken place on the previous evening. 'I seated myself at the table,' he wrote, 'together with the others, placing our hands on the table. At once the table started to move and skip about.' Knocking was heard under the table, raps answering other raps, 'directed,' Barthez said, 'by an intelligent entity.' An accordion, which Mr. Home held in one hand only, 'played a delightful tune.' All this, however, took place under the table. Presently, the medium being in a trance, a spirit spoke through him saying that there were too many in the party, and pointing out those persons to whose presence in the room he objected. Dr. Barthez was one of these. The doctor put this down to the fact that his face was wearing a mocking and incredulous smile. 'So I had to go,' he said. He heard the next morning that nothing remarkable happened during the rest of the evening, 'except that a table jumped up into the air with all its four legs.'

Speaking of these effects, Barthez said: — 'You will now be asking me what I think of all this. All these facts that I have seen and heard, they are true, exactly as true as the fact that I have just now had my breakfast. The facts do not comply with the common rule of things, and with that which allows me to judge them in accordance with my knowledge of physics. All this means that I cannot explain them.' But, he said, this was not to admit that they were the result of spirit activity. Between the facts and that explanation of them there existed a yawning chasm, which, for the moment, he found it impossible to bridge. This was a clear-sighted and rational assessment; but Barthez went on: 'I am altogether ignorant as to how they occur, but as they always occur under a table (where one is not allowed to feel or examine) I claim the right to disbelieve in spirits and to suspect the existence of very natural methods, which I cannot discover.'

It is remarkable that Barthez should say sitters were not allowed to investigate under the table. He had been present at one séance only, where he clearly had not attempted investigation, since if he had attempted it and been prevented, he would undoubtedly have said so; while on various celebrated occasions it is on record that the sitters took to themselves the right of investigation and dropped on their knees or lay flat on the floor. Adolphus Trollope and Sir David Brewster had done this at Ealing, (to say nothing of the latter's having been frequently invited to do it at Cox's Hotel). Napoleon III had searched beneath the table when the hand of the great Napoleon had appeared before the company's eyes, and some years later, Prince Murat meeting Home in London asked the latter if he remembered the meeting at the Tuileries when he had gone under the table and laid hold of Home's feet, declaring he would 'find out his tricks'. 'Was I not a saucy little dog?' the Prince said, and Home laughed and said yes! The Prince said that after Home had left the room, 'the Emperor leant forward with his arms on the table and said, in the most impressive manner: Whoever says that Home is a charlatan *is a liar*.'[5]

Nonetheless, Barthez had inaugurated, or strengthened, an atmosphere of denigration of Home, in which Home's lowered health obviously played its part. In the passage of *Incidents in my Life*,[6] in which he described the foreboding of misfortune which he was to encounter at Biarritz, Home does not mention Barthez, but he gives some account of the rumours about his methods of simulating phenomena, and from their position in the work, it seems probable that these *canards* were put about at this time: 'A very popular idea in Paris is that my legs are so formed as to be capable of elongation and that my feet are like those of a baboon. Many people suppose that when I go to a strange house, my tables have to be sent first . . . that they are always copiously draped and that I take with me wax hands and arms to show at the proper moment . . . others have stated that when I am said to rise in the air, it is only a balloon filled with gas in the shape of a man.'

Dr. Barthez presently felt that he had received tangible satisfaction, settling disquieting doubts and resolving enigmas. On 25 September 1857, he wrote to his wife, saying that at least one of

Home's methods had been exposed. 'The thing is quite simple. Mr. Home wears shoes of thin leather, easy to put on and take off, he has also, I believe, socks cut in a manner that leave his toes naked. At the moment he thinks fit, he slips off one of his shoes and with his foot he pulls a dress here, a dress over there, he rings a bell, knocks on this side or that, and once the thing has been done, he quickly puts on his shoe again.' Barthez then cited the source of this information, a member of the French Court. 'This has been seen by Monsieur Morio, who has written out and signed a fine report, giving all necessary details to authenticate his discovery. Home saw that what was behind his spirits act was guessed, and I assure you that he cut a pitiful figure.'

This being the only instance in which a definite and detailed accusation of fraud was brought against Home by anyone approaching respectable authority, to people interested in him, Dr. Zorab's comments on it are of great importance. He first makes the point that Barthez himself was not present at the sitting at which Morio is said to have guessed Home's fraudulent method. (Barthez, he says, used the word 'deviner', to guess.) This sitting was not the one from which Barthez was excluded, for as he told his wife afterwards, he heard that on that occasion nothing much occurred after he had gone, except a complete levitation of the table. The date of the séance at which Morio claimed to have made his discovery must have been between 4 September and 24 September 1857. He called Morio's report a fine one, but Zorab demonstrates that he had not read it himself. He does not say that he had, and his not having done so is borne out by the sentence: 'He has, I believe, socks cut in a manner that leave his toes naked.' Zorab further urges, that had Morio exposed Home during a séance, some one or other of the sitters would have undoubtedly spread such sensational news. As it is, no statement supporting Morio's discovery had been produced by anyone. Not only was the report not seen by Barthez himself: it was not, so far as can be ascertained, seen by anybody. When there was so much hostility towards Home among the Imperial ministry, such as was, for instance, entertained by Count Walewski, it is not possible to believe that a document so damaging to Home's credit and influence should not have been produced if it had been available.

Barthez said that Morio came forward with what he claimed was his discovery some time in the second half of September, and that Home, as a result of this exposure, declared himself ill and retired to the villa where his Polish friends were taking care of him, 'where they lodge him, look after him and coddle him.' The Empress, alarmed by the report of Home's condition, asked the doctor to visit him. Dr. Barthez must have been a competent physician but his own report of how he behaved to the patient hardly suggests that he was. He found

Home's pulse normal and therefore he paid no attention to the fact that he was excited and torpid by turns, that his eyes were reddened and his face swollen. Home began to say that the spirits were troubling him and then, Barthez said, 'pretended' to go into a trance in which his eyes turned upward and were fixed. Barthez, in his own words, 'took him by the arm and shook it rather roughly.' 'Come, Mr. Home,' he said, 'let all the spirits be. You know I don't believe in them.' According to him, then Home came out of this trance at once. Dr. Barthez did not credit the reality of a trance state, and in his own view was merely acting with common-sense, but anyone with experience of dealing with mediums has been taught not only to keep silence but to avoid any form of noise at all as the medium comes out of trance, so that the transition from one state of consciousness to the other may be effected as gently as possible. Barthez' own account of how he shook Home roughly by the arm makes painful reading. Zorab has pointed out that in the autumn of 1857, a few weeks after, according to Barthez, Home's credibility had been exploded by Morio's report, Home gave several séances in Paris which exhibited remarkable mediumistic powers, once more working at their height. One of these was with the Baron Du Potet, who had, from his youth, been engaged in the study of 'animal magnetism', otherwise known as mesmerism or hypnotism. Du Potet's query was the one which confronts every investigator who has reached the stage of accepting that Home's phenomena were supernatural. 'Do Home's phenomena prove spirit intercourse, or is there some other power, some other faculty, possessed of some living men, at work to make tables rise up in the air, move furniture, etc?' Home believed that they proved spirit intercourse, and that this was what he had been sent into the world to show. It was the strength of this belief that caused him to accept a great deal of the misrepresentation and abuse that came his way with passive unhappiness rather than anger.

Home's enemies had said, during his visit at the Villa Eugénie that the Empress was now disappointed in him, that he was no longer the Home of former days. On her own showing, she was a firm believer in his powers to the end of her days. At the close of her life, she was visited at her villa at Menton by M. Le Roy Dupré, who had many conversations with her about the past. He said her mind was still active and her memory clear. He brought up the matter of Home and his alleged exposure. This seemed so important to the parapsychologist Dr. Osty, that he asked M. Le Roy Dupré for a very careful repetition of what the Empress had said. The note the latter made for Dr. Osty, dated 26 November, 1934, said:[7] 'She admitted at once the reality of paranormal phenomena, quoting precise and detailed examples ... She confirmed that the anecdote propagated about Home was false

. . . Home in the course of a séance at the Tuileries, was said to have placed his foot, after first having taken off his patent-leather shoe, in the Emperor's hand, according to others, on his knee. The Empress even seemed to be somewhat shocked that people could believe it to have been possible that such an audacious and crass want of respect for the Sovereign could have taken place.' This account of M. Le Roy Dupré speaks of the incident as having taken place at the Tuileries, whereas Dr. Barthez places it at the Villa Eugénie when he himself was in attendance there. In spite of the confusion, one fact emerges unmistakably: the Empress was convinced of Home's integrity.

Perhaps the most effective vindication of Home on this matter comes from Frank Podmore.[8] Podmore had a strong prejudice against Home and says that we are 'entitled to assume' that he was 'a practised conjuror'. He gives no evidence whatever for this assertion, only a string of unconvincing suggestions as to how Home might have produced his effects by conjuring. From such a source, any tribute to Home's honesty, however wryly conceded, is valuable; and when one has read Dr. Barthez' account of Morio's report, it is satisfactory to find that Podmore said: 'There is no evidence of any weight that he was ever privately detected in trickery.'

# XII

## Marriage

The widespread desire to investigate the supernatural, and the rising star of Home, the medium whose powers were the greatest on record, caused an extraordinary activity in America, England, France, Italy, Germany, the Netherlands and Russia.

In Holland a group of hard-headed rationalists had bound themselves together in a society they called De Dageraad, the Dawn. Its members repudiated all belief in a spirit world, miracles, divine intervention, heaven and hell. They ran a paper, also called *De Dageraad*. A Dutchman, Baron J. N. Tiedemann Martheze, had lived for a long time on an estate outside Paris and was an ardent Francophile, but he wanted to keep abreast with the intellectual life of his own country. He took in *De Dageraad*, and having met Home in 1857, he wrote to the paper's editors, offering to bring Home to Holland at his own expense, that proofs of spirit communication might be offered to them. The offer was readily accepted; as one of the writers in *De Dageraad* had said: 'One should not lose sight of the fact that there exist natural forces which science is still unable to explain.'

In the February of 1858, Tiedemann brought Home to The Hague. When his arrival was known, Queen Sophia of Holland invited him to give a séance at the Palace of The Hague. Home sat with the Queen two or three times and nothing occurred. This was the first of three sets of sittings he gave in Holland. The second series was in Amsterdam to the directors of *De Dageraad*, the third in The Hague again, at the house of Major Revius, the commander of the Royal guard, who was himself a spiritualist.

The directors of *De Dageraad* had arranged for Tiedemann and Home to stay at a hotel in Amsterdam, which, Home said,[1] was perishingly cold. The month was February and 'the cheerless cold of the rooms with their bleak walls and beam-bare ceilings' was not much mended by the fire, 'which was but the ghost of such as we are accustomed to in England.' The body of inquirers arrived, ten professional men of keen and sceptical intelligence, and the first séance began. Dr. Zorab has explained the fortunate chance by which an eye witness account of the three Amsterdam sittings was made available. After the third series of sittings at the house of Major Revius, the latter published an account of them, and this was answered by an anonymous pamphlet, declaring that all the phenomena described by Major Revius could be accounted for by 'induced hallucinations' and unconscious muscular action. The *Dageraad* directors were incensed by this slur on their faculties, particularly as some of them, during the sittings, had put themselves through various mental tests, to prove to themselves that they were in normal possession of their senses. They did not subscribe to the theory of spirit communication, but they insisted on their opinion of the genuineness of the phenomena. A report of all three séances held with them was written by one of them, F. C. Günst, a doctor of philosophy, who owned a printing and publishing establishment.

The first séance was held in the evening, the next at midday and the third in the evening again. The occurrences were largely those which Home's mediumship usually produced: the table 'made sliding movements which the sitters on one side or the other tried to check but could not control; it tilted so that it looked as if the lighted candelabra must fall off, and it rose into the air in spite of all efforts to hold it down.

One of the doctors present took a light in his hand and got under the table to see if any machinery were to be discovered, but in vain. While he remained on the floor, Home asked for the table to become light, and it was then as easily moved as a feather; he asked for it to become heavy, and it was suddenly immovable by their united efforts.

The next day the sitters numbered five and as the great table used before was too large for the company, the hotel waiters were asked to bring in a kitchen table. The chief feature at this sitting was the answering by raps of questions mentally asked by the sitters. That evening the third séance was held, consisting of seven sitters, of whom one was a lady. This meeting was the occasion of really alarming disturbance. There were, first, soft raps all over the room, which changed to loud knockings, and these were accompanied by 'a complete rocking movement of the floor, which became so violent that, together with the chairs on which we were seated, we felt ourselves going up and down as if on a rocking horse. We experienced the same sensation and movement as when sitting in a carriage on springs while driving along the high road.' And now, the report continued, 'phenomena were produced which would make those who possessed weaker nerves than we had, believe there indeed existed a world of spirits. Here are the facts. One of us suddenly asked his neighbour if he had touched him.' His friend said No. The questioner declared that something had touched his cheek. The sceptics laughed loudly, saying they too would like to be touched. Hardly had they spoken when they felt touches on arm, hand, knee, cheek. 'In the case of one of us, this touching and contacting went on continuously for twenty minutes. Another man was so violently clutched that he jumped from his chair.' The report went on to describe handkerchiefs, wrapped round a sitter's finger or wrist, and tugged away by an unseen force. 'After this, many experiments were conducted, observed and tested with the greatest coolness. But all was in vain. We saw the phenomena happening but could not explain them. And nothing could be observed that could give rise to even the slightest suspicion that Mr. Home was acting in a fraudulent manner.'[2]

Major Revius in his account of the sittings at his house in The Hague described happenings very similar to those experienced in Amsterdam and he added a personal note; he had imagined that Home would turn out to be a powerful mesmerist, but in this he had found himself mistaken. The young man was polite, friendly, melancholy; so far from giving the impression of conscious power which Revius had expected, he looked like a sleep-walker.

The *De Dageraad* directors had accepted the honesty of Home's mediumship but had refused to accord it a spiritualist interpretation. The Queen of Holland believed in both its aspects. The first séances Home had held at the Palace had been without result, but before his departure he was asked to pay one more visit. This time the Queen asked him to choose the room in which the séance should be conducted. Accompanied by the Queen, a lady in waiting and some members of the Royal family, Home passed through the range of lofty state apartments till he paused outside a door. It proved to be locked. The room had been the nursery of the Queen's dead child, Prince Mauritz, and as a rule no one was allowed to enter it except herself. The door was unlocked and the party went inside. Home never gave any account of what then happened, he only said, when writing of the affair twenty years later in the *Spiritual Magazine*, that when the séance was over the Queen's eyes were full of tears and that she took from her finger a sapphire and diamond ring and gave it to him. In saying so, he perhaps made the presentation a little more dramatic than it actually was. Madame Home's account of it, made from working on her husband's papers,[3] says that the Queen sent him the ring, with a note saying: 'I send you a grateful reconnaissance.'

A series of engagements had been made for Home in Brussels, and as he was to leave the following day, he was obliged to refuse an invitation from a deputation of students from Leyden University; but when he arrived at Brussels, the engagements had to be cancelled. He had taken a chill at the hotel in Amsterdam, and this, acting on the condition of his chest, made his seriously unwell. He found that his power had forsaken him, and spirits told him that it would be some time before it was restored, and that before it was, events of great importance to himself would have come upon him.

He went back to Paris, where the doctor he consulted told him to get into a warmer climate at once and recommended Italy. Home was most unwilling to go, 'in as much', he said, 'as every time I left Paris, some silly stories were put into circulation, such as my being ordered away by the Emperor or that I went to fly from the law. I remained there for two or three weeks, growing daily worse.[4] The baseless stories, with their painful irritation, began even before he left, and one of them was serious.

Home at last departed for Italy; he went to friends in Turin but there the snow was thick on the ground. He went south to Pisa, but there the cold was still intense, and he went south again, to Rome. On 13 March, 1858, a friend telegraphed to him, asking for a letter to confirm that he was in the Holy City. Home sent this at once and presently received the explanation: 'Scandal says you have been arrested and that you are in prison at Mazas.' The Mazas Prison, which stood on what is now the Boulevard Diderot, was one of the largest in Paris. 'The Parisian newspapers,' Home said, 'took up the report, and it was confirmed by them that I was truly in prison in the Mazas — Persons, even in official positions, told their friends that they had seen and spoken to me in that prison, and one, an officer, went so far as to say that he had accompanied me there in the carriage.' This, though much more sinister than the offensive but ludicrous narrative of the *Court Journal*, was of the same *genre*: a circumstantial story, apparently vouched for by respectable people, without one word of truth in it. Home's friend sent the former's letter, with the Roman address and postmark to *La Patrie* and *Le Nord*, and the slander was officially stopped, at least as regarded the Press. Home said:[5] that he knew 'the origin and cause of this intrigue.' He did not disclose it, but it appeared so dangerous to some of his friends that Prince Murat, at great trouble and expense to himself, sent to Germany, Italy and England to investigate the foundations of the libel, 'and generously gave me his public and private testimony to its entire untruth.'

In Rome, Home tried to nurse himself back to health; he refused almost all social invitations, but one afternoon he was walking with a friend on the Pincian Hill, and the latter was telling him earnestly about a Russian family, that of Count de Koucheleff Bessborodko, then in Rome, who wanted very much to meet him. Home said he was so unwell he must be excused; but at that moment a carriage pulled up beside them, and before Home knew what was happening, his friend presented him to Countess de Koucheleff. The Countess asked Home to come to supper that evening, saying that they kept very late hours. So, in this unpremeditated way, began the events of great importance to himself which the spirits had promised him.

At ten that evening Home presented himself at the Koucheleff party. For the first two hours he saw only the Countess and her guests — but at midnight he was taken into the supper-room, and there he saw for the first time a girl, to whom the Countess introduced him as her sister. Alexandra de Kroll, known by the diminutive Sacha, was seventeen, of a small figure and a most winning, gentle gaiety and sweetness. Home said, that at the sight of her, 'a strange impression came over me at once, and I knew she was to be my wife.' He was seated at the supper-table between the Countess and this charming girl, who said to him laughingly: 'Mr. Home, you will be married before the year is ended!'

'Why?' he asked. She said that that was the saying in Russia, when a person sat down at table between two sisters. Home said: 'I made no reply.' Indeed, the moment was too weighty for speech. In twelve days' time, so far as it rested with themselves, they were engaged and waiting only to gain the permission of her mother, who was in Russia. The rash, the altogether extraordinary rapidity with which the engagement was formed, was justified by the serene and perfect happiness of the marriage. The attraction which Alexandra de Kroll exerted over Home needs no explanation, but it is interesting that his charm for her seems to have owed, overtly at least, nothing to his psychic influence. This may, subconsciously, have strengthened the mutual sympathy, but during the twelve momentous days which ended in their engagement, Home seems to have said to her little or nothing of his mediumistic powers, although the Countess had sought the introduction to him because of them. At the evening party given to announce the betrothal, the guests were dancing, while the engaged pair sat on a sofa, and Sacha said abruptly: 'Do tell me about spirit-rapping, for, you know, I don't believe in it?' Home said: 'Mademoiselle, I trust you will ever bear in mind that I have a mission entrusted to me. It is a great and holy one. I cannot speak with you about a thing which you have not seen, and therefore cannot understand. I can only say it is a great truth.' The lights and the music, the dancing figures moving in front of them and her sensibility enhanced by great happiness, combined to bring a glowing moment of perception. Her eyes filled with tears; she took his hand and said: 'If your mission can bring any comfort to those who are less happy than we are, or be in any way a consolation to mankind, you will always find me ready and willing to do all I can to help you in it.' Home wrote that she was faithful to this promise to the last moment of her short life.

It was understandable that the young man and the girl fell in love; but it is a matter of some astonishment that Alexandra's family should so readily have accepted Home as a husband for her. She was very young and most attractive; the de Kroll family were well-to-do and moved in the highest social circle of St. Petersburg; Alexandra herself was a god-daughter of the late Emperor, the Czar Nicholas, while her brother-in-law, de Koucheleff, was an aristocrat and one of the richest men in Russia. Home's financial resources, whatever they might be, were obviously very slender, he came of a humble family and though his state of health was not then considered as alarming in a prospective bridegroom as it would be today, even so it might have been expected to make the girl's family uneasy. He was tubercular and looked it, but so great was his celebrity now in the eyes of people who were interested in his powers, that not only was Madame de Kroll's consent forthcoming, but Count and Countess de Koucheleff welcomed the approaching marriage with a family sympathy and warmth.

The party, taking Home with them, went to Naples where they stayed six weeks; this was one of the few occasions when Home's monetary affairs were mentioned; he presented a letter of credit to the Bank of Naples, which made some delay in cashing it. They then returned to Florence and Mrs. Browning was agog at the news of the engagement. To placate her husband, she had long since undertaken not to renew the acquaintance made at Ealing Villa, but she was avidly interested in any gossip about Home. She had heard that his betrothed was about twenty five and rather good looking; in fact Alexandra was not twenty and of a most beguiling attractiveness. Mrs. Browning exclaimed in a letter to her sister that she did not envy the bride:[6] 'Her taste must be extraordinary ... Imagine the conjugal furniture floating about the room at night, Henrietta!

In Florence, a family, friends of the de Koucheleffs, who were returning to Russia, were asked to take Alexandra back to St. Petersburg with them so that she could rejoin her mother and make preparations for the wedding. Home meanwhile sent to the authorities in Scotland for a copy of his birth certificate, but when this reached him he saw that his name had been spelt, as it was pronounced, 'Hume' instead of 'Home'. So important did it seem to him to have the correction made decisively, that he travelled from Italy to Scotland to supervise the alteration himself. Such at least was the reason given for this long journey; it is not possible to determine what subconscious leanings he may have felt to visit the place where he was born.

He returned to Paris to rejoin the de Koucheleffs at their hotel, Les Trois Empereurs. A party of Home's friends gave a banquet in his honour, and the gaiety and hospitality of the de Koucheleffs themselves was unceasing. Their dinner parties went on till five in the morning and were attended by throngs of old and new acquaintances, of the most fashionable and celebrated kinds.

One of these was Alexandre Dumas, *père*, whose preposterous notoriety and brilliant success made him a guest worthy of the barbaric splendours of the parties at Les Trois Empereurs. The son of a mulatto general, whose negroid appearance he had inherited, Dumas, now fifty-five years old, was at the height of his fame. Writers do not always look as if they were the authors of the books they write; Dumas was one of those who do. His theatrical manner, his overpowering emotional energy, his child-like vanity, and when he was not crossed, his enormous good humour, with his exotic appearance and the richness of his dress, made him recognizable at once as the creator of Porthos, Athos and Aramis and their leader d'Artagnan.

Count de Koucheleff was delighted with him and he invited Dumas to come with the wedding party to St. Petersburg and act as Home's best man. Dumas accepted the offer and his account of some parts of the expedition in his book:– *De Paris à Astrakhan* which he published in 1860, is very lively reading and singularly interesting for the picture he gives of Home. He came upon the latter, by himself in the hotel, playing, as a child would, with a little cat, a pet of the De Koucheleff family, which was going with them in a basket on their formidable journey to Russia. Home, he said,[7] had a pale complexion with a tinge of pink, pale lips, beautiful teeth and hair of a hue between fair and sandy. He had effeminate, well-kept hands, loaded with rings. He wore what Dumas called a Scotch bonnet: the forage cap fashionable for men's informal wear in the 50's and 60's. The Frenchman said:[8] 'Il parla français très bien.' The fluency in French which Home had acquired through Dr. Hull's arrangements for him while he was at Newburgh had proved more than useful. It had enabled him to move freely in Parisian society and to carry on his courtship of Alexandra, since like all the Russian aristocracy, she spoke French as her second language. Dumas, said Madame Home[9], regarded Home with respect and wonder, but as a magician, not as a spiritualist. He had begged Home for an account of his early years and this he had put into his book, but as Madame Home said: 'There are natures to whom veracity is impossible, and history as treated by Dumas becomes fiction, biography becomes romance.' Home himself said of the account that it was 'amusing.'

The de Koucheleff family owned numerous estates in Russia; the chief of these was at Polonstrava, outside St. Petersburg, which had been given to their ancestor by Catherine the Great. Here the wedding was to be celebrated. The Czar Alexander II was extremely interested to hear of Home's arrival. His father, the Czar Nicholas had been a figure of awe and dread; when he visited Queen Victoria, the Queen told her Uncle Leopold of Belgium, that in spite of his dignity, his polished courtesy, 'the expression of the eyes is formidable and unlike anything I ever saw before.' But the Czar Alexander was not only a contrast to his father in himself; three years later he was to bring about the emancipation of the serfs; meanwhile he was eager to open the frontiers of his empire to the influence of European thought, and the interest in spiritualism which was abroad in Europe made this a propitious moment for Home's arrival in Russia. The Czar sent a message to Polonstrava, inviting Home to an audience at the Winter Palace of St. Petersburg, the Peterhof. An invitation from the Emperor was a command, but it was characteristic of Home, that much as he enjoyed and valued social success, he replied that he could not wait upon His Imperial Majesty; his mediumistic powers were in abeyance. In the same way he had declined Count Branicka's invitation to Italy; he had no scheme for hoodwinking an audience, he did not even trust to luck that the power might return when it was called on. The Czar returned a most gracious reply; he would be glad to make the acquaintance of Mr. Home as a private gentleman. Home was extremely gratified, but he again, respectfully, declined the invitation; he had, he said, so much to attend to in connection with his forthcoming wedding. It was natural that he should not wish to enter the Czar's presence except with the distinction that his famous powers conferred on him. Meanwhile, a month later the Scottish civic authorities had still not sent the necessary papers in their completed form, and as the regulations governing the marriage of Russian aristocrats were very strict, it looked as though the marriage which had been arranged for 1 August, would have to be postponed. One night in July, however, Home believed that his mother stood by his bed. She told him to tell the Czar the following day that the power had returned. This Home did, and at once received an invitation to spend a week at the Winter Palace; this was the first of his several visits to the Winter Palace at St. Petersburg and the Summer Palace at Tsarskoe-Selo.

The Winter Palace, erected in all its grandeur over the small, primitive abode originally built for himself by Peter the Great, was in the classical European idiom of the XVIII century: the terraces with fountains playing on them, the avenues of evergreens, the obelisks, were reminiscent of Versailles, but the building combined European taste with the native Russian one, which was richer, more massive, more ornate. Similarly the great Summer Palace at Tsarskoe-Selo, which had been decorated for Catherine the Great by the Scottish architect Cameron, combined the outlines of European architecture with the Russian feeling for the colours of their own materials and semi-precious stones: malachite, rose-quartz, amber and lapis lazuli. Cameron had panelled one saloon with sheets of translucent amber; in a room upholstered with yellow silk, he had put a chimmney piece and a table made entirely of lapis lazuli. The Empress's bedroom showed purple glass pillars with bronze capitals; her boudoir was lined with opalescent white glass ornamented with gold, its doorway was framed in columns of blue glass[10]. These effects were in harmony with the Russian interest in jewels, and the instincts that made the gold, silver and jewelled icon, rather than painting, their national expression.

The stimulus and happiness that his returning gift brought with it, and the Czar's sympathy and kindness made Home's week at the Winter Palace delightful to him. The details of the séances he held with the Czar are not published, but their result was the unalterable confidence and friendship of Alexander II, which ended only with his assassination in 1881. The visit also saw the beginning of the warm liking for Home of two members of the Court, the Chamberlain Count Schouvaloff and an officer of the Imperial Guard, Count Alexis Tolstoy, the great Tolstoy's cousin and then well-known as a poet. The Czar was so graciously disposed towards Home that he waived all the difficulties which the incompleteness of Home's personal papers seemed to threaten, and the date of the wedding was confirmed. After Home had left the Winter Palace, Count Schouvaloff sent him a ring set with diamonds, 'que Sa Majesté vous a destinée comme une marque de sa bienveillance.' Of all the jewels given to Home, this was to be the most famous. The hardness of a very fine diamond produces an extraordinary glitter called by jewellers its 'adamantine lustre', and this ring, mounted with several stones, ('enrichie de diamants' as Schouvaloff said) in its amazing brilliance was a gift worthy of the Czar.[11]

Home had come back to Polonstrava full of happiness and satisfaction. The member of the bridal party who was angry and disappointed was Dumas. He felt that he, as well as Home, should have been invited to the Winter Palace; but he presently composed his feelings, saying: 'There are several crowned heads in Europe. There is only one Dumas.' In spite of his childish pique, Dumas made some sensitive and percipient observations on Home. While the latter was still bereft of his powers, Dumas had said that Home had lost the power to make himself feared, but he still had the power to make himself beloved. Now that Home had come back from a week spent in the Winter Palace, having gained a social réclame at the highest level, Dumas might have seen him with jealous eyes as a figure of the most enviable celebrity; but he wrote: 'Home, l'homme à la mode, l'homme du jour, l'homme indispensable, l'homme envié, était, en effet, l'homme le plus malheureux du monde.'

This unexpected insight is explained by a letter Home wrote to his fiancée while he was in the Winter Palace. At first, he said, some of the company had not known how to 'place' a medium; now they knew that a medium could be a gentleman, some of them had expected that he would prove to be merely a conjuror; they had seen their mistake, and after that he had been astonished as well as charmed and delighted, by the general attitude of interest and sympathy. It was especially soothing, because, he said: 'Ma vie est assez triste, car toute personne qui a un pouvoir incomprise est nécéssairement soupçonné dans ce monde.'[12] The consciousness of animosity and contempt caused him a suffering which his attackers would greatly have enjoyed if they had known of it. To this was added the sheer strain of the medium's function. Sir William Crookes wrote several years later[13] when Home had been co-operating with him in some experiments: 'After seeing him lying in an almost fainting condition on the floor, pale and speechless, I could scarcely doubt that the evolution of psychic force is accompanied by a corresponding drain on vital force.' It is protracted, energetic activity which exhausts most people. Home said[14], of these experiments: 'The continued effort to be passive became a kind of nightmare.' This was the result of stress working on a volatile temperament with a childish capacity for happiness, and the marriage now entered on was exquisitely happy. The wedding ceremony was very long, as it was performed first according to the rites of the Greek Church in the de Koucheleffs' private chapel at Polonstrava, and then since Home was at least nominally a member of the Roman Catholic Church, in the church of St. Catherine. Beside Dumas, Home had two other groomsmen: one was Count Bobrinsky, the other, Count Alexis Tolstoy. The bridal pair spent the late summer and autumn in visiting Count de Koucheleff's estates, some in the Crimea, some inland.

The sympathy with which his young wife enfolded him was not founded on affection only; she soon developed a mediumistic capacity herself. 'A short time after our marriage,' Home said, when they were in bed and Sacha was asleep, 'I saw the spirit of my mother come into the room, followed by one who, though I had never known him on earth, I knew to be my wife's father.' Home was at first thankful that his wife was asleep; she had never had any pyschic experience and he had been afraid that the sight of the two figures might frighten her. Then, to his surprise he heard her say: 'Daniel, there is someone in the room with us, and I am not afraid.' But she moved towards him in the bed, trembling violently. Her first experience of this kind was alarming but presently the experiences became second nature.

When they came back from the honeymoon, the de Koucheleffs' town house in Moscow was put at their disposal. Here they stayed six weeks, coming back in November to St. Petersburg, to the de Koucheleffs' house on the Quai Gargarines. In the winter months, daylight in St. Petersburg lasted only five and a half hours. The river Neva, which Dumas had calculated was three times as wide as the Seine at its widest reach, was frozen almost solid, the great, paved quayside street, the Nevsky Prospect, was so thickly mantled in snow that the traffic was silenced. The horse-drawn sleighs were not allowed to use bells, and in the deep twilight they whirled silently about, guided with consummate skill by their drivers, whose hoarse shouts were the only sounds that broke the eerie stillness. Indoors, the houses were heated by such an excellent system of stoves that delicate plants filled the rooms and the rigours of winter were not felt.

In the middle of January, 1859, however in spite of so much protection and comfort, Home became alarmingly ill with what he called 'internal inflammation'. This term was used for abdominal afflictions; a swelling appeared and was so acutely painful that the friction the doctor prescribed had to be given up. Home then underwent a crisis of a kind seemingly unbelievable, but paralleled in some modern works on spirit healing, which describe the cure by spiritual means of cases which would otherwise require surgery. George Chapman, for instance,[15] describes the removal by 'spirit surgery' of a malignant brain tumour and a cancer of the breast. Sacha Home and their friend Count Mayendorff, one of the officers of the Imperial Guard were at Home's bedside when, he says, his hands 'were suddenly seized by spirit influence' and he was made to beat them violently on the sensitive spot. Sacha was terrified by what appeared to be a dangerous seizure, and tried to hold his hands still, but Mayendorff who had had more experience of spirit manisfestations, prevented her. Home continued to strike himself blows which shook the bed, but after five minutes, the swelling was seen to be subsiding and the involuntary movements of his hands became gentler. In an hour's time he was asleep, and when he woke next morning, though he was very weak, the inflammation had disappeared. Home said:[16] 'The expression of the doctor's face baffles my description, when he visited me early in the morning ... and felt my pulse and saw that a great change must have occurred, beyond his skill to account for.'

## XIII

## The Shade of Cagliostro

On 8 May, 1859, at 7 in the evening, while the snow was still falling, the Homes' child was born. A few hours afterwards, the father, the mother and the nurse heard the warbling of a bird, as if it were singing over him. The room was dimly lit by a night-lamp, and that night and the two or three following ones they all saw a bright light like a star which remained for some time poised over the child's head and then, moving towards the door, disappeared. Home believed that these manisfestations were the result, not of his mediumship, but the child's. During the last months of Sacha's pregnancy, he had thought it better for her not to take part in séances, because when raps were heard, the child in the womb made movements in unison with them. A fortnight later the baby was christened; he was named Gregoire after his uncle de Koucheleff, and the Czar sent a christening gift of a magnificent emerald surrounded by diamonds. A week later, the family party removed to another of the de Koucheleff houses in the neighbourhood of St. Petersburg. On the anniversary of their wedding day, Home and his wife were on a steamer bound for Dunkirk, to visit Madame de Kroll who was lying ill at Ostend. As Home embraced his mother-in-law, the touch gave him a clairvoyant vision such as had been given to him twice before, once by a drop of rain on the back of his hand, once by the touch of a woman's hand as he helped her out of a carriage. He said: 'I had another of those singular impressions which so often come to me at the moment of external contact.' He knew that when he and Sacha left Ostend, they would not see her mother again on earth.

They arrived in Paris in August and after a brief visit to Switzerland, returned to Paris where M. Tiedemann gave them the use of his house, the Château de Cerçay. Here they stayed two months and in October they came to England.

Though Home's power had been weak and was not yet returned in full force, a large circle was waiting to welcome him and his charming young wife. Sacha had the attractions of an emotional, affectionate nature, combined with simplicity, gentleness and the beautiful manners of her upbringing. Some idea of her is found in the reproduction of a photograph which Home, after her death had enclosed in a medallion and printed at the head of his writing paper. A letter from him on this writing paper (now in the Harry Price Library), written to an unnamed 'Dear Friend' says: 'My wife liked you much and that is why I send you her portrait.' It shows a small, oval face with dark hair parted in the centre. A much more telling impression is given by the memorial articles[1] written by Mrs. S. C. Hall and Mrs. Howitt printed by Home. By the time Home brought her to England, her English was 'no longer broken, but accented.' She was delightful to talk to; her ordinary mood was one of radiant joy, in her husband, her baby, and the happiness of her life among Homes's friends; sometimes she was wildly gay; but if an appeal were made to her sympathies, 'her eyes grew deep and dark, her sweet lips quivered; the girl became the deep-hearted, tender, earnest woman.'[2] Where the Homes stayed immediately on their arrival is not recorded. It may have been at Cox's Hotel. Home was in close touch with Mr. and Mrs. Cox; they always knew his address and were able to forward letters sent to him at 55 Jermyn Street. At this time Home's power had been absent for several weeks, so it was the more surprising that one evening when he was out, Sacha and the nurse, sitting with the baby, heard raps overhead which, since Home was not there, they thought must be sounds of people walking over-head. When it became clear that they were spirit-produced, Sacha demanded in surprise, who was the medium. The reply transmitted was, that the medium was the sleeping baby; but Home says that the spirits added that though they had the power to manifest through him, they would not do so any more, 'as the atmosphere which they made use of, was necessary for his physical development in the natural world.'

Towards the end of November Home's power returned in great force and he began a series of séances which became more numerous as their fame spread. One of the most interesting to be described was held at the house of Benjamin Coleman, 51 Pembridge Villas, Bayswater.

Two commodities, now extremely expensive, the Victorians enjoyed at a very cheap rate; one was domestic service, the other, desirable house property. People of modest means could occupy a whole house, maintaining it with two or three servants, in a pleasant neighbourhood, which it would now require a considerable income to keep up. Pembridge Road, of which the further reach is called Pembridge Villas, is an area behind Notting Hill Gate, which, in spite of shabbiness and traffic, has kept much of its charm; its trees, its wide street, its pavements with their broad, worn flagstones, its good, solid houses with pillared porches. Coleman was so great an admirer of Home, so devoted to him as a personal friend, and his house the scene of so many séances with him, that the quiet pavement in front of it, over which the medium so often passed, is, for the sympathetic, invested still with a strange, attracting power.

This séance was held for the benefit of Mr. Wason, a Liverpool solicitor who came down to London for it, and brought with him, by permission, a hitherto hardened sceptic, Mr. J. G. Crawford. The latter left a detailed account of one of Home's levitations, that phenomenon which was perhaps the most extraordinary of all that he produced, since it could not be explained by telepathy, clairvoyance, thought-reading, all of which means were sometimes stated to be the source of what was claimed as spirit-communication.

Either Home defied the laws of gravity and rose into the air, or he did not. The descriptions left by people who actually saw him do it are therefore of particular interest.

Mr. Crawford's account is not one of the most valuable, because the room in which the levitation took place was almost dark but Crawford both heard and felt. Home exclaimed: 'I feel as if I were going to rise. I am getting up.' Crawford says: 'As I was only a few feet from him, I put out my hand to him. I indubitably felt the soles of both his boots some three feet above the level of the floor. On my doing so, he said: Don't touch me, or I shall come down. Of course I instantly desisted, but down he came. In less than three minutes, he said: I am again ascending.' From his voice, Crawford said, 'they could but infer that he was actually rising towards the ceiling of the ante-room. He then appeared to rise to the cornice of the room we were sitting in and to float under the archway. They heard the scraping sounds of his drawing three marks on the ceiling besides doing some other writing. Then he came softly down and lay stretched out on his back on the table in which position we found him when the gas was lighted.' This is not one of the most valuable pieces of evidence for Home's levitation as it was not performed in full light; but the impression is clearly given of his position in the air above their heads as he moved about; and though the noise of the marks being drawn on the ceiling may be ascribed to ventriloquism, it is not so easy to account for the marks themselves being seen afterwards, or for Mr. Crawford's feeling the soles of Home's boots as he rose beside him three feet into the air. Home's comment on the affair was: 'Mr. Crawford mentions my immediately coming to the ground again on his touching my feet. I have observed that this is invariably the case when I am touched, or even anxiously gazed at, until I have risen above the heads of those who are in the room, but after I have attained that height, their looking at me or touching me has no effect on me.'[3]

On the evening of their engagement party, Sacha had promised that she would do anything she could to help Home in his psychic life; this sympathy had resulted in her allowing her own mediumistic gift to be developed and some of the deep affection her husband felt for her was obviously based on her readiness to share his experiences. In April 1860, Monsieur Louis Blanc was in England; he had been exiled from France by Napoleon III as a socialist of subversive views, and had been welcomed among the English intelligentsia. One the evening of 3 April he was giving a lecture in St. John's Wood, on 'The Mysterious Persons and Agencies in France towards the end of the Eighteenth Century.' Home went with some friends to the lecture; Sacha had a very bad headache and had gone to bed.

It turned out that Blanc had much to say about Cagliostro. This man, whose real name was Joseph Balsamo and who lived from 1743 to 1795, is one of the figures who are so perplexing in psychical research; he was undoubtedly the possessor of psychic gifts, he was undoubtedly a charlatan. His career had taken him to Greece, Egypt, Arabia and Rome, and everywhere he had gathered secret lore; as a student of the occult he was eminently distinguished. He had made money by marketing an Elixir of Perpetual Youth, which, though no doubt stimulating as a tonic, was naturally discovered at last not to do what it claimed to do. On the other hand, during his two seasons in London, where he initiated a group into Masonic rites, he had remarkable success in predicting the winning numbers of lotteries. He had acquired considerable medical knowledge and was also a faith-healer: a powerful combination of qualities. Although he was unscrupulous, he was uncommonly good to the poor, giving them medical aid and food, saying he had been sent to minister to them. Among his fraudulent schemes he professed that by alchemy he could enlarge the size of diamonds, producing a stone of immense value from a very small one. In France, in 1785, he was thrown into the Bastille as a confederate in the affair of the Diamond Necklace, in which, however, he was only slightly concerned. When he was released, he was told to leave France, and instead of going to Germany or Russia where he had already been successful, with extreme and fatal rashness he went back to Italy, where his chief crime was not fraud or magic or necromancy, but the political one of being a Freemason. The Papacy showed the utmost rigour towards this cult which was recognised as antagonistic to both Church and State. In 1738, it had declared excommunication for anyone who practised it. The authorities arrested Cagliostro, and he was convicted and sentenced to death, but the sentence, most unhappily for him, was commuted to life-imprisonment. He was condemned to a dungeon in the castle fortress of St. Angelo. Here, in one of the most ghastly imprisonments in the annals of man's inhumanity, he spent three years in an underground hutch, 'without air, movement or intercourse with his fellow creatures.' He was afterwards transferred to the fortress of San Leone, where he could look out from behind bars. When Napoleon's troops were known to be approaching, a terrific thunderstorm broke; the prisoner thought the peals were the noise of French gunfire, and shouted wildly: 'Me voici! A moi! Me voici!' In 1795 he died, it was said of apoplexy. This story, so lurid, so painful and so terrifying, was bound to affect anyone of human sympathies, and to be particularly harrowing to Home.

He said[4] that while the lecturer was speaking of him, 'I had the strongest impression of the presence of Cagliostro and the lady who was sitting next to me was also aware of some strong spirit presence.' When he came home his wife was still in the throes of headache but she asked him how he had liked the lecture. When he said: 'I have been haunted all the evening by Cagliostro,' she exclaimed: 'Pray don't use that word "haunted", it sounds so weird-like and quite frightens me.' Home had put out the light and was in bed when a sudden flash of light filled the room. Thinking this might have been visible only to him by spirit perception, he said: 'Sacha, did you see anything?' She said no; her head was buried in the pillow; bad as her headache was, he begged her to be on the alert, then he asked, mentally, that if the light had been external, it might be reproduced. Instantly the light filled the room again, 'so distinct and with such brilliancy, no noonday was ever brighter.' Sacha had conquered her fears. She asked if this were the spirit of Cagliostro? And the affirmative reply of three signs was given by three flashes of light, so vivid as to be almost blinding. They both put questions to which the flashes of light answered 'yes.' Then at a question, came a musical tinkle, 'as if a silver bell had been touched directly over our heads.' Through these sounds they carried on a further conversation. Then they both heard a footstep, approaching very gently as if of someone anxious not to disturb them. Sacha courageously asked that it should come nearer and the step approached till they had the impression that a form was leaning over their bed, they felt the pressure on the bedclothes. Home asked the visitant if he had been a medium on earth? And the result was the very rare phenomenon, a 'direct voice' answer, heard by both of them:[6] 'My power was that of a mesmerist, but all-misunderstood by those about me; my biographers have even done me injustice but I care not for the untruths of earth.' Accustomed to spirit communication though he was, Home said that not only his wife, he himself was so much impressed by the 'startling and almost terribly real evidence of this presence' that for a few moments they were deprived of speech. Then they felt someone placing a hand on their heads. Sacha seized her husband's two hands and held them up in her own. With an earnestness inspired by pity for the dreadful story, she cried: 'Dear Spirit! Will you be one of my guardian angels — watch over me with my father?' About four yards away from the bed, a signet ring that had belonged to General de Kroll was lying. The unseen hands gently separated her left hand from her husband's, and the ring was slid on to one of its fingers. Again they both heard the voice: 'Good night dear ones, God bless you.' Their nerves had been much shaken, but Sacha's headache had disappeared and they soon fell into a sound sleep.

However willingly his wife gave herself to these experiences, it seems that she knew what it was, sometimes at least, to be a little scared of them, and when living with him exposed her to these sensations, it is interesting to read in one of Bulwer Lytton's stories, his impression of Home's charm and the antidote it conveyed to gloom and fright. Madame Home says[5] that Lytton writing *A Strange Story* in this year 1860, made the hero a young man called Margrave, who was not Home, but possessed Home's type of charm; even Madame Home admitted that the picture was a little exaggerated, 'as it was the habit of Bulwer Lytton to exaggerate.' She said that when Home was not in pain from illness, 'all who knew him were struck by the joyousness of his nature and the gaiety and sweetness of a temper that no wrong could embitter and no suffering sour . . . he had the bright cheerfulness of a child and that keen joy in living that charms us in young children.' Lytton had remarked on these traits, and in the description of Margrave he makes another character say: 'Never have I seen human face so radiant as that young man's. There was in the aspect an indescribable something that literally dazzled.' Madame Home thought the charm of Margrave's conversation was described in a way even more evocative of her husband than the attractiveness of his appearance. 'Nothing could be more frankly cordial than Mr. Margrave's manner. In a few minutes the narrator found himself conversing as familiarly as if they had been brought up together. His vein of talk was peculiar, off-hand, careless, shifting from topic to topic with a bright rapidity.'

# XIV

## The Hyde Park Place Séances

A London suburb that, in the 1860's, still preserved its charm, was Sydenham and the adjoining district of Norwood; both were to be associated with Home. The neighbourhood was being built up with modest but substantial villas, with fields still behind them, and quiet, tree-shaded streets. The growth of the neighbourhood had been encouraged by the fact that in 1854, a company had been formed to buy the Crystal Palace and remove it from Hyde Park; it now stood on the summit of Sydenham Hill and intermittent gleams from it could be caught for miles around. It had been reconstructed on an even larger scale. The Glass Fountain had been reinstalled, but to take the place of the merchandise which it had been its original function to display, there had been set out a range of Fine Arts Courts: Grecian, Roman, Assyrian, Byzantine, Pompeiian, Chinese and Renaissance. There was an Aquarium, a Picture Gallery, a Theatre, a Concert Hall and Library, and parts of the vast, luminous building were available for congresses, receptions, exhibitions and bazaars. An improvement on the original lay-out in Hyde Park, was the setting up around the Palace of ten enormous fountains, whose tiered cascades rose one hundred and fifty feet into the air. Two of them, immense and sparkling, stood, wide apart, in the foreground, and between them, in the middle distance, the Palace could be seen in its glittering length. While the mid-Victorian era was producing heavy and elaborate furniture and interior decoration of an ornate and gloomy caste, it was unexpected and incongruous that this airy, brilliant, transparent creation, with its tossing, coruscating fountains, should now crown Sydenham Hill. The magic of the scene was enhanced by the marvel of ascending balloons, floating away over the landscape of the Surrey hills, and as evening came on, by ravishing displays of fireworks; fountains of silvery flame, aerial festoons of jewels, swarms of gold and silver fire-flies. The character of the place was echoed in some of the musical entertainments. In *The Times* of 16 April, 1863, it was announced that 'Mr. Sydney Smith will play his popular piece,

Morning Dewdrops, and his Grand Brillant Waltz, Gaieté de Coeur, in his pianoforte recital at the Crystal Palace this day.'

A railway line now brought the patrons out to Sydenham, and the Crystal Palace railway station had been opened halfway up Anerley Hill, the long hill that led up to the Crystal Palace Parade. On the morning of 29 May, 1860, Sacha Home was, in her husband's words, 'then engaged at a bazaar held at the Crystal Palace.' She was in considerable anxiety about her mother, whom they had left in weak health at Ostend, Home, at least, with the certainty that they would never see her again. In the middle of May, Sacha had had a letter from her mother who was back in St. Petersburg. It said that on the next day she was to undergo an operation. 'I have seen my confessor; I have taken the sacrament and I now feel quite happy. Do not be alarmed, but do as I do — trust in God.' Home may have accompanied his wife as far as Sydenham, as he had made an appointment with a friend for that morning to visit Barclay and Perkins Brewery in Southwark, a district immediately to the north of Sydenham. 'We drove there', he says, 'and had gone over nearly all the establishment when, in the barrelling room, one of the workmen proposed our tasting the porter.'

Pots were brought to them and his friend drank, but when Home's fingers touched the metal, he received another of those clairvoyant impressions which the sense of touch had caused him before. He shuddered and knew that his mother-in-law was dead. He refused the porter and his friend took him home. He looked so miserably ill that the friend wanted to stay with him, but this Home would not allow; he wanted to be alone, to decide how best to conceal the news from his wife so that she might learn it by natural means. A few days afterwards, Sacha came running upstairs. She opened the door but even before he saw her, he exclaimed: 'Why, Sacha, I knew it last Monday.' In her hand was a letter from the Countess de Koucheleff, containing a telegram announcing their mother's death. Two nights later while a séance was being held, Home said: 'Her dear spirit came and her hands were made visible, resting on her daughter's head and afterwards on mine. She wrote in her own peculiar hand-writing: You will love her always, won't you? Natalie.'

Mutual love, a child they both adored, freedom from anxiety about money, and, above all, tremendous success in his chosen career, would have made this an entirely blissful era in Home's life. What sometimes worked against his happiness was the dawning of an anxiety about his wife's health, and the strain of his abnormal existence—the usual condition of victims of tuberculosis: spells of high spirits alternating with deep depression. His social success was indeed extraordinary. Some of it was no doubt due to the infectiousness of a fashionable

110

craze, but most of it was accounted for by the fact that when the increasing pressure of materialism was driving people to a frantic search for reassurance, their need was met by the appearance on the scene of a medium of unrivalled powers. Dr. Zorab has said of this period of Home's career: 'His mediumistic performances were at their height with regard to their versatility, great power and the ease with which, day after day, they were conducted.' Those who sat with him longed to do so again and besought to be allowed to bring friends with them. Madame Home copied down lists upon lists of the names of people in high society, asking Home to lunch, to dine, begging him to hold séances at their houses. Home enjoyed meeting the great, and the courtesy, sympathy and admiration with which they received him. He appears never to have refused, when he was in power, to hold a séance except when physical exhaustion made one impossible, but he invariably maintained that he could not undertake that any phenomena would occur, and sometimes, a sitting would pass without any. He had a remarkable power of making friends, and at this time he formed two friendships of permanent value. The poet Shelley's son, Sir Percy Florence Shelley, like his father in appearance but with a vacuous expression in his large eyes instead of the intense, penetrating light that filled his father's, was living at Boscombe Manor, outside Bournemouth. His wife was a short and stout but attractive woman of prodigious energy. She worshipped the poet's memory; when her mother-in-law Mary Shelley left her the journal she had kept during her marriage with Shelley, Lady Shelley had this precious document printed with somewhat high-handed editing by herself. Under the title, *Shelley and Mary*, it became one of the most discussed literary works of the nineteenth century. Mary Shelley had also given her a ring worn by Shelley, mounted with a gold coin bearing the heads of Nero and his wife. Lady Shelley had taken this to a psychometrist, Mrs. Wagstaffe, who had first said that she saw a mighty city, Rome in the time of Nero. Seeing the nature of the ring's mounting, this was not very wonderful, but Mrs. Wagstaffe went on to say, that she saw a tall, slim youth, 'he was sad and sorrowful, full of love for his race and pity for their afflictions. He was a great poet.' She then said, 'I see one walking by his side but unlike him in every way,' and she described Byron, 'going on to tell me of their respective characters and life . . . She knew nothing of me . . . I went as a complete stranger.'[2] With this interest in the occult, Lady Shelley became deeply interested in Home. A woman of her warm-heartedness, vigour and self-confidence, once her sympathies were engaged, would be a staunch supporter. Her friendship was an advantage to Home in itself, and it brought with it one even greater. She introduced to him Dr. James Manby Gully, who, as a doctor and a friend, was to prove invaluable.

Dr. Gully had begun his practice of hydropathy in the 1840's, when he and his friend Dr. Wilson had been in revolt against the rapidly developing use of drug medication. They held that every time a purgative or a stimulant or a sedative was administered, it postponed still further the all important task of making the body able once more to do its own work. They developed the theory that the water cure in its various forms of douches, sitz baths, compresses, packings in wet sheets, restored the power of the circulation and so effected the cure of chronic diseases which were caused by the viscera's being starved of blood or engorged with it. Wilson said that they must find a place beyond London to establish their practice, and Malvern, under the shelter of towering hills, with beautiful scenery, inspiring air and water of diamond purity was an admirable choice of scene. Their success was rapid and surprised even themselves. Their fame turned a hillside village of two thousand inhabitants to a flourishing country town of eight thousand, with its complement of hotels, houses, lodgings, livery stables and shops. The partnership did not survive the strains of this success. They separated and Dr. Gully with the practical intelligence which made him the obvious choice for civic appointments, became much the more important of the two. He had acquired two houses, side by side, on the hillside road above the town, one for resident patients, the other for himself and his family. By 1847, the demands of his practice were so heavy he had given up the latter to patients as well, and removed to The Priory House at the bottom of the town, a Regency house surmounted by crockets, pinnacles and ornate chimneys. It stood in a large garden with evergreen trees on the lawn; high above it rose a great range of hills. His first wife had died in 1840, leaving him with two sons and a daughter; his sisters Anne and Ellen now lived with him and took care of the children. In 1841 he had made a disastrous second marriage with a rich widow, seventeen years older than himself, and the mutual miseries this entailed led to a separation eighteen months later. This had cleared the way for his removal to Malvern.

By 1850 he was established there without competition as the most celebrated physician in the district. The system he practised was a sound one and he had, to an unusual degree, the qualities of a born doctor. By 1860, patients were coming to him, not only from all over England, but from America and Russia. Many doctors had now come to Malvern to glean after him and Dr. Wilson, but Florence Nightingale who was there in 1860, had written to Edwin Chadwick: 'Of all the Malvern doctors, Dr. Gully has the most genius.' Though he preferred homeopathy because it used the smallest possible quantity of drugs, he maintained that the doctor should never be prevented by professional prejudice from using any remedy that would help the patient. He used hypnotism to promote sleep, and the services of a clairvoyant where he would now demand an X-ray. In the summer of 1860, he was not a spiritualist, but he was much interested in psychic phenomena. He had been very glad to avail himself of Lady Shelley's introduction to Home.

Of the hostesses who entertained Home, the most eminent socially was the Duchess of Sutherland, whose town house was Stafford House, at the bottom of the Mall, overlooking both St. James' Park and Green Park. The Duchess had made 'its noble suite of drawing rooms' famous as the meeting place 'of ladies and gentleman . . . interested in social reforms[3],' and her reception in 1853 of Mrs. Harriet Beecher Stowe had been of great value in publicizing *Uncle Tom's Cabin* in England. Mrs. Beecher Stowe described the Duchess as 'tall and stately, with a most noble air, a fair complexion, blonde hair and full lips.' She was deeply interested in spiritualism and became a cordial, sympathetic friend of Home and his young wife. But in spite of the Duchess's unrivalled social distinction, the most energetic and successful of Home's hostesses was Mrs. Milner Gibson. Her husband, Thomas Milner Gibson, was Secretary to the Board of Trade. He was on excellent terms with his wife and made no objection to her entertaining whom she pleased, but he let it be known that he was never present at any of her parties at which séances were conducted. He was absolutely determined that none of the contempt and ridicule so frequently attached to spiritualism should injure him in his parliamentary career. He was not always, altogether, successful in this intention, as Madame Home showed.[4] On one occasion in the House, Mr. Milner Gibson began to say: 'I have been a medium——' he meant to say, 'of communication between so-and-so and the Government', but the rest of the sentence was drowned in cheers and laughter. On another occasion he stated that he had nothing to say against Home . . . all he himself wanted to be able to say, was that 'he knew nothing of spiritualism'.[5] When Home published the first volume of his autobiography, *Incidents in my Life*, he used at least one of Mrs. Milner Gibson's accounts, kept in her journal, of séances, but though he had her permission to put her name to it, he decided in the end to publish it anonymously. He knew only too well that certain members of the Press would accuse him of himself having written any evidence that was not signed, but Mrs. Milner Gibson had been his warmhearted, generous supporter, and the forbearance of her husband had been taxed by the notoriety of the séances held in her drawing-room. Home therefore decided, at last, that he would not risk causing the couple any further domestic discomfort by the publication of Mrs. Milner Gibson's name. Madame Home acknowledged that this was characteristic of her husband's consideration for his friends, but it was exacerbating to her patience.

The Milner Gibsons' house, which was to be the scene of one of Home's most famous manifestations, was No. 3, Hyde Park Place. This row of solid, rather gloomy houses lies in a stretch of the Bayswater Road, between the mouths of Albion Street and Clarendon Place; some of the houses, including Number 3, are still standing. A pair of massive fluted columns flanks the front door, which is approached by a flight of ten marble steps. Large sash windows light the ground and the first floors, and the wrought iron balcony over the porch gives a pleasant outlook on Hyde Park, whose railings are just across the road. The drawing room was said to be forty by thirty feet. The séance in this room at which Home levitated has attracted so much celebrity because it was described by Robert Bell who was present at it, in the August number for 1860 of the *Cornhill Magazine*, but at least one which took place before it was the most remarkable because of the detailed evidence with which the levitation was described by the witness. This was the Liverpool solicitor, Mr. James Wason, who had already been present at the levitation in Benjamin Coleman's house in Pembridge Villas. Mr. Wason on this visit was invited to 3 Hyde Park Place for séances on two separate occasions. On the first one, the phenomena were merely those of the floor's shaking and trembling, and the table, 'a very large and heavy one', rising a few inches from the floor and again subsiding, till at last it rose at least three feet and remained suspended in the air for about a minute. This, though inexplicable, was a commonplace feature of Home's sittings; but on the second occasion, 'Mr. Home', said Wason, 'crossed the table over the heads of the persons sitting around it. By standing and stretching upwards,' he went on, 'I was enabled to reach his hand, about seven feet distant from the floor, and laying hold and keeping hold of his hand, I moved along with him five or six paces as he floated above me.' When Madame Home examined her husband's papers for the period culminating in Robert Bell's article in the *Cornhill*, she found evidence of many more séances than she had room to describe and had to choose among them. She chose two described in letters to his wife by Count Alexis Tolstoy, who had been groomsman at Home's wedding. The Countess had sent Madame Home the letters to add to her husband's memoranda, and she had translated them herself from the Russian. Alexis Tolstoy had begged Home to come again to Russia, and as this had not been possible, the Count had come to London; with him he brought Count Steinbeck Fermor, as interested in spiritualism as he was himself, and Dr. Botkine, who, at the time of the party's arrival in England, was a profound sceptic. The Russians

114

spoke fluent English and there was no difficulty in presenting them to Mrs. Milner Gibson.

The letter describing what was much the more remarkable of the two séances was written by Alexis Tolstoy at two in the morning of 17 June, 1860. 'I have just left Home and in spite of the pain it gives me to be away from you, I do not regret my journey to London, for this séance has been overwhelming . . . Botkine is converted and wishes to shut himself up and stay the whole day indoors to meditate on what he has seen.' He described the events of the evening; Home is said never to have sat in the dark, but he sometimes asked to have the light lowered, and this was, and is, often used to discredit altogether the account of the phenomena, but Tolstoy said: 'the light being reduced, every article of furniture took to moving about of its own accord. A table placed itself on another table; a sofa moved out into the middle of the room; a bell rose in the air and went all round the apartment, ringing as it floated. Finally the remaining lights were put out and we sat almost in darkness. There was only the faint light that came through the window from a gas-lamp outside.' During this spell a bracelet fell from Mrs. Milner Gibson's arm, 'and lay on the table surrounded by a luminous appearance.' Then came the climax: 'Home,' said Tolstoy, 'was raised from the ground and I clasped his feet while he floated in the air above our heads.' As in Mr. Wason's experience, the evidence of sight might be dismissed on the grounds of dim light; the evidence of touch seems unassailable.

Other phenomena came upon the sitters. Tolstoy said a piano began to play, a faint voice was heard singing, on a piece of paper the words were written: 'Love her always' with the name Natalie Kroll written after them. The table under Botkine's hands emitted loud raps like the blow of a hammer. 'Hands laid themselves in my hands,' Tolstoy said; 'when I sought to retain one, it melted in my grasp.' This, he said, was what would have convinced him if he had been a sceptic. After this séance he found that Home's hands were burning hot and his eyes full of tears.[4]

These events were intensely interesting to a circle which, though large, was a private one; but in August, the subject gained, suddenly, a wide publicity; the *Cornhill* for August 1860 carried Robert Bell's account of a séance at 3 Hyde Park Place, which had occurred in June or early July. The latter limit is fixed by the fact that Home took his wife abroad on 14 July.

The *Cornhill*'s editor was now Thackeray, of whom it was remarked that the author of *Vanity Fair* was not easily duped. When Bell's article, 'Stranger than Fiction', appeared, Thackeray added a footnote: 'As editor of this magazine, I can vouch for the good faith and honourable character of our contributor, a friend of twenty-five years' standing; but, as the writer of the above narrative owns, "that he would refuse to believe such things upon the evidence of other people's eyes," his readers are therefore free to give or withhold their belief.'

The evening was, apparently, one of those all too usual in an English summer, of veiled light in a grey, watery sky. A gas-lamp outside gave some illumination through the three sash windows. These were draped with heavy curtains and fitted with spring-blinds. The space before the middle window was empty; in front of the other two were stands filled with geraniums. The spacious drawing room was furnished with sofas, ottomans and a large round table. In the hearth at the far end of the room a low fire was burning. The company included doctors, lawyers, and scientists. One of the latter was Robert Chambers, the founder of *Chambers' Encyclopaedia*, to whom Darwin had paid tribute in his introduction to *The Origin of Species*; Chambers in his work, *Vestiges of Creation*, published in 1844, anticipated Darwin by maintaining the theory of the evolution of species in animal life. This accurate observer of scientific detail was one of the witnesses to the séance; another, equally trained but in medical observation, was Dr. Gully. Among the collection of faces, however, Bell described the most interesting one. Home, he said, 'looks like a man whose life has been passed in mental conflict. The expression of his face in repose is that of physical suffering, but it quickly lights up when you address him and his natural cheerfulness colours his whole manner. There is more kindliness and gentleness than vigour in the character of his features.' Serious conversation was the last thing to be expected of him. His appearance and manner would never have led you to suppose who he was. 'He not only cannot call up spirits . . . he tells you that whatever happens, happens from causes over which he has not the slightest influence.' After a relation of telekinesis experienced at other séances, where he does not name the medium, Bell then comes to the events of the famous evening.

Some sheets of paper were strewn on the table and an accordion was lying on the floor. He says that 'through the usual channels of communication' (by which he presumably means raps corresponding to the letters of the alphabet), a message was received asking for the lights to be lowered. Those on the walls, chimney piece and consol table were put out. Bell now gives a careful and extremely important description of what light there actually was, and his whole relation is accompanied by detailed references to the state of visibility. 'We must now have been in utter darkness but for the pale light that came in through the window, and the flickering glare thrown over a distant part of the room by a fire which was rapidly sinking in the grate. We could see, but scarcely distinguish our hands upon the table. A festoon of dull, gleaming forms round the circle represented what we knew to be our hands. An occasional ray from the window now and then revealed the hazy surface of the white sheets and the misty bulk of the accordion. We knew where these were placed and could discover them with the slightest assistance from the cold gray light of a watery sky.' One of the blinds began to descend; the tassel on the cord could be seen going up and down jerkily as if an effort were being made to lower the blind; at last it descended and covered that window. Bell then felt a large hand 'come under the table cover and with fingers clustered to a point, raised it between me and the table. I seized it,' he said, 'but it went out like air in my grasp ... it was as palpable as ... velvet or pulp, and seemed as solid, but pressure reduced it to air.' He heard the accordion begin to play where it lay on the ground; 'the air was wild and full of strange transitions with a wail of the most pathetic sweetness running through it ... the sounds rolled through the room with an astonishing reverberation ... then sank to a strain of divine tenderness.' There were other sounds, as the sheets of paper were moved about, and twigs of the geranium plants were snapped off and thrown towards the sitters. Proceeding to the climax of the séance, he described the event which those present found the most thrilling, and those who had not been present resented the most violently when it was made public. Bell said: 'Mr. Home was seated next the window. Through the semi-darkness his head was dimly visible against the curtains and his hands might be seen in a dim white heap before him. Presently he said in a quiet voice: My chair is moving — I am off the ground — don't notice me — talk of something else. I was sitting opposite Mr. Home and I saw his hands disappear from the table and his head vanish into the deep shadow beyond. In a moment or two he spoke again. This time his voice was in the air above our heads. He had risen from his chair to a height of four or five feet from the ground. As he ascended higher he described his position, which at first was perpendicular and afterwards became horizontal. He said he felt as if he had been turned in the gentlest manner as a child is turned in the arms of a nurse.' The following sentence is the most important in the whole narration, and it is invariably omitted by those who deny the truth of the event: 'In a moment or two more, he told us that he was going to pass across the window, against the gray, silvery light of which he would be visible. We watched in profound stillness and *saw his figure pass from one side of the window to the other, feet foremost, lying horizontally, on the air*. He spoke to us as he passed and told us that he would turn the reverse way and re-cross the window, *which he did*.' Bell said that it was Home's own freedom from any sign of fright which kept the sitters tranquil, but even so, 'it was impossible not to be conscious of a certain sense of fear and awe. He hovered round the circle for several minutes and passed, this time, perpendicularly over our heads. I heard his voice behind me in the air and felt something lightly brush my chair. It was his foot, which he gave me leave to touch ... I placed my hand gently upon it, when he uttered a cry of pain and the foot was withdrawn quickly and with a palpable shudder ... it was floating and it sprang from the touch as a bird would. He now passed over to the farthest extent of the room and we could judge by his voice of the altitude and distance he had attained ... an incident which imparted a strange solemnity was that the accordion, which was supposed to be on the ground under the window close to us, played a strain of wild pathos in the air from the most distant corner of the room.'

After reading Bell's exact description of the various conditions of the light, it is extraordinary to read Horace Wyndham's comment[6] on this levitation: 'As the narrator points out that this occurred in pitch darkness, his story takes some swallowing.'

# Conflicting Evidence

Thackeray was castigated by people who had not seen the levitation for allowing Bell's account of it to be printed in the *Cornhill*, since, they said, it was clear that the whole affair was a farrago of impudent and ridiculous falsehoods. C. R. Weld, the assistant Secretary of the Royal Society[1], was at a dinner party where several scientists taxed Thackeray with having failed in his duty as an editor by allowing it, and Thackeray had answered: 'It is all very well for you, who have probably never seen any spiritual manifestations to talk as you do, but had you seen what I have witnessed, you would hold a different opinion.' He then, said Weld, 'told us that in New York, at a dinner party, he saw a heavy dinner table, covered with decanters, glasses, dishes, plates . . . rise fully two feet from the ground. No possible jugglery, he declared, was or could have been employed . . . and he felt so convinced that the motive force was super-natural, that he then and there gave in his adhesion to the truth of spiritualism and consequently accepted the article on Mr. Home's séance.'

There was another person who had seen some of the phenomena in Hyde Park Place, whose views were not made public till much later. Mrs. Lynn Linton was a formidable lady of an extremely positive cast of mind, whose assertiveness had been increased by her success as one of the early woman journalists. Her most famous production was her article: 'The Girl of the Period', which the *Saturday Review* published in 1868. The girl, of any period, is liable to be extravagant and perverse, but a hard-favoured elderly woman is not the person best-placed for telling her that she is. No consideration of this sort, however, deterred Mrs. Lynn Linton. She laid about her with a fearful zeal, and raised a commotion which, though she said it was painful to her as a private person, could not but be gratifying to a journalist.

Mrs. Lynn Linton and Mrs. Milner Gibson, different though they were and holding widely divergent views on Mrs. Milner Gibson's favourite topic, were and remained close friends. The former had once wished very much to be able to believe in manifestations from a spirit world and had attended séances at 3 Hyde Park Place, but had come to the conclusion that such a belief was impossible to anyone of sense. She stated[2], 'I have never seen anything whatever that might not have been done by trick and collusion, and I have seen almost all the mediums. Never, anywhere, has there been allowed the smallest investigation.' From someone who had sat with Home, this can only be called the same sort of reckless mis-statement into which Sir David Brewster's feelings had hurried him. It so happens that one séance which Mrs. Lynn Linton refers to was described in some detail by another sitter; this was the Mr. Jones of Peckham who had pursued the exhausted party consisting of Mr. and Mrs. Rymer and their guest to Sandgate in August 1855. Mr. Jones was completely devoted to spiritualism and had a passionate belief in Home as a medium; he was also of a naive disposition; and yet his account of two séances at 3 Hyde Park Place, written on 1 May and 10 May 1860, appear on the whole to be more credible than that of Mrs. Lynn Linton, which, written many years later, shows puzzling differences in the details of the room and appears to throw together the episodes of two séances, which Jones carefully described within a short time of their taking place.

Jones says[3] that at the séance on 1 May, there were present Mr. and Mrs. Home and seven other sitters. From Mrs. Lynn Linton's account one can identify four of these:- Mrs. Milner Gibson herself, her companion Mademoiselle Galeer, Jones and Mrs. Lynn Linton. Jones says they sat at a round table 'in the large drawing-room'; this room, estimated by Mr. Wason as about forty by thirty feet, must in all probability have been the front portion of the double drawing room that ran the depth of the house, the front half overlooking Hyde Park. Mrs. Lynn Linton appears to have remembered the sitting as taking place in the back drawing-room, as she speaks of light from a gas-lamp coming through the window that gave on to a mews. Jones says that as they were sitting, the table began to move away from them. (Mrs. Lynn Linton does not record this.) When it was asked whether they should move it to the window, the reply was yes. It was moved to the vacant space in front of the centre window (mentioned by Bell). Spirit direction caused them to put out the candles and unclose the shutters. The fire burned brightly. The communication was: A little too much light, and two gentlemen of the party screened the hearth. 'The moon and the gas-light from the street then lighted up the table, but did so completely as the moon was very bright.' Mrs. Lynn Linton, however, says: 'The room was almost pitch dark, lighted only by the lamp in the mews which this window faced.' Jones describes various phenomena; music, messages addressed to the sitters, the appearing of a female hand among others, with light streaming from it. Mrs. Lynn

120

Linton dismisses this as: 'the usual array of luminous hands.' It was known to the company that she had had an adopted child, whose death had caused her great grief. Among the luminous apparitions of hands, she says, 'there came a round, shining thing, which Mademoiselle Galeer and Mr. Home both cried out was a child's head.' Jones says: 'Then came a dear baby hand and then the baby (Mrs. L's adopted child) showed its head, and finally spirit hands held up the little child so that all nine of us saw her shoulders and waist.' Home exclaimed that this was the spirit of her adopted child. What enabled Mrs. Lynn Linton to determine that the whole exhibition was a fraud, was that Home spoke of the child as Eliza, whereas she had always been called Lizzie. 'This,' said Mrs. Lynn Linton, 'saved me from all after-dangers of credulity.'

Jones then says that Home went into a trance and, as is recorded of several occasions when he was in this state, supernatural light was produced. 'As he fell back in his chair, a gleam of most vivid light fell over my shoulders and gleamed on my right hand, and came from a direction whence no earthly light could have come.' No one but Jones saw this light, but as he had before, in this drawing-room, felt that the spirit of a dead friend was standing behind him, he looked behind him now. Home said: 'Yes, he is there.'

Mrs. Lynn Linton speaks of being present in the house when Home 'was said to have floated to the ceiling.' This seems to refer to the second séance recorded by Jones, of 9 May, 1860. After several manifestations, of moving furniture, music, detonating raps, the sounds of geranium twigs snapping, and sprigs of geranium being thrown into sitters' laps, Mr. Home said he felt as if he were about to be lifted up. He moved from the table and said: 'I am rising,' but Jones says: 'We could not see him.' Jones asked that he should be brought as near as possible to the window, 'and at once he was floated with his feet horizontally into the light of the window, so that we all saw his feet and a part of his legs resting or floating on the air like a feather, about six feet from the ground and three feet above the height of the table. He was then floated into the dark, and he exclaimed: They have turned me round and I am coming towards you. I saw his head and face at the same height as before and as if floating on air instead of water. He then floated back and came down and walked up to, and sat, on the edge of the table we were at, when the table began to rise with him on it.'

Mrs. Lynn Linton's account is, that a sound was heard as of a chaise-longue moving away from the wall, where upon Home left the table and went to it, saying: The spirits want me to sit on this. Mr. Jones, she says, exclaimed: 'let me come with you and went and sat beside him,' but his presence was found inconvenient and he was soon sent packing. Jones' own version[4] says:- 'He was then taken behind to the settee next to me . . . feeling a pressure against my chair, I looked and saw that the ottoman had been brought along the floor, about six feet, no one touching it, and close to Mr. Home (Mrs. Lynn Linton remembered it as a chaise-longue.) He said: 'I suppose it is for me to rest on — he lay down and the ottoman went back to its original position.' Home said: 'Oh, I am getting excited, let some one come and sit with me. I went and sat beside him; he took my hand and in about a minute and without any muscular action, he gently floated away from me and was lost in the darkness. He kept talking to let us know where he was. We heard his voice in various parts of the further end of the room as if near the ceiling . . . I saw the shadow of his body on the mirror as he floated along near the ceiling. He said: I wish I had a pencil to make a mark on the ceiling. I have made a cross with my nail. He came down near the door and after a pause he was again taken up; I did not see him but heard his voice as if near the ceiling. Again he came down and shortly returned to the table we were at.'

Jones says three times that he did not see Home for the darkness, and three times that there were moments when he did see him in the air. Mrs. Lynn Linton goes painstakingly to work to explain, not how Home engineered a fraud, but how he might have done.[5] 'There was nothing to have prevented Mr. Home from drawing the chaise-longue to himself by means of a string round the two front legs, moving it by his own feet and muscles; standing on the centre-piece of the ottoman, and with a knife tied to the end of a stick, scratching a cross on the ceiling. The rest was easy to ventriloquism and certain to credulity.' She speaks of the room, faintly lit by the gas-lamp in the mews outside which implies that this room was the back drawing-room, but she also, as Jones does, speaks of a mirror. There could, of course, have been a mirror in each drawing-room; but then she makes an enigmatical statement: 'We could see that a dark body was between us and the mirror.' But where? At what level? If Home had been standing on the floor, this would have been so strong a point in her favour, she would hardly have omitted to say so. If he were standing on the ottoman and were seen standing on it, then it would have been possible to see him mounting it. Podmore's statement about the unreliability of evidence being in proportion to the time which had elapsed since the experience, was made with a view to discrediting as many accounts as possible of psychic phenomena. Those of Mr. Jones and Mrs. Lynn Linton, taken together, form a rare instance of the sceptic's evidence being vaguer and more unsatisfactory than that of the devotee. On the appearance of Robert Bell's article, the outcry in certain sections of the press was virulently hostile. It was declared that the only genuine proof of Home's power to levitate would be his announcement that he would perform this feat on a particular occasion and then for him to rise into the air in front of a multitude of spectators. The fact that Home did not know when he was going to rise until the process of levitation was actually about to begin unfortunately made it impossible to fall in with this suggestion. On the publication of *Stranger than Fiction*, *Punch* produced one of the numerous attacks which Home's celebrity drew from it:-

> With a lift from the spirits, he'll rise in the air,
> (Though as lights are put out, we can't see him there.)
> He can make tables dance, and bid chairs stand on end,
> (But of course it must be in the house of a friend.)

All this was natural enough; but when one correspondent said that he looked forward keenly to seeing Home levitate, 'at the end of a hempen rope', this was an early sign of that peculiar vindictiveness, of which Browning had shown some and was to show more, demonstrated by a section of society who were goaded, not merely by contempt for what they thought was stupidity and indignation at what they supposed was fraud, but by some alarmed, deep-seated instinct which they themselves could not have recognized.

Though the people who had seen the levitations were much calmer than those who had not, there was a feeling among them that some defence should be made of their honesty and their mental balance. Benjamin Coleman said in a letter to the *Morning Star* that someone who had witnessed the phenomena should publish a straightforward account, either confirming Robert Bell's or refuting it. Coleman had now become a friend of Dr. Gully, and whether at his suggestion or not, Dr. Gully wrote from his house at Malvern a letter which the paper published in October, 1860. He stated that several of the sitters, including himself, were professional men. He mentioned, though without naming, Robert Chambers, and a solicitor, William Martin Wilkinson, brother of Dr. Garth Wilkinson. These two, with Dr. Gully himself, made a dependable trio of witnesses to the fact that what was said to have happened did happen. Dr. Gully dismissed the theory that Home had risen into the air on a hydrogen-filled balloon. A balloon that could raise a man would be so large that it could not have been concealed in a room, which, for some of the time was in 'a blaze of light' and all the time was partly illuminated by the gas-lamps in the street.[6] 'Between which gas lamps and our eyes Mr. Home's form passed, so that we distinctly perceived its trunk and limbs . . . his foot touched my head when he was floating above.' Dr. Gully, who was passionately devoted to music, described some of the musical phenomena in detail much greater than Bell's. The accordion was a favourite instrument of the time; it had a wide variety of notes, some

123

sounding like strings, some like those of a flute. Henry Blagrove, who had conducted the music in the Abbey at Queen Victoria's coronation, was a past master of the accordion. On this occasion, in Mrs. Milner Gibson's drawing room the accordion played of itself more exquisitely, Dr. Gully said, than we had ever heard it played, even by Blagrove, 'that master of the instrument'. Robert Chambers believed that his father's spirit was present, and asked that the accordion should play the air of what had been his father's favourite ballad. Chambers said: 'The accordion was not invented at the time of my father's death, so I cannot conceive how it will be effected, but if his favourite air is not played, I promise to tell you.' The accordion stood by itself on the floor; immediately the flute notes began to play the air of: 'Ye banks and braes of bonny Doone'. When it was finished, Chambers said that had been his father's favourite air, and the flute his favourite instrument. Dr. Gully concluded his letter by saying that though he bore testimony to the truthfulness of the facts related by the writer in the *Cornhill*, and that the phenomena could not have been produced by any contrivance or trick, he was quite unable to say what had produced them: 'I believe that we are very, very far from having accumulated facts enough upon which to frame any laws or build any theory regarding the agent at work in their production . . . many gaps must be filled up before the bridge between the spiritual body's life here in the flesh and its life elsewhere, out of the flesh, can be finished.' Respecting purely physical phenomena, such as the levitation of tables or human bodies, 'it may be' he said, 'that we are on the verge of discovering some physical force hitherto undreamed of; who shall say that we know all the powers of nature?' Dispassionate enquiry must be pursued in this direction also, 'regardless of . . . ignorant and malicious prejudice.' He himself by writing this, he knew, must come in for his share of pity and abuse. 'Let it be so' he said, 'if it helps on a truthful search.'

Mrs. Browning was to die in 1861, and it is interesting that the very number of the *Cornhill*, that published Bell's *Stranger than Fiction* in August 1860, printed one of her last works, 'A Musical Instrument'. This describes the god Pan, trampling the river bank into mud, breaking the water-lilies, to choose and pull out a reed for making a pipe.

> High on the shore sat the great god Pan,
> While turbidly flowed the river,
> He hacked and hewed as a great god can,
> With his hard, bleak steel at the patient reed,
> Then drew the pith like the heart of a man

Steadily from the outside ring
And notched the poor, dry, empty thing
In holes as he sat by the river.

Then, laughing with satisfaction, he begins to blow. The music,
'blinding sweet', makes the sun stay his setting, the lilies revive and
the dragon flies come back.

Yet half a beast is the great god Pan
To laugh as he sits by the river,
Making a poet out of a man;
The true gods sigh for the cost and pain,
For the reed that grows never more again
A reed with the reeds in the river.

Mrs. Browning had been married to a great poet for fourteen years.
This, it seems, was her opinion of the effect of poetic genius on the
balance of the mind.

## XVI

## The Death of Sacha

When Home took his wife abroad after the famous séance in Hyde Park Place, they travelled in France and Italy and on their return journey to England they stayed with Baron Tiedemann, who had introduced Home to the Dutch savants, at the Château de Cerçay. There were many tall trees in his park; one, a 'northern poplar', stood in the angle of a hedge where the game used to fly for refuge when the Baron's guests were out shooting. Home, an indifferent marksman, thought this would be a good place to bring down a bird. As he was approaching the hedge, he was surprised to hear a voice call out, in English: 'Here! Here!' He did not alter his position as he was already taking aim; suddenly he was seized by the collar and lifted forcibly from the ground. At that instant he heard a loud crash. He thought his gun had gone off and that he was already on the other side of life. Then he saw that in front of him a huge branch was lying on the ground. It had split off from the trunk of the poplar under which he had been standing. He ran to fetch the rest of the party. They found that the branch was fifty feet long and three feet in circumference. It had fallen from a height of forty-five feet, making as clean a severance from the bole as if it had been sawn off. Home was told that these trees were liable to such mutilations, of great suddenness and with fatal results to anyone standing within range of the falling bough. Without supernatural intervention his death would have been certain. A slice across the thickest part of the branch was made for him; he gave it a place among his keepsakes.[1]

They returned to London in November 1860. Sacha Home was now very unwell. Several doctors had seen her and they all agreed that she was not suffering from tuberculosis, but from another disease which Home does not specify. Her death was not thought to be imminent but her expectation of life was said to be very uncertain. Continual illness did not impair her sweetness and gentleness; and Home's devoted friends were hers also. A new one of these was now added to what Thomas Moore called 'love's shining circle.' In 1860, No. 7 Cornwall

Terrace was the home of Mrs. F. C. Parkes, the widow of an Indian judge. If Regent's Park is entered by Clarence Gate, Cornwall Terrace is the first on the right hand side of the semi-circle of classical terraces whose pale, pillared façades stand out against the Park's greenery. Built by Decimus Burton in 1822, it is altogether superior in elegance and grandeur to the heavy Victorian houses of Hyde Park Place. The first-floor double-drawing rooms are, for a private house, enormous. In each front drawing-room three sash-windows give on to wrought-iron balconies with motifs of crossed spears. The front doors open on to the pavement, and just across the road is the bowery foliage of the Park, in spring and summer a translucent green. For grace, beauty and quietness, the scene is matchless.

Mrs. Parkes had been present at a séance in Hyde Park Place in December 1860, after the Homes' return from France. She had written in her diary: 'I returned home from this my first séance with Mr. Home, convinced of the truth of our being permitted to hold intercourse with those who have passed to the spirit-land.'[2] From this beginning, a friendship grew rapidly, and by the summer of 1861, the Homes and their child were staying with her in 7 Cornwall Terrace. Home was in very great power during the years 1860, 1861. No. 7 Cornwall Terrace, without superseding Hyde Park Place, became another centre of psychic manifestations, with its own group of sitters who were friends of Mrs. Parkes, or had been introduced by her friends.

Mrs. Adelaide Senior, sister of Tom Hughes, the writer of *Tom Brown's Schooldays*, was a widow who had suffered deeply from the loss of her husband, Henry Senior. Her first séance gave her the reassurance, the comfort, of being again in touch with him, for which her whole being was longing. She wrote,[3] 'I had never seen anything of spiritualism before, but had heard a good deal of it from the dear friend who introduced me to Mr. Home. My own experiences that night were far more wonderful than anything I had ever heard or read of.' Home had described his vision of her husband, his handsomeness, his powers of mind. He said to her: 'You forgot to wind up his watch, and how miserable that made you!' Mrs. Adelaide Senior said that on the night of her husband's death, she had wound his watch, determining never to let it go down again, but one night, on her return to their old home, she forgot it; next morning the watch was motionless. 'My agony was great . . . but I never mentioned it, even to my husband's sister who was in the house with me.' At a second séance, Home, in trance, said that her husband and his mother were standing behind her, longing to comfort her. Then he went on to say that eight months before her husband's death, she had had a conversation with him. He blessed her for that conversation now. They had been sitting in their drawing-room, he in his arm-chair and she in hers, with the little round table between them, and she had just read a chapter of the New Testament. Their conversation after this had been unforgettable. 'These are facts for which I can vouch', she wrote. 'To me, the comfort has been unspeakable'. Her husband's brother, Nassau Senior, was the Professor of Political Economy at Oxford, a member of the Poor Law Commission, who has been described as the most distinguished political economist of the period between Ricardo and J. S. Mill. As he was of a placid disposition and liked to enjoy life, he avoided trouble where he could. He advised: study theology carefully, but if you form unusual opinions, don't mention them except to intimate friends. Nevertheless, he was much interested in his sister-in-law's experiences. He sat with Home several times to assure himself of the genuine nature of the phenomena, and in 1863, he negotiated with Longmans the publication of Home's first volume of reminiscences, '*Incidents of My Life*, Series I'.

Adelaide Senior was of course greatly interested in the experiences of other sitters. It was she who gave one of the best descriptions of the ambiance of 7 Cornwall Terrace, in recounting the conversion to spiritualism of Miss Catherine Sinclair. This lady was one of six tall sisters who were known in Edinburgh as Sir John Sinclair's six and thirty feet of daughters. Edinburgh in the nineteenth century was called the Athens of the North and Catherine Sinclair was a characteristic product of its society, intellectual, clear-headed and vigorous. In 1839 she had published a children's book, *Holiday House*, which became famous. The children in it, Harry and Laura Graham, had bursts of wildness and excitement amounting almost to dementia and were barely kept under by their brutal nurse Mrs. Crabtree who thrashed them continually with a tawse. Nonetheless, the work has an extraordinary purity and freshness, like the boisterous airs of Scotland, the violence of the action being accepted as the result, merely, of energy and high spirits on the part of everybody. Miss Sinclair was a friend of Mrs. Milner Gibson, but her first séance with Home was held, not in Hyde Park Place but in Cornwall Terrace. Mrs. Senior, describing it, says[4], 'We were all assembled in the summer twilight in a large drawing-room in one of those immense houses in the Regent's Park where Mr. and Mrs. Home were staying with the widow of an Indian judge.' The company had not formed a circle but were seated about the room. Home came up to Miss Sinclair and said, 'in that peculiar trance voice', 'You knew James Ferguson.' Miss Sinclair actually bounded to her feet, exclaiming: 'Yes, I did!' Home said: 'He wants to communicate with you, but he cannot do so — you are so surrounded by your friends'; and she answered bitterly — 'Aye, I daresay!' Mrs. Senior imagined that a love-story lay behind this, and was sure afterwards that she had been right. Home said: 'He wants you to do something for him.' 'Oh, what is it?' she interrupted, 'there is nothing I would not do for him.' Home then spoke of a message which Sir James Ferguson wanted her to send his son. 'But I do not know where he is!' she said. 'Can you tell me?' Home said, 'I will try to find out.' He turned away to walk about the room and Mrs. Senior saw a star glittering on his forehead. She cried: 'Oh! look at that star!' but, like the light which only Jones had seen when his friend's spirit stood behind him, the star was invisible to everyone except her. Home walked to the folding doors which were closed and began to pace up and down in front of them like a sentry; then, they all saw seven stars sparkling round his head. In a few minutes he came up to Mrs. Senior and said: 'No one saw the first star in my forehead but you — that was Henry's star.' Then he turned to Miss Sinclair and gave her an address in Baden Baden. Some time afterwards Mrs. Senior saw a notice in the paper that Sir James Ferguson's son had died there.

Mrs. Parkes, in describing this séance spoke of Home's 'trance voice'. It is she who records his own description of his sensations on going into this state. When he was asked what these were, he said: 'At first a heaviness in my feet comes on, I feel as if I were fainting away on the brink of a precipice — there is a moment of suffering, and then all is agreeable.' In the diary which she made available, Mrs. Parkes[5] said that on 7 July, 1861, four people including herself were sitting in the centre window of the front drawing room when spirit-raps were heard on the floor. It was a fine summer evening, she said, and the room was perfectly light. 'Mr. Home fell back in his chair and went into the deep trance for some time.' Presently he got up and walked about the room; he looked as though some one were leading him. 'A very large, bright star shone on his forehead, several clustered on his hair and on the tips of his fingers.' Home now passed in front of a very large mirror, 'a sea of glass'. Reflected in it, Mrs. Parkes saw Home, being led by a figure, entirely veiled in a bluish covering which showed the shape of the head and shoulders and came down to the ground. She saw them both in the mirror; Home's head, hair and face were perfectly distinct; the features of the other figure were veiled. Then two more figures appeared in the glass — a female figure veiled in white and rather higher up, a man in oriental costume. The startling vision faded away, and the great mirror remained empty, filled only with the light from the windows which streamed upon it.

Mr. W. M. Wilkinson was a solicitor with a large practice, with offices at 44 Lincoln's Inn Fields. His house, Oakfield, was at Kilburn, then such an outlying, sparsely inhabited neighbourhood, it hardly had its own identity: Wilkinson described himself as living at Hampstead. He was one of the people who had a great concern for Home, as well as a deep interest in his psychic powers. Later, after Sacha's death,

Home was to stay with Mr. and Mrs. Wilkinson at Oakfield, and Wilkinson helped him very greatly in the compiling of 'Incidents of My Life, Series I'.[6] Wilkinson and his wife were present at the séances at 7 Cornwall Terrace, and Wilkinson gave Home his report of them for the 'Incidents', I, p. 186 et seq. The oriental figures which Mrs. Parkes described as appearing in the looking glass, were in harmony with her having spent much time in India, and with her having, in one corner of the drawing-room, a shrine on which were displayed several metal figures of Indian deities, in front of which she usually arranged flowers. Wilkinson said that at these séances, the music supernaturally produced was particularly moving, because of the presence of young Mrs. Home: 'from our knowing the sickness, even unto death, of one of the party, the youngest and the happiest, in her bright longings for this second life.' The most interesting event of this séance was that, with a crash, the largest figure was thrown down and tumbled across the floor to come to a standstill under the table. A metallic rattle was traced to the fact that the ornamental canopy over the idol's head had become unscrewed and was knocking against it. The figure first pushed itself up under the table cloth, then rose 'naked' above the table. Some of the flowers in front of the shrine were carried by invisible means across the room and distributed among the party. Wilkinson and his wife were given a rose and several pinks. He concluded his statement much in Dr. Gully's manner: 'It is not yet fashionable to believe in these impossible things, and as some one must begin and put up with the necessary ridicule I willingly submit my name for as much as can be made to stick to it.'

The wide range of people, aristocratic, professional, private, who were magnetized by Home's powers, included two literary couples, most of whose work has not survived though it enjoyed much popularity and success in the life-time of its authors. William Howitt and his wife were serious-minded, industrious writers, who gauged effectively the growing public eagerness for information of a straightforward kind about interesting people and places. Howitt's magnum opus, *A History of Spiritualism*, is a work of thorough research, of which Brian Inglis has said[7] that it 'showed impressively how enormous was the range of evidence for psychic phenomena', but the rest of his work was, though serious, of a more generally popular kind. *Visits to Remarkable Places, Rural and Domestic Life in Germany, The Boys' Country Book, Ruined Castles and Abbeys of Great Britain*, were some of the titles that served to build up his fame with a large reading public. His wife Mary collaborated with him in much of his work; she made one of the first English translations of some of Hans Andersen's stories, and wrote verse for children, including the unforgotten 'Will you walk into my parlour, Said a spider to a fly.' The Howitts were living in the late

1850's in West Hill Lodge, on West Hill, Highgate, above the misty, romantic Highgate Ponds. Here they frequently entertained Home. Their circle was a large one, including painters and writers. Among the latter was another married couple, like themselves writers and journalists. Samuel Carter Hall was a popular writer more prolific even than Howitt. His output, as editor, reporter, journalist, was enormous. His industry and energy, his commitment to his profession, made him respectable, and it is disconcerting to learn that when Dickens published *Martin Chuzzlewit* in 1844, it was said to be recognized by some people that he had used S. C. Hall as a model for Mr. Pecksniff. This would seem to be over-stating the case. Charles Osborne who had known S. C. Hall well, gave a clear assessment[8] as to what Dickens had taken from him: that he was tiresomely voluble, overflowing with moral platitudes and had a tendency to humbug. But Osborne makes the point that there was nothing criminal about him. He was marked by 'inordinate egotism and self-complacency' but not by depravity. Bearing in mind Phiz' drawings of Mr. Pecksniff, pot-bellied, bland and smug, Osborne declared that these bore no resemblance to S. C. Hall whatever. The latter was tall and thin, extremely good-looking with classical features and long, wavy white hair. He was a kind, genial and amusing host, and enjoyed a joke, providing he were not the subject of it. Whatever might be his short-comings, there was clearly a good deal about him which made him agreeable as a sympathetic and affectionate friend, but the charm of the acquaintance was no doubt his wife. Anna Maria Hall was a most attractive woman, tender-hearted, intelligent and sincere. She was very actively charitable. She and Mary Howitt were both devoted to Sacha Home, but Mrs. Hall had, perhaps, a special impulse towards her; one of the former's most pressing charitable concerns was the Brompton Hospital for Consumption.

The circle of people around Sacha suffered keenly from the certainty that they were going to lose her, and their grief was equalled by their astonishment at the calmness and joy with which she, a young, happy woman, loving and beloved, looked forward to her death. Its rapid approach was recognized as inevitable. Only in the last fifty years, have the drugs been available which might have warded it off. Hers would appear to have been a case of 'galloping consumption' which runs the most rapid course in adolescents and young adults, in which, it is said, the highest mortality occurs after twenty. At the time of her death she was twenty-two. Home was consumptive himself and it is often taken for granted that she caught the disease from him, but she seems to have had the temperament typical of the tubercular subject, which used to be called the 'spes phthisica', in some victims a reckless, overbearing optimism, in gentler ones an almost supernatural serenity and brightness. Home, in despair, took her to Bournemouth for April and May of 1861, and Mrs. Parkes went with them to take care of her. After many consultations in London, it was here definitely diagnosed that her left lung was affected, that she was suffering from consumption and not from the un-named disease which Home had feared, which was probably cancer. He said[9] that before their marriage they had promised to keep nothing from each other, and he told her now what the verdict was. She had felt before that her mother's hand was on her forehead, blessing her; she said: 'I feel she is here now, I feel a continuation of the same thrill.' She asked for her writing desk, and set about writing letters to be given to her friends after she was dead. The three year old Gricha came to her knee and said: 'Mama is too good to be ill', and this was the only time Home saw her cry. 'There were musical sounds in our room every night', he said, 'and the singing of a bird more than once, from more than an hour over her bed.' With a patient so much oppressed in breathing, it was felt that any change of air was worth trying. The soft, heavy climate of Bournemouth was not favourable, and the Coxes urged Home to bring her to Stockton House. This, though still in Hampshire, was many miles inland, near Crondall, outside a village called Fleetpond, where two great ponds flowed into each other, forming a mere. The luxuriant greenery and the rhododendrons made it a paradise, but one that was of no avail. Brighton was tried, and Folkestone, but in December 1861 they came back to London. The last doctor to attend her in England was Dr. Hawkesley, a celebrated consultant for lung trouble. When he sounded her chest, Dr. Hawkesley saw that there was no hope, but he attended her several times. He was astonished and impressed by her attitude. He said: 'With my other patients, I have to give them hope that they are going to stay, and you are always asking me for hope that you are going to go!' In February 1862, Home took her to France to the Château la Roche near Périgueux, a house belonging to the de Koucheleffs. Here she died on 3 July. He says[10] that it is needless to go over the harrowing details of their parting, but the Bishop who visited her deathbed, the servants of the Château, the peasants who poured flowers on her coffin when it had been lowered into the grave, were all deeply moved by her seraphic sweetness. 'In God's loving mercy we shall meet again and find our lasting habitation in the inner world.'

When, the following year, he prepared his first volume of *Incidents of My Life*, Mary Howitt and Anna Maria Hall both contributed a paper on their recollections of Sacha Home to the chapter he called In Memoriam.[11] They each stressed the point that she was 'a deeply believing spiritualist'. Mrs. Howitt says: 'She had been permitted to solve the great, perplexing and mysterious riddle of the hereafter'. She was speaking of the dying girl's absolute conviction that she was visited by the discarnate spirits of her father, her mother and her husband's mother; that she would soon join them 'in the inner world' and, with them, would remain in touch with her husband, her child and her dearest friends; that in the continuity of existence, there was no parting. Her calmness in the face of death was, therefore, understandable by the older woman, yet she was astonished by it. She said that though weak and exhausted from her long and painful illness, Sacha 'made constant exertions to see her friends', not to see only, but to take part in séances for them. These were held at 7 Cornwall Terrace; it sounds surprising, but Home said she wanted them to be held and they seemed to do her good. The Duchess of Sutherland was one of the visitors who longed, but was afraid, to ask to see her.[12] 'Dear Mr. Home', she wrote, 'I hope you will not think me intrusive on your great anxiety if I tell you how anxious I am to know how Mrs. Home has been since you wrote. Should you think her well enough, and *quite inclined* to see me — or not, if I went to her this evening? . . . I would not for worlds be the cause of any over-exertion to her.' A second letter says: 'As regards what I saw and heard, I was made very happy in feeling that a deeper ground of belief had been given me.' Madame Home says:[13] 'From the dates of the letters, the séance was evidently that of 5 June, 1861, at which Mrs. Parkes' diary shows four persons only to have been present, three of whom would be the Duchess, Mr. and Mrs. Home, and the fourth, Mrs. Parkes herself. Many communications, according to the diary, were received that evening, but none are contained in it — a sufficient indication of their intimate nature.'

Mrs. S. C. Hall's paper is longer and details arguments and expositions of spiritualism, but her picture of the last days of Sacha Home is identical with Mrs. Howitt's; she also gives an insight into the state of the patient, dying without the help of pain-killers and sedatives.[14] 'Suffering wearied the young, fragile form, and she longed to be away, she desired freedom from the body's pain, from the perpetual endurance of restlessness . . . She enjoyed beyond description a séance with those she loved. One of her pleasures was tying up little bouquets of flowers with one of her long dark hairs, flinging a bouquet under or on the table, or into the room, and expressing a wish that a spirit would give it to one or other of her friends. This was invariably done. I preserve these flowers and shall do so while I live.' Sacha, she said, was longing to leave the body and to be with them in the spirit. 'She never doubted that this would be permitted, and she loved to dwell upon the delight it would be to her to be with us . . . I never saw a more perpetual belief in the soul's immortality.' Sometimes, Mrs. S. C. Hall said, they would see her eyes: 'illuminated by a bright light, wandering round the room, while her whole face smiling as if recognizing some spirit friend.' At their betrothal in August 1858, she had told Home she did not believe in spiritualism. Four years had led her through a strange, unexpected path.

The sculptor, Joseph Durham was one of the several artists among Home's friends; he had been converted to spiritualism by Home and he wanted to do something to comfort him. Durham had begun a bust of Sacha before she was taken away to Périgueux. His busts of Jenny Lind, done in 1848, and of Queen Victoria in 1856, had brought him so many commissions that he had almost no time to spend on any private project; but he was so anxious to finish the bust of Sacha so that Home might have it, that, unknown to anyone in his household he was getting up at daybreak to work on it. When Home came back to London, the S. C. Halls, then living at Barrow Lodge in West Brompton, were often the host and hostess at séances given by him. At one of these, Durham was present. A message was given to him: 'Thanks for your early morning labour; I have often been near you.'[15]

## XVII

## 'Impossible to Believe'

The child Gricha had two distinguished playmates while living in his parents' household. Madame Home says[1] that Turgenev made Home's acquaintance while on a visit to London and that when calling on him, took great pleasure in playing with the little boy. Another visitor was Thackeray. The latter had shown his goodwill towards Home in publishing *Stranger than Fiction* and in afterwards defending the publication. When he visited the Homes, he played with Gricha delightfully.

His mother's death now made some arrangement for Gricha an urgent necessity. Several of Home's friends took charge of the child in turn; the first was Dr. Gully who had Gricha and his nurse at The Priory. The doctor's sisters, Anne and Ellen, now forty-eight and forty-five, were unselfish, capable and kind. They had brought up Dr. Gully's own children Susanna, Charles and William; the latter, who eventually became Speaker of the House of Commons, remembered his aunts' care with particular affection and gratitude. Dr. Gully himself was very fond of children and the motherless little boy could not have found a better refuge. Home was grateful for his wife's death had left him not only in a domestic, but in a financial plight. His sister-in-law, the Countess de Koucheleff, remained his friend, but her husband and another member of the family, the Countess Pouchkine, claimed Sacha's estate, and refused to allow Home any of his wife's money. Since this situation arose before the passing of the Married Women's Property Act, Home was entitled by English law to all of it, except what might have been exempted by settlement but the income was derived from Russian sources, Home was in England, and possession was nine points of the law. The estate was not restored to him till 1871, when the Czar intervened on his behalf.[2]

This period though one of grief, anxiety and ill health, was marked also by extraordinary exhibitions of Home's power. Early in the New Year of 1863, he was in Paris as the guest of his faithful friend Count Waldemar de Komar and the séances are recorded in the memoirs of

Princess Pauline Metternich and Princess Caroline Murat. These, unlike so many which were frightening or at least awe-inspiring, were exciting and brilliant. The portrait painted in 1861 of Princess Metternich, shows her as most attractive and typically French, with a small, dark, strongly marked, vivacious face and hair drawn up and then released in ringlets. She is *en grande tenue*, with bare shoulders, a four-fold rope of enormous pearls, pearl bracelets and a voluminous, gauzy scarf: very much as she must have appeared on an evening in January 1863, when she and her husband came to the home of Monsieur and Madame Janvin d'Attainville in the Rue de Paris. The drawing-room, she said, was very spacious, richly furnished and bright as day. During the whole evening the lamps and chandeliers were in full blaze: 'nothing could escape our eyes.' Fifteen guests were assembled and a little after nine o'clock, 'the door opened and at Prince Murat's side we beheld the mysterious, long-awaited hero of the day, the man who inspired fear and uneasiness alike: Dunglas Home.'[3] She said he was fairly tall, slim and well-built and in his dress clothes he looked a gentleman of distinction. 'He was not handsome but his face was attractive in its gentle, melancholy expression.' He was pale, with light, china blue eyes and thick reddish hair. He spoke fluent French.

Prince Murat introduced him to the hostess, then to all the guests. The company seated themselves irregularly about the table, Home sat in an arm chair, three or four yards distant from it. He said hoarsely: 'I don't know if they are here, if they will come.' He leaned back in his chair becoming paler and paler, and Prince Murat exclaimed: 'The trance has begun.' Suddenly Home cried out in English: 'Bryan, Bryan, are you here?' Two raps sounded on the table which was altogether out of Home's reach. He said: 'Bryan comes nearly always when I call him. He is my best friend.' (The spirit Bryan has been identified with the poet William Cullen Bryant who had befriended Home in his early days in America, but Bryant did not die till 1878.) 'At the same instant the crystal hangings of the lustres were agitated; moved by an invisible force, a chair travelled up from the end of the room and halted in front of us. Home remained motionless in his chair.' Suddenly he cried: 'They have come, they are around us!' The Princess said that the sitters now felt as if an iron hand gripped them on neck or arm. The table cloth was raised as if hands were underneath it. Some of the party pounced on the cloth to seize what they supposed to be hands, all of which melted in their grasp. The cloth was pulled off and revealed that there was nothing on the table. Some of the men crept under it to keep watch there while Home remained sitting motionless in his chair. 'They might look and search where they would,' the Princess added, 'they could not find the slightest indication of anything suggesting fraud.' After a few moments the gentlemen reappeared from under the table and went and seated themselves in their chairs. Home cried out that the spirits were now around them and the sitters felt a cool breeze blowing over their shoulders and hair. Now occurred the most charming event of the evening. Home said: 'There is a spirit approaching the piano. I am going to ask it to bring you the bunch of violets that one of you placed there.' His head fell against the back of the arm-chair. 'At that very moment we saw the bouquet beginning to move, or rather, to slide along the polished surface, raise itself in the air, and with a swaying movement, cross the space between the piano and the table around which we were gathered. Then the bouquet dropped upon my knee. At once my husband took hold of it to examine it and see if it was not fastened to a thread. He found nothing of the kind, and, greatly disappointed, he returned the bouquet to me. He really was at his wits' end.'[4] The liveliness and brilliance of the scene: the marble, gilding and looking-glass of the Second Empire drawing room, the blazing lamps, the chandeliers with their trembling, tinkling crystal pendants, are in complete contrast with the summer twilight in the lofty, simple elegance of 7 Cornwall Terrace, or the solidly furnished, half-lit drawing room in Hyde Park Place. The character of the French scene is repeated in Princess Caroline Murat's memoirs. At their suppers after the Opera, the enchanting gaiety and excitement began: 'a noise as if every window and mirror in the room was ringing with sounds, that told us Home was coming, was in the house.'

His circle of distinguished admirers grew continuously, but as he invariably refused to take fees for a séance, it was necessary for him to find some means of making an income by normal means. He had abilities which he had never thoroughly developed, in the spheres of music, acting and art. His association with Durham led him to think he would take up sculpture. Durham gave him some lessons and thought well enough of his talent to recommend him to the American sculptor William Wetmore Story. The latter had been working in Rome since 1856 and had gained great *réclame* by his statue, 'Cleopatra', shown in London at the International Exhibition of 1862. He was a member of the Anglo-American society of Florence and Rome in which everybody knew each other. When Thackeray was in Italy in 1853, the Storys' little girl Edith was ill, and Thackeray, sitting by her bed, invented a story to amuse her which he afterwards published as *The Rose and the Ring*.

Another artist whom Home had met in the S. C. Halls' circle was Thomas Heaphy, who had painted a portrait of Sacha. His friendship with the Homes had led him to a wavering indeterminate belief in spiritualism. His friendship, however, was of a positive kind. When he knew that Home meant to study sculpture in Rome, he gave him an introduction to John Gibson, an English sculptor, once famous. Gibson had executed a tinted bust of Queen Victoria and had exhibited three tinted statues at the International Exhibition: the Tinted Venus, Cupid, and Pandora. It was perhaps Gibson's success in this *genre* which had made Powers say to Hawthorne[5] that he disapproved of colouring marble statues. 'The whiteness,' he said, 'removed the object represented into a sort of spiritual region, and so gave chaste permission to those nudities which would otherwise suggest immodesty.'

Home meant to make a leisurely approach to Rome. He first went as far as Dieppe, where he was joined by Mrs. Milner Gibson and some of her friends, and here a remarkable event took place, of the kind which, unforeseen, alters the course of life. Dr. John Elliotson had had a highly successful but a tempestuous career. He had been one of the founders of University College Hospital, and the first to introduce Laennec's stethoscope into hospital practice. He had been the professor of the Practice of Medicine at London University, but he had aroused violent antagonism by his examination and promoting of mesmerism, which he thought very valuable as a means of relieving pain in the era immediately before the introduction of anaesthetics. He explored the matter in all its bearings in his paper, *The Zoist*. When University College Hospital imposed a ban on the use of mesmerism, Elliotson resigned the chair of the Practice of Medicine. His private practice, at first injured by this reverse, became afterwards increasingly, spectacularly successful. Thackeray, whom he attended in an attack of cholera, drew him as 'Dr. Goodenough' in *Pendennis*, published in 1850, and dedicated the novel to him. Writing to Mrs. Brookfield, he said that, riding in the Park, he met 'dear old Elliotson, thundering along with his great horses at ten miles an hour.' Thackeray trotted up to the carriage on his little horse, and they shook hands, 'at a capital pace.'

Elliotson was interested in mesmerism on a purely scientific basis. He was a materialist, who declared: 'We have no miraculous powers nor can anything we do be miraculous.' This view caused him to abhor the notion of spiritualism, an attitude which led him to a bitter and, as it seemed, irreconcilable quarrel with his former friend Dr. Ashburner. The latter, once a sceptic and a rationalist, had altered his views after sitting with the American medium Mrs. Hayden, who had come to London in 1852; these séances convinced him that 'the manifestations of the presence of unseen intelligences were undeniable.' He was a neighbour of Mrs. Milner Gibson and attended several of Home's séances in Hyde Park Place. At this volte-face on the part of his one-time friend, Dr. Elliotson's scientific convictions were reinforced by unbounded personal rage. He had never seen Home, but he both wrote and spoke of him as a cheat and a scoundrel.[6]

Walking one autumn morning with Mrs. Milner Gibson in Dieppe, Home heard from her that Dr. Elliotson was in the town. Hardly had Home said, to her surprise, that if so, he would like to meet him, than they came upon Dr. Elliotson himself, sitting on a seat on the sea-front. Mrs. Milner Gibson made the introduction, and Home said, with childish candour: 'Dr. Elliotson, you have written and said very hard things of me. Now, don't you think it was very wrong of an old man like you, to make such accusations as you have done against me, and to call a man an imposter of whom you knew nothing whatever?' He added, that should Dr. Elliotson like to take the chance of seeing some instances of spirit manifestation, Home knew that Mrs. Milner Gibson would make him welcome that evening. The old doctor was perhaps too much surprised to demur. At all events he came to the séance. Afterwards, he exclaimed that it was wonderful and convincing, but that it was too much of an effort for him suddenly to change the convictions of seventy years. Might he come again and bring a young friend with him whose powers of observation could aid his own? This was readily agreed to and Elliotson came the next evening, bringing with him two young men, the sons of his friend Dr. Symes. The results of this séance confirmed the impressions of the previous one. On his return to London, he sought out Dr. Ashburner. 'Can you forgive me?' he asked. The writer of an obituary on Dr. Elliotson repeated this episode, saying that, as would be expected by all who knew Dr. Ashburner, it was followed by a perfect reconciliation.[7]

Home records that while he was at Dieppe, he experienced one of his prophetic visions of death. A Russian gentleman asked him if he had ever seen visions in a crystal? No, Home said. The Russian, eager to see as much as he might of Home's powers, produced a crystal and asked him to look into it. Home did so. He saw a group of people and in the middle of them, a man falling forward from his chair. He said: 'That is Abraham Lincoln. Within a year he will be assassinated.' This was the autumn of 1863. Lincoln was murdered on the night of 14 April, 1865. The time given in the prophecy was out by something like eighteen months; clairvoyant predictions are frequently inaccurate as to times they mention, but the vision of the fatal act was all too true. Home said: 'I do not attempt to explain these things. I only give the facts.'

He had very early received warning that his wife's family meant to sequestrate her estate, and before taking up the idea of making a living by sculpture, he decided to earn some money by writing a memoir; he intended to produce a sequel to it, so he called this, *Incidents in my Life*, Series I. It was felt by people interested in the subject that there was a widespread longing to hear more about it, and that Home, by his integrity and his extraordinary powers, was uniquely fitted for the work. He was given help and encouragement of considerable value; Robert Chambers wrote an arresting introduction, though he did not sign it; Professor Nassau Senior, as already mentioned, introduced him to Longman's, the publishers, and W. M. Wilkinson gave what was, in its way, important assistance; he says[8]: 'I wrote very nearly the whole of it, Home staying with us at Hampstead, and producing all the letters and documents, and giving me the necessary information. Some of it he wrote himself, but very little.' Mr. Wilkinson clearly was of great use in putting the material together, but it could be wished that the lawyer's help had taken the form of encouraging Home to do his own writing. At the same time, the rapidity with which the work was produced (Sacha Home died in July 1862 and the book was published in March 1863) shows the handiwork of a man if not of literary experience, at least of a professional discipline. There is no saying how long it might have taken Home, unaided, to complete the work.

The reviews came out while he was in France, staying with his sister-in-law at the Château de la Roche. He gave extracts from them in his second volume[9] which appeared in 1872. The papers from which he quotes show an attitude of mind which is hardly surprising, including a degree of gross inaccuracy in even non-controversial matters. Home collected some of the mis-statements in the letter which he sent to *The Times* on 13 April, 1863, first thanking them for the fair-minded review they themselves had given him. He then said it was hard that critics 'should condemn a book they had not taken the trouble to read.' 'One,' he said, 'kills my child, another my father, a third calls me an American,' though, as he said, the first sentence of the book told the reader that he was born in Scotland. He went on to the serious offence of sheer untruth. *The Critic* had stated, on the authority of 'a gentleman,' that Home had declared a message must be true, because it had come through the spirit of his father. 'My father is alive and well and the whole story is without a syllable of truth.' 'Why,' he asked, did not the 'gentleman' who supplied the anecdote to *The Critic*, come out and tell them his name?' He answered his own question, 'I have found,' he said, 'people who, to sustain a pre-conceived idea, would not hesitate at the most gross untruths in vindication of it.'

Prejudice and personal rancour were freely expressed. The *Saturday Review* of 21 March, described Home as 'a weak, credulous, half-educated, fanatical person,' whose witnesses were few in number and unknown. It said that the producing of evidence from people referred to only by initials, was 'an insult to the court.' Home supplied the names for which the initials stood and gave his reasons for having originally omitted them. *The Critic* made a statement even more extraordinary than mere untruth. 'It is not so much the spiritual element we object to,' they said, 'as the bad taste exhibited throughout, and the impudent treatment of Sir David Brewster.' The exposé of Sir David Brewster unwittingly supplied by his daughter was not yet available and was reserved for Home's second volume. The *Athenaeum* of 14 March said: 'This impudent and foolish book criticises itself.'

But some critics admitted that the subject might have an importance and that if it had, then the importance was extreme. The *Morning Herald* of 4 April said: 'The matter has grown too great for laughter.' The *Spectator* of 14 March said: 'The facts of this book, whether facts or not, all drive at our conclusion, that the gates between the world of the living and the departed are always open.' The writer's comment, however, on the accounts of Sacha Home's death would express the feelings of a great many people: 'It would be brutal to ridicule and yet it is quite impossible to believe.'

# XVIII

## Expelled from Rome

Home arrived in Rome in November 1863 and presented Durham's letter to Story. The latter could not, or at least did not, accept him as a student, but he recommended lodgings to him and found him a studio. When Robert Browning heard this, his frenzy against Home broke out afresh. He wrote to Isa Blagden on 19 December, that Story had refused to admit Home as a student but had felt obliged, by the letter Home brought, to find a studio for him. 'Of course', wrote Browning, 'Home immediately wrote to England (to Dr. Gully, a Gull indeed), that S. had taken him as a pupil — it is Story's own business if he chooses to take this dungball into his hand for a minute, and he will get more and more smeared.' It is not discernable through whom Browning had heard that Home had written to Dr. Gully, but the latter had several acquaintances in Rome; nor can it be learned what Home had actually said. He may have said only, on the strength of Durham's letter, that Story was going to accept him. At all events, in the dealings with the Roman authorities in which he was presently engulfed as in a whirlpool, he made no use of Story's name.

For nearly two months he led an existence of visiting galleries and working in his studio. Then on 3 January, 1864, he received a summons to the Palazzo Citerio, the chief Police Station in Rome[1]. Home asked his friend M. Gautier, the Greek Consul at Rome, to go with him. Snow was on the roofs, and they were kept waiting half an hour in a fireless room, unfurnished except for some straw-seated chairs. They were admitted at last to the office of the Police Chief, Signor Pasqualloni, who was seated at his desk. This room also was scantily furnished; if Home had had the opportunity to conceal any machinery in it, he could not have done so. Signor Pasqualloni began to examine Home as to his family and their characteristics, the dates of his previous visits to Rome and what he was doing there now. Home answered calmly and candidly. He said he had been in Rome since 15 November last. 'Nay', said the Police Chief, 'you have been here since 1 November.' Home replied: 'Here is my passport, which shows you that I have been here only since the 15th.' Pasqualloni relinquished this point and went on to other questioning. 'You say you are a medium, that you become entranced and see spirits?' 'I have said so, and it is true.' 'And you hold communication with spirits?' 'When they think proper.' 'How do you summon them?' 'I do not summon them. They manifest themselves of their own accord.' 'How do they manifest themselves?' Home was about to answer, sometimes in one way, sometimes in another, when raps were heard on a table, 'close to him and far from me.' 'What are those?' exclaimed Pasqualloni. Monsieur Gautier now said: 'These are the spirits, and it must be evident to you that Mr. Home has no volition in the matter.'

'Spirits!' repeated the Police Chief. Then he said: 'Let us continue our examination.' He mentioned 1856, the year Home had been admitted to the Church. 'Have you', he said, 'never exercised your power since that time?' Home replied: 'Neither before nor since, seeing that I am passive in these manifestations which are spontaneous.' Pasqualloni referred to certain works of healing which Home had recounted in his book. 'How did you accomplish them?' he demanded. 'I know nothing about it', Home answered. 'I am only an instrument.' 'Do you see spirits when you are awake or asleep?' 'In both states.' Pasqualloni then questioned him very closely about the religious status of people connected with him. Home had said that at present his child was at Malvern, in the household of Dr. Gully. 'Has he a nurse?' 'Yes.' 'Is she a Catholic?' 'No, she belongs to the Greek Church.' 'Is Dr. Gully a Catholic?' 'No, sir.'

The result of this examination was that Home was told that he must leave Rome in three days. At this, he sought the English Consul, Joseph Severn, who had brought Keats to Rome in 1820, and nursed him till he died. Severn had the capacity which was called for by the ordinary duties of his position, but Home's case was something altogether outside his experience. However he saw, more clearly than Home, why the Catholic Church and the Roman government adopted towards him the attitude they did. He promised to see the Governor of Rome, Cardinal Matteuci, and meanwhile an influential friend of Home's obtained an interview with the Cardinal on his behalf. The Cardinal said there was nothing at all against Home, except the fact that he was a sorcerer, and the practice of sorcery was absolutely forbidden by the Church. Severn was told next day that Home might remain if he signed an undertaking that he would not conduct any séances while he was in Rome. He agreed, and signed a document to say so. This was on Monday, 4 January.

The following Saturday afternoon, at half past five, he was summoned again to the Palazzo Citerio. At quarter to six, he presented himself, accompanied as before by Monsieur Gautier. This time they saw Signor Pegallo, who examined Home's passport, said that it was in order and would entitle him to stay in Rome for a year. Next morning, he was sent for yet again, by a policeman who told him that he must come at once as he had not obeyed the summons for the previous evening. Home said, he had obeyed it and had brought a friend with him. The policeman said: 'Your friend came, but you did not.' Home made off at once to recruit Monsieur Gautier. Together they went to the same office, where, at the same desk, they found the same Signor Pegallo. The latter said: 'I waited for you last night till quarter to eight, and you did not come.' Home cried in exasperation: 'I tell you, I did come. You took my passport, and told me that I might remain for a year.' But Signor Pegallo had now had his instructions, that Mr. Home must be outside the gates of Rome by three o'clock that afternoon, and waiving anything that might seem inconsistent in his own conduct, he gave this dictum to the visitors.

Once out of the office, Home found Severn, who had apparently heard that there had been instances of rappings since Home's signing of the undertaking, and assuming that these had been voluntarily produced by Home, reproached him indignantly with having played the fool, broken his promise and put at risk Severn's attempts to help him.[2] Home was now very angry. He said: 'Mr. Severn, I have come to you as an English subject, not to speak to you either as to my beliefs or the phenomena which happen through me.' He went on: 'Since my promise, no manifestation has taken place, though in undertaking not to give séances, I am unable to promise that no manifestation shall occur.' Severn, who though annoyed and perplexed, showed unfailing energy and goodwill on behalf of this British subject, went once again to the Cardinal, but again the reply was that though there was nothing to say against Home's conduct, he exerted a dangerous fascination by his powers, and as he was unable to avoid spiritual manifestations taking place in his presence, he could not be allowed to stay in Rome any longer. Home had been told that he might stay till the following Wednesday, but he made his departure on the Monday. He took a train for Naples. A crowd of vociferous well-wishers attended him to the station. The *Spiritual Magazine* reported that in Naples he had been 'received with great distinction'.[3]

Weld commented on the affair in his *Last Winter in Rome*.[4] He said: 'If Mr. Home be a vain man he must have been gratified by the excitement he occasioned.' Weld had foreseen, from the moment of Home's arrival, that he would not be allowed to stay in the Papal dominions. Not only was his book, already placed on the Index, full of surprising revelations but these were outdone by the rumours about him. It was said that he called up spirits, that he was able to foretell the winning numbers in the Government lottery (as Cagliostro was known to have done) and, this story no doubt arising from his work as a sculptor, that he had made a statue and animated it. It was said also that he floated in the air. Either this was the echo of his past success, or he had held séances in Rome at which he levitated, before the prohibition of the Cardinal. Weld had heard that influence had been tried to get the sentence of banishment rescinded, but afterwards Home had been ordered to depart. The Government, it was said, had invited him to submit to them a list of the expenses he had incurred in making arrangements for his studio. This he had done, but he had heard no more of it.

It so happened that Dr. Gully, who had been very ill in the previous year, was taking an Italian holiday in the spring of 1864. He arrived in Rome in March, two months after Home had left it for Naples. Here he found among other letters waiting for him, one from Lady Shelley, asking him to see that £2 were given to the *custode* to repay him for the care of Shelley's tomb. Dr. Gully wrote in his journal that the grave was very well kept, that the whole cemetery was full of the scent of flowers, and that the dark yew trees made a beautiful contrast with the camellias underneath. To discharge Lady Shelley's commission he called on Severn, and then had a conversation with him about Home. Severn said: 'It was all settled satisfactorily that Home might remain, but Home was indiscreet enough, after that, to go into English and Italian society, and state that the Roman government *dare* not send him away'. Home was again, and finally, ordered to go, the Pope himself insisting on it, Severn said. He added that 'people here all thought Home exceedingly and absurdly vain!' This, said Dr. Gully, led us to the subject of spiritualism, and we talked for more than an hour, Severn giving credence to the likelihood of the mode of existence exhibited or announced by the spirits. He seems a good sort of man: spoke with great affection of Italy. That *all* the people in Rome thought Home 'exceedingly and absurdly vain', is not borne out by the enthusiastic crowd of well-wishers, who went to the station to see him off to Naples; but Severn had had his trials, and his situation had been one of unique difficulty for a consul.

Home returned to England in May, and on his behalf, a complaint was addressed to the Prime Minister, Lord Palmerston, of his treatment at the hands of the Roman government: of his unjust expulsion and the loss he had incurred of the money spent in setting himself up in the studio he had been forced to abandon. Lord Palmerston handed the business to the Foreign Secretary, Lord John Russell. The matter was not a simple one. A state of tension had been created when, that spring, Garibaldi, the foremost enemy of the Papacy, had come to London, been presented with the Freedom of the City and received with tremendous enthusiasm by the crowds whom he addressed at the

Crystal Palace. The English Catholics had resented his presence strongly, and the report of Home's petition gave the Protestant press an opportunity to make hostile criticisms of the Papacy. Lord John Russell declined to act and the affair was dropped.

# XIX

# The Blot on Browning's Scutcheon

Mrs. Browning died in 1861 and in 1864 Browning published *Dramatis Personae*. This collection contained one of his greatest poems: 'By the Fireside', and several characteristic of his genius:— 'Confessions', 'May and Death', 'Prospice'. It also contained 'Mr. Sludge the Medium'.

In May 1860, Mrs. Browning had written to Miss Haworth:[1] 'Robert has been writing a good deal this winter, working at a long poem which I have not seen a line of.' It is assumed that this poem was 'Mr. Sludge', and that Browning, anxious not to wound his wife's feelings, did not show it to her or publish it during her life-time.

It need not be said, seeing who wrote it, that the poem is a work of very considerable power. It depicts a ruthless and diabolically clever swindler who pretends to be a medium, growing rich through the public's determination to be hoodwinked, but reserving to himself a faint possibility that there might be something in spiritualism after all. The main body of the poem displays, at length, how he exploits humanity's deep-seated longing to be deceived. His cheating has been detected by Hiram Horsfall, his client and one-time dupe, and in a vindictive and inordinately lengthy monologue, he confesses how he entered on his career of fraud, how he developed it, how he was not only encouraged, but driven on, by the demands of his victims, whom he despises with a burning and poisonous rancour. He grovels on the floor at his patron's feet, imploring Horsfall not to expose him. When the latter gives him a fistful of five-dollar notes and scornfully dismisses him, he goes off snarling, wishing he had the courage to burn the house over his benefactor's head, but consoling himself with the reflection that there are plenty more fools in the world and that he may as well cross the Herring Pond and find them.

If the work stood by itself as the study of a charlatan, exceptionally gifted with histrionic ability and psychological insight, it would be a brilliant demonstration. There are scoundrels in every walk of life, and Mr. Sludge is accepted as the classic example of a scoundrel pretending to be a spiritualist; as a portrait of Home, it is not libellous only, but absurd.

Browning nevertheless made a deliberate attempt to establish a link between Home and Mr. Sludge. The milieu is Boston, where Home had a reputation as a medium of extraordinary gifts and where he counted among his friends and believers Judge Edmonds, an eminent and highly respected member of the United States Supreme Court. Judge Edmonds had given the leisure time of three years to examining the claims of spiritualism and had come to the conclusion that they were justified. Browning introduces him with vitriolic contempt:—

> Well, Judge Humgruffin, what's your verdict, sir?
> You, hardest head in the United States.

The poem is no doubt full of allusions to contemporary figures now lost to sight, but one can be detected to be Lord Lytton:

> Who draws on his kid gloves to deal with Sludge,
> . . . flavours thence, he well knows how,
> The narrative or the novel, half believes
> All for the book's sake —

a judgement on Lytton not borne out by the latter's letters to Home:— 'Let me introduce to you my eldest brother . . . he is seriously interested in the extraordinary phenomena which are elicited by your powers.'[2] Browning refers to the famous jewels given to Home and worn by him:— 'the spirits . . . see rings on his hands with pleasure,' and he caricatures the attitude to religion which Home maintained was the inspiration of spiritualism:—

> As for religion, why, I served it, sir!
> . . . with my phenomena
> I laid the atheist sprawling on his back,
> Propped up St. Paul, or at least Swedenborg

The most important passages are those which describe how a rogue gains his effects:— 'manage your feet, dispose your hands aright,' by the uncanny skill that comes with practice, the surreptitious gleaning of personal details, to be brought out as if by spirit communication. Browning also introduces as instances of trickery, the various phenomena associated with Home's séances: the child voice, the messages from dead relatives, spirit-writing, starry lights. As an indication of Sludge's powers, Hiram Horsfall is shown as still part-influenced by him, even while exposing him; but he attempts to throttle Sludge who whines and prostrates himself in a paroxysm of rage and servile fear.

On the poem's appearance, Home made the entirely proper comment,[3] 'There is nothing whatever to connect his portrait of Sludge with myself, and no one who was even slightly acquainted with me could discover our point of resemblance.' He added:[4] 'Mr. Sludge is supposed to have been led into his confession by an over-dose of champagne and to be sustained during it by continual potions of egg-nog. Had Mr. Browning known anything practically of spiritualism, he would have been aware that indulgence in intoxicating drink has a strong tendency to destroy medium power.' Browning might logically have argued that there was nothing inappropriate in Sludge's intemperance, since the poem denied that he had any medium power; but Home went on: 'I believe Mr. Browning did intend his portait of Mr. Sludge to represent me, for he once remarked of me that I was in the habit of being brought home drunk by the police every night.' This accusation as applied to Home himself, who was known to be very temperate, was as wildly inaccurate as the picture of him clutching Horsfall's bank notes, when it was well attested that he never took money for a séance.

In America, the work was declared to be a vicious libel. The inhabitants of Boston may well have wondered why their city should have been singled out as the scene of these disreputable and preposterous doings, when Florence, Rome, Paris, London, were just as much connected with Home's activities. The most effective protest in an American newspaper was made by Helen Whitman. Twenty years before, her classical features, pale face, dark eyes and dark ringletted hair had aroused Poe to an understanding of Grecian art, and inspired his hopeless love:[5]

> Lo, in yon brilliant window niche
> How statue-like I see thee stand,
> The agate lamp within thy hand,
> Ah, Psyche, from the regions which
> Are holy land!

Her family had obliged her to part from him because Poe was drinking himself to death, and the horror and anguish she felt at the sight of his sufferings make it clear that she would feel keenly the brutality and injustice of Browning's attack on Home: a man whose gifts filled her with awe and of whose integrity she was certain; writing to the editor of an American journal, she said:[6] 'If you will take the trouble to read the poem of Mr. Browning to which I have referred, you will understand why it is regarded by some of Mr. Browning's warmest admirers as "A Blot on the Scutcheon."'

It might be argued, as the types of phenomena which Home produced were now widely known, might not a picture of a fraudulent medium naturally show him as counterfeiting them? Since, as a personal likeness of Home the picture is altogether wide of the mark and bears no resemblance to him in the opinion of any impartial reader, why should it be said that Browning deliberately meant it for Home?

Browning himself said that he did. When Allingham[7] lunched with him in Warwick Crescent in 1864, Allingham told him that Tennyson had said the poem was too long. Browning answered: 'I hope *he* thought it too long, that is, Sludge, when the confession is forced from him. Sludge,' Allingham said, 'is Home the medium, of whom Browning told me a great deal that is very amusing.' Allingham had heard nothing of the matter except what Browning told him.

When Madame Home worked over her husband's papers in writing *D. D. Home, His Life and Mission*, she was most careful to supply, wherever she could, the names of the people whose letters she quoted. In a very interesting letter of 1870, apropos Browning's own attitude to 'Mr. Sludge', she does not, for once, give the writer's name, speaking of him only as 'an old friend, a well-known English medical man.' It should be remembered, however, that when F. W. H. Myers, on behalf of the Society for Psychical Research, visited her in Paris, and was shown the originals of the letters she had used, he examined their envelopes, post-marks, official stamps, crests, monograms, and his opinion was that in her use of material she was entirely trustworthy. The letter she quotes without naming the writer says[8]: 'Since I saw you, I have been in the Isle of Wight, I went to lunch with Alfred Tennyson and had two or three hours' talk with him . . . he says he is much more inclined to believe than to disbelieve. He had all those tales about you from Browning, including one that you went on your knees, wept and confessed your imposture in a certain thing. I told him Browning was mad about the matter, and he admitted that Browning's manner led him to credit his prejudice more than his statement.'

It is possible that the old friend, the distinguished English medical man, may have been Dr. Gully. Tennyson had been his patient at Malvern and had given him a copy, in his own handwriting, of the first version of 'Come not, when I am dead, to drop thy foolish tears upon my grave.'

Three years after Home's death, and within six months of Browning's in 1889, the Society for Psychical Research printed the following statement:[9] 'Mr. Robert Browning has told to all of us the circumstances which mainly led to that opinion of Home which was expressed in "Mr. Sludge the Medium." It appears that a lady (since dead), repeated to Mr. Browning a statement made to her by a lady and gentleman (since dead), as to their finding Home in the act of experimenting with phosphorous for the production of "spirit lights" which (so far as Mr. Browning remembers), were to be rubbed round the walls of the room, near the ceiling, so as to glow when the room

1.    DANIEL DUNGLAS HOME

2. (a) SIR DAVID BREWSTER

(b) SIR WILLIAM CROOKES

3.    DR JAMES MANBY GULLY

4.　SACHA HOME – The only known photograph of her, reproduced from a letter to D. D. Home, to which it was pasted.

was darkened. This piece of evidence powerfully impressed Mr. Browning, but it comes to us at third hand, without any written record, and at a distance of nearly forty years. We may add that few, if any, of the lights seen at Home's séances, could (as they are described to us), have been contrived by the aid of phosphorous.'

When Browning produced this piece of so-called evidence, which had not even the merit of agreeing with what he had been in the habit of saying before, he was an old man within a few months of his death, and should not, perhaps have been considered as altogether responsible. A much more serious case is brought against him by Andrew Lang: 'The Case of Daniel Dunglas Home.'[10] Lang says that several years before, an eminent writer, whom he does not name, published in a newspaper a statement to this effect: Browning told him that, when he and his wife were sitting alone with Home (a sitting not recorded anywhere else), he saw a white object rise over the table. This Home declared was the phantom of a child of Mr. and Mrs. Browning which had died in infancy. Mr. Browning seized the phantom and it proved to be Home's naked foot.

Lang comments, first, that the Brownings had no child which died in infancy, and secondly, that whatever the circumstances claimed for the hypothetical sitting, 'Mrs. Browning's faith survived the shock'. Browning had obviously repeated some form of this story often, with a reckless disregard for truth. Stirred up by Mr. F. Merrifield's letter to *The Times Literary Supplement*[11], the Brownings' son, Penn Browning wrote to that paper on 2 December that 'Home was detected in a vulgar fraud, for I have heard my father repeatedly describe how he caught hold of his foot under the table.' As Lang says: In the other story the foot was *above* the table; in the new version, no infant phantom occurs ... Why did not Mr. Browning tell this, instead of quite a different story to Mr. Myers?'

The answer seems plain enough. His cruel rage and spite had quite early interfered with Browning's power of accurate remembrance. At last they carried him to the point where he neither knew nor cared whether he were telling the truth. The séance at Ealing which he had carefully described to Mrs. Kinney, and the second séance which he had asked for, and not been granted, had by degrees evolved in his mind into a malignant but chimerical growth. His imagination had produced 'Mr. Sludge the Medium' which ended with the medium writhing at his patron's feet. Browning having lived intensely in his own creation, then transferred the episode from fiction to real life and declared that Home had grovelled on the ground before him. In spite of a low personal opinion of Home, Mrs. Browning had maintained her opinion of the genuine nature of his psychic powers; but Browning put about a story that in a hitherto unheard of séance with the pair of them, Home had produced his naked foot to represent the spirit-head of a child which Mrs. Browning had not borne. Browning, in his son's presence, had frequently told the story of catching Home's foot under the table, though he had declared in his letter to Mrs. Kinney that he had no idea of how the effects of the séance had been produced. But when he was invited by members of the Society for Psychical Research to give his evidence for the accusations in which he had persisted for over thirty years, he had not liked, it seemed, to bring out this farrago to courteous but experienced examiners. He had taken refuge in a story which he said had been told him by a lady, who had heard it from another lady and a gentleman that Home had been discovered painting walls with phosphorus. His monstrous charges had dwindled to these pitiable and ludicrous remains.

> When all its work is done, the lie shall rot.
> The truth is great, and shall prevail,
> When none cares whether it prevail or not.[12]

## XX

## Trouble at Willis's Rooms

Home came back to England from Italy in the summer of 1864, and
left for America almost at once. Being, for the time, deprived of his
wife's fortune and remaining immovable in his determination never
to take money for his work as a medium, he was very anxious to find
some means of livelihood. His talent for acting had been so far unused;
he now decided to give public readings. The Civil War was raging,
and his most effective numbers were recitations of contemporary
American verse. Though his object was to make a living for himself,
in Norwich, Connecticut, he gave a reading for the Soldiers' Aid
Fund[1], for the 'ghastly human wrecks', whom the war had returned
to almost every town and village in the Union. Home's sympathy with
physical pain was acute; a Philadelphia newspaper speaks of his
visiting the improvised hospitals in that city where the influx of
casualties was very heavy and giving readings 'to the great delight of
the sick and wounded soldiers.' On this visit to America there were
many calls on his mediumistic powers. Helen Whitman wrote to him
from New York on 11 May, 1865. 'I shall not forget the evening
passed with you in 35th St ... If we do not meet again on earth, I
trust we shall hereafter.' Poe had met his terrible end sixteen years
before. Whose spirit had manifested, during the evening that she would
not forget?

A scientific development of the mid-nineteenth century which bore
a relation to the power of the dead to return, was photography. Sir
John Herschel, the astronomer and scientist whose work contributed
to the art, was the first to call it photography: 'written by light'. The
memory of the dead achieved a new vividness when the bereaved
looked at a telling photograph of the face, a sensation difficult to
estimate to-day, when photography has been a commonplace for over
a hundred years. As the art has become more sophisticated and
aesthetic, something seems to have been lost of that sheer power of
presenting a likeness, which strikes one so forcibly in many early and
mid-Victorian photographs. Among mid-nineteenth century photo-

graphers, one of the most successful was John Mayall. He established a chain of photographic studios in London and the provinces; his speciality was the *carte de visite* photograph, small and intensely characterized; it was estimated[2] that his studios issued half a million of these in one year.

Mayall was a friend of Dr. Gully and had photographed him in his Regent Street studio, sitting at a writing desk with bent head. In January 1865, Mayall wrote to Home in America:[3] 'My dear Home, Many thanks for your kind letter which reached me a few days ago . . . the Doctor is looking better than I ever saw him, and so are the Miss Gullys. It must be cheering to you to be so loved by intelligent men and women . . . We all join in praying for your safe return.' Mayall by this time had made a fortune. He went on: 'I shall now disincumber myself of business and devote the remainder of my life to spiritual investigation.' He was writing from The Grove, Pinner, 'I need not say that my house is yours whenever you can avail yourself of it. Your loving friend, J. E. Mayall.'

Home returned briefly to England in May. In July 1865, he went to Russia. Several people there were anxious to see him again, including the Czar; Count Alexis Tolstoy and his family had written affectionate letters, saying: 'Come, come, come!' Home's purpose on this occasion was one of important business; he had to set in hand negotiations for claiming his wife's estate; but he looked forward to being with his friends again. He was in the train approaching St. Petersburg and thinking about those whom he longed to see, particularly Alexis Tolstoy whom he believed to be an infinity of miles away, on one of his estates in central Russia. His intense concentration on the Tolstoy family brought about a strange instance of the phenomenon of the wraith or doppelgänger. No one knew that his arrival at St. Petersburg was imminent, except Baron Mayendorff, whose guest he was to be. He reached St. Petersburg at seven o'clock and had himself taken to Mayendorff's hotel. There he found awaiting him a note from Alexis Tolstoy. It said, 'I am so glad you are here. Come, at any time, day or night. You know how glad we are to see you.' It turned out that at four o'clock that afternoon, three hours before his arrival, the Countess Tolstoy said that she saw Home in St. Petersburg, in the Arcade; she had told her husband, adding that it was very strange, but Daniel had not seemed to see her.

Something in the climate of Russia seemed favourable to Home's extraordinary physical constitution, and caused him not only to be exceedingly successful in his mediumistic practice but to give involuntary signs of it, which are not recorded of him elsewhere. The appearance of his wraith was one instance; another was the turning on a powerful electric current which seemed to be dormant in his body.

The evidences of luminous appearances in his presence are numerous: of light appearing on his head or sitters' heads, of walls bathed in light, but what occurred on the threshold of Baron Mayendorff's house, in the darkness, reads like a recognizable display of electricity. One night he came back alone and was let in by a servant, who at the same time handed him a letter. As Home took it from the man's hand, standing in the dark at the street door, vivid sparks shot from his fingers, and the servant fled, uttering cries of terror.[4] From Baron Mayendorff's house, Home was transferred by the Czar's command to one of the Imperial palaces where he was lodged, attended on and had a carriage and horses at his disposal. The Czar's brother, the Grand Duke Constantine, invited him to his palace at Strelna but on a day for which the Czar had already summoned him to the English Palace at Peterhoff. On 18 August, 1865, Home wrote a long letter to Mrs. S. C. Hall.[5] He told her that he had held several séances with the Czar, at which the manifestations were very interesting and beautiful and had comforted the Czar very much; Home said that he was truly glad to have been of use to him, but he could not disclose any details of the sittings. He was only sorry, he told Mrs. Hall, that when the Czar appointed to meet him at the English Palace, the Imperial Guard was of course drawn up outside the Palace to await the Czar's arrival. This meant that the meeting was made more public than Home would have liked, but he hoped that the publicity would dignify the cause of spiritualism.

The Grand Duke and Duchess Constantine had arranged another day for him to visit them at Strelna. They had both treated him with the utmost kindness and the Grand Duchess was sending to Warsaw for a picture of herself and her children to give him.

Meantime the calls upon him for séances were innumerable. Sometimes, even after a sitting with the Czar, he was begged to hold another one by people already waiting for his return. Count Steinbock-Fermor who had come over to London with Alexis Tolstoy to attend the séances at Mrs. Milner Gibson's, had now heard that Home was at St. Petersburg, and had travelled from the midst of Siberia to see him. He found Home almost at the point of exhaustion, and took charge of him. The Count brought him away to his country seat at Nijni Novgorod, where the famous fair was in progress. Novgorod, the great Slav merchant city of the middle ages, had been Russia's outlet to the west centuries before the founding of St. Petersburg. As it lay on the river Volkhov, it was said to be 'on the water-road between Scandinavia and Byzantium.' The enormous trading area of its past, embracing West and East, still sent a brilliant variety of merchandise to the Fair. It was a spectacle to do Home all the good in the world; of simple entertainment, kaleidoscopic gaiety and crammed with joyous folk.

But, as he told Mrs. S. C. Hall, his material prospects were, for the time, bleak. Count de Koucheleff, having procrastinated in the matter throughout the three years since Sacha's death, now, urged on by the rapacious Countess Pouchkine, absolutely refused to pay over to Home his wife's money. Fortunately, Home said, he was in possession of all the legal documents necessary to prove his claim; there was no doubt of his gaining his suit in the end, but he foresaw that it would take five or six years; it did, in fact, take six years. 'During that time', he said, 'I shall be very poor, as indeed I am at this moment.' He was now considering whether he should not remove altogether to America; he had proved that he could earn a living there as a public reader. He did not think he had the courage to give readings in England. 'It may be', he said, 'that this arises from a false pride, but there the feeling is.'

In the autumn Home came back to London. The winter months of 1865–66 were ones of suffering caused by depression and illness. It was at this time that Pickersgill painted his portrait. William Pickersgill, who had been an R.A. for thirty years, was said by now to have almost a monopoly of painting the portraits of celebrated sitters. In 1864, through the invitation of S. C. Hall, he had had two sittings with Home.[6] He was anxious to paint his portrait, 'though I wish you were in better hands', he said. The picture now hangs in the lecture room of the College of Psychic Studies. Of life-size, it has an arresting quality. The pale face, sandy hair, lean but broad-shouldered frame, are what one would expect to find, but the air, at once ill, oppressed and visionary, gives an insight into what it was, actually to see Home. He is leaning his left elbow on the plinth of a bust, incised with the word 'Sacha'. Home said this was the bust executed by Durham. With the small photograph reproduced on Home's writing paper this is the only available likeness of her, but the background is murky, and the drooping head with a veil over the hair is not clearly seen.

Home had many friends among painters. The most famous was Landseer, the artist of great technical capacity, who endowed animals in his pictures with the emotions of love and suffering experienced by human beings; the death agonies of a hunted stag, a dog sitting beside a coffin: The Old Shepherd's Chief Mourner, a dog wounded and dying, The Last of the Garrison. Such an attitude naturally appealed to Home; there was a mutual sympathy. Landseer sat several times with him, first at 14 Wilton Place, the house of Mr. James Grant, the editor of the *Morning Advertiser*, whose editorial policy had always been favourable to Home; and afterwards at Landseer's house in St. John's Wood Road. Among her husband's papers, Madame Home found a drawing of a dog, signed by Landseer, with: 'This is my little dog' written underneath it.[7]

156

The ill health plainly to be seen in Pickersgill's portrait of 1865 was a matter of great concern to Dr. Gully. He had Home to stay at The Priory in December. The air of Malvern and the care of an eminent doctor did something for Home, but as Dr. Gully had said in his book, *The Water Cure in Chronic Disease*, 'For pulmonary consumption there is, of course, no cure.' In 1845, he could have said nothing else; but he explained that the water-cure treatment would make the symptoms much less distressing: 'the hectic, the sweatings, the bad sleep, the languor, these can be in great measure avoided, notwithstanding the unceasing onward progress of the miserable malady.' He had said that if a patient recovered from an illness, it would be, not as the result of any treatment, but because of the strength of his own constitution, and therefore it was the business of the doctor not to administer drugs to perform the body's work for it, but to husband the body's strength so that in the end it would be able to do its own work once more, and he used all the authority which his position and his personality could exert, to prevent Home from exhausting himself by giving too many séances. He had held some at The Priory House, of an extraordinary nature, but Dr. Gully, faced with the great danger to the patient of overtaxing his strength, now felt that he ought not to have allowed so many to take place, and when Home had gone back to London in January, he wrote: 'My conscience went against the frequency of our sittings down here.' 'You must, on no account', he said, 'for no person whatever, have more than two sittings in a week, it will destroy your health altogether if you do. You must be firm in this, and, if you like it, quote me, your medical friend, for it.' But the prohibition could not make its mark. Home, as his second wife despairingly recorded, was incapable of refusing to sit with people who earnestly wished it; and a séance often started, with raps or sounds, when he had not courted it, did not expect it. Père Ravignan and Dr. Gully, from opposite motives, had both said that these experiences must be controlled, and both received the same reply:- I do not bring them on, and when they come, I cannot stop them. Meanwhile, he conquered the reluctance he had had when he wrote to Mrs. Hall from Russia, and began to investigate the possibilities of a career of public reading in England. Before entering on this, he arranged to give a lecture on spiritualism in Willis's Rooms.

This building, in King Street, a turning at the bottom of St. James's Street, was well known as the scene of public lectures, but it had once been more famous still. Under the name of its original proprietor, Almack's, it had been the assembly-rooms, during the reign of George IV, for the balls, parties and gaming of an exclusive circle. When Charlotte Brontë went there to hear Thackeray lecture in 1851, the lecture hall was still the great painted and gilded saloon where balls

157

had been held and the seats were still the long sofas which had once lined its walls. In 1863 the premises were bought by Mr. Willis and were known from then as Willis's Rooms.

Home delivered his lecture there on 15 February, 1866. One of the people who abominated Home and traduced him without ever having laid eyes on him, was Charles Dickens, now at the summit of his resplendent fame. He had never attended a séance of Home's, but as he had written to Mrs. Lynn Linton in September 1860, it would not be worth his while to do so, because the conditions (of which he had no first hand knowledge) 'were preposterously wanting in the commonest securities against deceit or mistake.' He had never met Home, but he said: 'Mr. Home I take the liberty of regarding as an impostor.'[8] In 1859, Dickens had started a weekly paper, *All the Year Round*; in 1866 this was being edited by Mr. H. G. Wills. It is however undeniable that whatever a journalist may write, the responsibility for printing it rests with the editor and in the last resort, with the proprietor of the paper in which it appears. The episode of Home's lecture as it actually took place, and as it was reported in *All the Year Round*, is astonishing.

The lecture was covered by reporters from several papers; one of them, from the *Evening Star*, gave what Home accepted as a fair account of the lecture, but it described his personal appearance with that slightly acidulated zest which is meant to stimulate the reader's attention. The audience, it said, was filled with ladies and gentlemen deservedly well known in the literary and dramatic world, who had given convincing proof of their belief in spiritualism as they had paid for their entrance tickets. It described Home as tall, slim and pale with light hair, only erring in calling his eyes 'small and dark', when they were large and light. It gave a, no doubt, recognisable picture of Home's somewhat finicking and self-conscious manner in front of an audience — 'with dainty white fingers he spread out his manuscript, displaying the neatest of wrist-bands while on his left hand sparkled a lustrous diamond every time he lifted his pocket handkerchief.'

Home delivered what sounds from the extracts of his speech which he printed himself,[9] a calm and reasonable assessment on the spiritualist position. He mentioned the researches of Professor Hare and Judge Edmonds among others, he mentioned spiritualist drawings as 'conveying some lesson by symbol and correspondence': (a very interesting comment apropos some automatic drawings by Lady Shelley's twelve-year old niece, which were afterwards published under Dr. Gully's auspices; the child had produced, inter alia, a column of symbols of which she had added the explanations, all without the least idea of how she had done it). Home said: 'To an investigation of the laws and principles, as well as the phenomena, of spiritualism, I earnestly invite your serious attention.' He said of the matter of being misled by spirit communication: 'Abuses are possible, but God gave every man the power of reason and this it is in no way the province of spiritualism to supersede.' He made a point of great moment: 'All spirits are not perfect and the moment we give up our reason, either to men or spirits, we wrong ourselves and insult our loving Father.' The absurd slanders about himself, he said, were numerous. It was said that he had prehensile toes, and some people had asked to be allowed to see his naked feet. The phenomenon of electricity which had shown itself in Russia, had got about, and it was said that while he was there, he had a great number of cats sleeping with him, who so charged him with electricity that rapping noises were heard in his presence. But he emphasized the fact that many men of scientific repute, while denying the spiritualist origin of phenomena, accepted that the phenomena themselves were genuine; he would urge that the communications were our links with the other world. The essential message of spiritualism, he said, was: 'God is love, and there is no death.'

It might seem that there was not much here to give grounds for ribald hilarity, but anyone who thought so would seriously underestimate the powers of the reporter briefed by *All the Year Round*.

He began[10] by saying that he was called on to pay half a guinea for his seat 'Are there no five shilling seats left? I asked. The answer was, no they are all gone, only a few half-guinea seats left.' When he got into the auditorium, he found, he said, that there were plenty of five shilling seats left, only a few half-guinea ones remaining. He accused the door-keeper of deceiving him. The man said, it was not his fault: he had been told to say there were no five-shilling seats. It transpired later that he had been told to say so because it was so. Two weeks later,[11] the *Spiritual Times* announced: 'We have taken the trouble to enquire of the management about this matter, and we learn that all the five shilling tickets were sold, and that those seats the writer saw were half-guinea ones. And we are assured that a seat would have been offered him gratis if he had only shown his card and stated that he was one of the Press.' The *All the Year Round* reporter, settled in his seat, looked about him and said that he counted fifteen members of the audience fast asleep. The *Spiritual Times* said: 'Is there another person beside this writer who will state this?' The *All the Year Round* reporter then turned his attention to the lecturer, who, he said, was 'a tall, thin man with broad, square shoulders, suggestive of a suit of clothes hung on an iron cross. Hair long and yellow, teeth large, glittering and sharp, eyes pale grey with a redness round the rims that comes and goes as he talks ... his hands were long, white and bony, and you knew, without touching them, that they were icy cold.'

The reporter now achieved a feat of unscrupulous suggestion which amounted to a lie. In October 1864, the actor Dion Boucicault had held a séance at his house when the Davenport brothers, two young Americans who possessed paranormal powers of the most extraordinary nature, gave a demonstration at which, while they themselves were securely roped up in a cupboard, musical instruments outside it — guitars, tambourines, bells, brass trumpets — played of their own accord and created pandemonium. Boucicault had written a signed deposition which had been published in several newspapers, and as the Davenport brothers had afterwards given exhibitions of their powers in music halls, the public in general was familiar with the various details of their act. Home had declared in his lecture his view of the extreme importance of spiritualism in man's present and future life, and the reporter credited him with saying that: 'Spiritualism, founded upon table-rapping, rope-tying and banjo-playing in a cupboard, is a means of man's salvation.' Home replied: 'I never spoke such a sentence; I have never had anything to do with rope-tying and banjo-playing in a cupboard; least of all have I ever said that spiritualism was founded on such manifestations.' When Home was asked at a later date, what was his opinion of the Davenport brothers as mediums, he said: 'They are not mediums at all.'

The meeting did not close without spectacular interruption. John Henry Anderson, a celebrated Scots conjuror and illusionist known as The Wizard of the North, had conducted his profession on a grand scale. He was the lessee of Covent Garden theatre, and in March 1856, he organised a two days' saturnalia of continuous entertainment, eating and drinking. At five o'clock in the morning of the third day, the theatre had burned down, with such fury that the flames lit up the façade of St. Paul's and threw a flood of light over Waterloo Bridge. Anderson's career emerged, phoenix-like, from the ashes, and in the 1860's he was giving a series of acts satirizing and deriding spiritualism. When he heard that Home himself was speaking at Willis's Rooms, he turned up there, in a condition, as Home said, which made it painfully evident to all present, that he was not fit to address a public meeting. Pulling off his overcoat as if he meant to fight, Anderson stormed the rostrum, yelling:- 'Swindler! Humbug!' Home possessed a reasonable amount of personal courage but he did not want a bout of fisticuffs with a drunken man in front of an audience. He jumped down to the floor and left it to the ushers to see Anderson out. It was here that the *All the year Round* reporter told his most audacious lie. He asserted that Home went round among the audience distributing bills to them. It had rather startled him, he said, after his experience at the pay-place to hear Mr. Home announce during his lecture that he never had and never would receive money for his work. And besides

160

the sharp practice at the box office, Mr. Home had declared in a circular to his friends that he hoped they would support him, as 'much *of my own fortune* must depend on the issue of this experiment.'

Samuel Carter Hall had been in the audience and he read the report issued in *All the Year Round* on 3 March. He wrote to its editor, Mr. Wills, that the report was 'a mass of deliberate falsehoods', and the editor 'ought to know it.' Home, on coming down from the platform did not deliver bills. 'He had none to deliver'. As to the private circular which the reporter, admittedly with great sharpness, had contrived to see, this was not delivered to the public, but only to Home's personal friends. When quoting from it, the reporter had altered a word so as to convey a false and damaging impression. The wording of the original was, not 'much of my own fortune depends'; but 'of my own future.'

Whatever might be said against S. C. Hall by people who personally disliked him, he was widely known as a man who had followed a respectable literary career for over thirty years and his evidence against the *All the Year Round* reporter could not be set aside by any impartial judge; but if a protest is made against a newspaper, proving a statement to be untrue, and the paper does not intend to admit the charge but cannot refute it, the editor's best course is to behave as if the protest had not been made. S. C. Hall's letter was not acknowledged.

# XXI

## 'Triumphant Music'

Attacks on Home's mediumship published in the press, were as a rule ignorant and not seldom, downright untruthful. On one occasion, however, a devoted spiritualist published comments which, for criminal irresponsibility, would have done justice to Home's traducers themselves.

Edward Sothern, aged forty in 1866, was a well-known comic actor who carried 'waggishness and high spirits' into private life, and had a great turn for practical jokes. He was happily married and very successful in his theatrical career on both sides of the Atlantic. Tom Taylor's comedy, *Our American Cousin* was put on at the Haymarket in November 1861, where it made a slow start, but Sothern, who played Lord Dundreary, wrote a great deal into the part himself and made such a hit with it that the play became a long-running success, and the side-whiskers which he adopted for the role became the fashion and were known as Dundrearies. The play afterwards acquired a macabre interest: it was being played at Ford's Theatre in Washington on the night of 14 April, 1865, when the event Home had foreseen took place, and Abraham Lincoln was murdered in his box.

The *Spiritual Magazine*, the most interesting of its contemporaries, had been founded in 1860 and was edited by Thomas Shorter, assisted by the solicitor W. M. Wilkinson. A frequent contributor was Benjamin Coleman.

In 1865, Sothern, his wife and family, and the painter Frith were holidaying at Scarborough; in October 1865, Sothern published in a Scarborough newspaper an article describing how he and some friends in 'a private séance' had produced 'all the manifestations of floating about the room and so on, familiar to those who have concerned themselves with the ridiculous exhibitions of Mr. Home and the Davenports.' Coleman quoted this article in a letter to the *Spiritual Magazine*[1], and said that if Mr. Sothern and his friends had actually, in truth, performed the feats of which Home was capable, then they were involuntary mediums. In a further letter of December 1865, he referred to what were, in fact, some practical jokes Sothern had played in America; Coleman said he had there claimed to be a medium and practised as such. Sothern replied to this in the *Evening Citizen*[2] that he and his friends had investigated spiritualist claims in weekly meetings over two years. By constant practice: 'we outdid everything ever attempted or accomplished by Home or the Davenports or any other notorious spiritual exhibitors. Not the least of our discoveries,' he said, 'was that the whole thing was a myth ... We *did* produce spirit hands and spirit forms; people *did* float in the air, at least we made our audience believe they did ... How we succeeded in doing these things, I do not intend to explain. We *did* them ... but I have not the slightest hesitation in saying we did *not* do them by spirit agencies. I look upon every spiritualist as either an impostor or an idiot.'

Imitating the phenomena of spiritualism by clever conjuring can, up to a point, be successful, but Adolphus Trollope made a significant comment.[3] Maskelyne and Cooke held an exhibition of conjuring, with the object of exploding the credibility of supernatural phenomena. Trollope, who saw it, said he thought that the demonstration proved how the tying and loosening of knots in a dark cabinet might have been effected by normal means, but, he said, 'when the above-mentioned performer proceeded to float in the air, he only demonstrated the impossibility of doing, by any means known to his art, that which Home was declared, on the most indisputable testimony, to have done. Mr. Maskelyne certainly floated in the air above the heads of the spectators, but I saw, very unmistakably, the wire by which he was suspended. Nor is it possible that the gentlemen who saw, or supposed themselves to have seen, Mr. Home floating in the air above them would have failed to detect any such artifice as that by which the professor of legerdemain was enabled to do the same.' Another important consideration was, that Mr. Maskelyne had 'all the advantage of a locale in which he had abundant opportunities of making every preparation which his art could suggest to him,' while Home 'exhibits his wonders under circumstances absolutely excluding the possibility of any such preparation.' When, in 1869, the Dialectical Society were conducting a symposium on the genuineness of spiritualist phenomena, Adolphus Trollope submitted a statement made to him by the famous Italian conjuror Bosco, who was, he said, 'one of the greatest professors of legerdemain ever known,' and Bosco 'utterly scouted the idea of the possibility of such phenomena as I saw produced by Mr. Home, being performed by any of the resources of his art.'

This was a reasoned argument, which commanded, at least, respect, but Benjamin Coleman's reaction to Sothern's attack, was unfortunate to a degree. He had been goaded by Sothern's claim of have demolished the authenticity of spiritualism and was deeply indignant at the actor's impudent abuse of Home, and when he saw in the *New York Sunday Times* a statement that Sothern, on his last American tour, had mesmerized and raped a young actress and wrecked his own married life by his infidelities, he embodied it in an article and offered it to the *Spiritual Magazine*. That the paper accepted it seems to show that Mr. Wilkinson was very loosely attached to its editorial board; whatever his private sympathies, no solicitor would have sanctioned such a publication.

As it was, the article appeared in January 1866, and wreaked its damage with the speed of a forest fire. The *Spiritual Magazine* was advertized in several newspapers and these came out with such headlines as 'Extraordinary Disclosures concerning Mr. Sothern.' The actor sued Coleman for libel; he was not asking for damages or he would have sued in the civil courts; the action was for criminal libel and the case was heard on 3 March, 1866, at the Old Bailey, before the Deputy Recorder, Mr. Common Serjeant Thomas Chambers. Coleman asked for a postponement, to give him time to bring over witnesses from America, who, he felt, would give valuable support to his defence; the Deputy Recorder refused his plea, saying: 'when a man publishes a personal libel, he ought to be prepared to justify it at the moment.' He gave judgment against Coleman, censuring him for 'overstepping the bounds of philosophical discussion by a personal attack on private character.' He added that he, personally, 'was rather disposed to be a believer in spiritualism,' though, he said, 'I never saw anything of it;' and he imposed on Coleman a fine of £50, which, even in money of the time, appeared to some people nothing like enough. The *Daily Telegraph* exclaimed on 5 March: 'What could have induced Mr. Chambers to pass so absurdly inadequate a sentence we are at a loss to discover, unless we are to look for it in the impression he conveyed to his listeners while addressing the prisoner, that he was himself a believer in spiritualism. What the Deputy Recorder believes or disbelieves . . . is a matter of indifference to anybody but himself,' but, the protest concluded with words which amounted to a sinister prophecy: 'it is *not* a matter of indifference that justice should remain uninfluenced by the personal opinion of a judge on an abstract question.' Home himself was presently to suffer considerable injury from a judge's personal opinion on an abstract question. Meantime, Coleman had got off lightly and Sothern in the event was hardly wronged, though he and his public were indignant at the paltry nature of the fine. His charming wife accompanied him to the Old Bailey, effectively giving the lie to the libel that his infidelities had wrecked his married life, while on the evening of the trial day, 3 March, at the last night of the play, *Brother Sam*, in which he was appearing, his entrance was greeted with a great ovation.[4]

The Carter-Halls changed houses several times during their married life; from 1861–1863 they lived at Barrow Lodge, the Boltons, Brompton. It was here that Henrietta Mary Ada Ward, a painter herself and a painter's widow, wrote[5] of having seen Home. She disliked S. C. Hall and said that her children detested him and his rollicking approach. He would say: 'A kiss for the girls and a box on the ear for the boys,' as to which one of her daughters had said, the boys were more to be envied than the girls. But Mrs. Ward seems to have been one of those guests who, though they dislike the host, have no objection to his hospitality. She paid the Carter Halls several visits, one of which is worth recording.[6] She calls their house The Rosery, Brompton, but Kelly's Directories give the Carter Halls' addresses from 1851 to 1871 as: 27 Ashley Place, Barrow Lodge, 8 Essex Villas and 15 Ashley Place. Mrs. Ward therefore must have made a mistake over the name of the house, though it was probably the one at Brompton. She said that at 'The Rosery' a woman used to act as medium at Mr. Home's demonstrations. 'I remember she required two glasses of port and two of some other beverage, before she began her work.' Home is recorded as giving one demonstration in the presence of another medium. In 1871, he consented to be tested with Kate Fox, in a brightly-lighted room, when the events were reported by a special correspondent of *The Times*, on 26 December, 1872;[7] but this was not a case of Home's using Kate Fox's powers to support his own. Mrs. Ward's story is, it is safe to say, the only one of its kind related of him by anybody. That he would employ a woman who needed four glasses of stimulant before she could work for him, is improbable enough, but not so unlikely as his employing anyone at all. Home's touchiness and *amour propre* would be enough to put the story out of court, without the consideration of his unique powers. It is worth noting that Mrs. Ward's book came out in two editions; the first, published in 1911, says nothing of Home's female assistant; the latter is mentioned only in the second edition, published in 1924. This seems to bear out Podmore's view that reminiscences become more unreliable the further they recede into the past. This theory may invest with a certain doubtfulness S. C. Hall's remark with which she says he greeted her one day at The Rosery: 'You've just missed dear Daniel! He floated in triumph in through the window and out again, and I don't doubt that the day will come when he will float round St. Paul's!' In 1864, the S. C. Halls established themselves in Essex Villas, a broad, quiet street, parallel with Kensington High Street but on a higher level. The white-plastered houses on each side of the street are built in pairs, forming semi-detached units. Most of the original ones are standing, including the S. C. Halls'

No. 8, with its other half, No. 6. They are not of architectural interest, but plain, solid and convenient; No. 8 had a conservatory at the back. With its spear-headed iron railings, the elegant Victorian pillar box under a plane tree at the end of the pavement, the muted murmurs from Kensington High Street which lies below, Essex Villas made one of those scenes whose simplicity and tranquility meant that the human consciousness was enhanced instead of being fragmented and dissipated by a variety of distractions.

On Easter Eve, 1866, the S. C. Halls held a séance with Home, Mrs. Adelaide Senior and Lady Dunsany. Elizabeth Evelyn, her father's heiress, had married Lord Dunsany; there had been no children of the marriage, and in 1866 she had been a widow for fourteen years. She had found intense comfort in spiritualism. In a letter to Home of December 1865, she had said: 'My dear young friend, . . . no words can express how much consolation your wonder-working presence has poured upon my earthly life. God grant that the happiness you confer may rebound upon yourself . . . faithfully and affectionately your friend, Elizabeth Dunsany.'[8] Her affection for Home had drawn her into the circle of his friends. Beside the S. C. Halls, she was now on terms of close friendship with Dr. Gully and his sisters.

Home's séances on various occasions had produced sound pictures: an orchestration of the sounds associated with the scene evoked, as when a shipwreck had been called up by the noises of a ship labouring in a storm, the billows crashing over its decks. On this great Christian festival, the Easter moon overhead almost at its full, a sound picture was produced so extraordinary that Mrs. Senior not only wrote down a description of it, she got this signed by the three other sitters, the S. C. Halls and Lady Dunsany, to establish that they were all agreed as to what they had heard. She gave the writing to Home for his second volume of *Incidents of My Life*, with the sitters' permission for the use of names.[9]

Home came to the séance looking pale and ill, and they were afraid that there would be few, if any, manifestations. He sat down at the piano and began to play and sing. When he sang a little Russian song that his wife had been fond of a chair that stood at some distance, slid across the floor and came to rest at his side. The table was raised, and then an accordion gave out notes, and where raps demanded the alphabet, the message was spelt out: 'We will play the earth-life of one who was not of earth.' The accordion played an introduction but then sounds filled the room that the instrument could not have produced; Mrs. Senior said, it was like listening to a great organ. Through a passage of great volume and tragic character, the tramp of marching feet were heard, then the fearful sounds of a hammer on a nail, 'like two metals meeting'; 'A crash and a burst of wailing which

166

seemed to fill the room, followed; then there came a burst of glorious triumphal music, more grand than any of us had ever listened to, and we exclaimed: The Resurrection!' All this, Mrs. Senior said, took place in a room brilliantly lighted. Some time after the sounds had died away, it was decided to put out the lights in the room and have only the light of the hanging lamp in the conservatory. When this was done, the rest of the company saw S. C. Hall's face bathed in silver light. The accordion was carried round the room by invisible means and gently touched each member of the party except Home, who was never near it. Then Home levitated. He rose to the ceiling, hovered there and they heard him say he wished he had a pencil. He descended and S. C. Hall put a pencil into his hand, hoping he would rise again. Within five minutes he did, and they saw his face and chest illuminated with silver light. Home made a mark on the plaster and sank down once more. While this happened the sitters felt their hands and faces caressed by hands whose touch they recognized. The séance ended by knocks and sounds dying away in the distance out of doors. Mrs. Senior said: 'That burst of music was still thrilling on our hearts . . . The wondrous effects of the sound of the feet and of the hammer and nails running like a thread through the music, it is impossible that those who have not listened to it could understand; in the music itself there was a mixture of tones out of my power to describe.'

Home had come to the séance on Easter Eve looking very ill, and 1866 was a year when his health, always uncertain, was at a very low ebb. Anxiety about how to make a living made it worse, but as happened all through his life, his cares were lightened by unexpected help.

In 1852 he had been a guest of Mr. Ogden in the latter's house on Long Island. One of the daughters of the family, Cora Mowatt Ogden, had considerable theatrical talent. She wrote several plays which were put on with success in New York and other American cities, and at least one of them in London; *Fashion, or, Life in New York*. She had also a successful career as an actress in America, Dublin and London. In 1854 she married William Ritchie, a newspaper editor. He died untimely and she then settled herself in London, where she had already many friends. Her great charm was her vitality and warmth; Poe had spoken of 'her brilliant and expressive eyes and her radiantly beautiful smile.' In 1866, one of her English friends was anxiously seeking an introduction to Home. Remembering having known him fourteen years before, Mrs. Ritchie renewed the association, with the result that she became deeply interested in spiritualism herself and felt an affectionate friendship towards Home. With a characteristic eagerness to help and comfort, she took charge, for the time being, of the seven year old Gricha.

In May, Home was with Dr. Gully at the Priory House. The S. C. Halls were much distressed about his health and S. C. Hall wrote to him: 'We are very anxious about you . . . there would seem to us a dismal blank if you were removed . . . we claim to rank among the most affectionate of your friends, who have loved you and had faith in you from the day we saw you first.'

# XXII

## In Quest of an Occupation

As the founder of Malvern's prosperity, Dr. Gully was very influential in the neighbourhood; among other local offices he held those of a directorship of the Worcester City and County Bank and of the Worcester and Wolverhampton Railway Company. Malvern is near the county town of Worcester and it was natural that people in the district should hear that the famous Mr. Home was Dr. Gully's guest. The outcome was that the manager of the Theatre Royal, Worcester, engaged Home for the part of Guy de Neuville in his forthcoming production of Tom Taylor's comedy, *Plot and Passion*. The show opened on 1 May, 1866, and *Berrow's Worcester Journal* gave Home a very favourable notice: he had, it said, 'the advantage of a figure well suited to the stage, and a voice of the greatest flexibility . . . Mr. Home's first appearance was completely successful . . . his impersonation . . . a truly striking performance.' The *Birmingham Daily Post* said that he had appeared without any advance publicity; on the sheer merits of his performance 'he was very warmly received'.[1] It is not said for how many nights the play ran, but Home's success in it may have been the origin of a proposal which, though like many ideas started in the theatre, it came to nothing, was in itself very interesting. Charles Fechter, an actor of German origin, had had seasons in Paris and London. Dickens who had greatly admired his performance as Armand in *La Dame aux Camélias*, had persuaded him to return to London, and in 1863, Fechter as an actor-manager had taken a lease of the Lyceum Theatre. The friendship between Dickens and himself was very close. Dickens had lent him £3,000 to tide him over in a financial crisis, and it was Fechter who gave Dickens the little wooden chalet which was put up in the garden of Gads Hill. Fechter gained great applause by his own performance as Hamlet in 1864. Some idea of his imaginative scope can be gained from the sketch for the backdrop of the battlements prepared for him by the scenic artist Telbin. The keep of Elsinore crowns a towering hill, a yawning arch covers the roadway into the castle. At ground level, sketches of human figures indicate the vast height of the overhanging steep.[2] With his theatrical imagination on the stretch, it occurred to Fechter that a superb piece of theatre might be achieved if Home, with his reputation as a seer of spirits, were to appear as Hamlet. The exchanges of Marcellus and Bernardo:-

> Look, where it comes again!
> In the same figure, like the king that's dead.

would lead to a thrilling climax when this Hamlet demanded of the spirit why it had returned to trouble them, 'with thoughts beyond the reaches of our souls?' The coup, if it succeeded, would be immense:- but would it succeed? Whether, when it came to the point, Fechter would have brought out, in a West End production, an amateur, even a gifted amateur, in one of the theatre's most demanding rôles, must be doubtful, but it got about that he had made the suggestion to Home; Lady Loftus Otway, one of Home's eager supporters, sent him a pair of foils and begged him to have a box reserved for her.[3] Dr. Gully, with his usual commonsense, was against the project. In part of a long letter to Home written on July 21, 1866, he said that Home might well succeed in a theatrical career eventually, but 'the stage . . . is an arduous calling and requires all the perseverance a man can give; you would do well to *work up* and learn as you work; no man ever played Hamlet for his début.' It turned out that, given from another angle, Dickens' advice also was against the scheme. Home's name however, was in the air of the theatre world, and he received an offer from the St. James's Theatre, of the part of Mr. Oakley, the husband in a revival of George Coleman's *The Jealous Wife*; but his health made the effort impossible to him. His name was advertised twice and twice withdrawn. Dickens wrote a letter to Adolphus Trollope on 25 July, 1866.[4] He said: 'after trying to come out as an actor, first at Fechter's, (where I had the honour of stopping him short) and then at the St. James's Theatre . . . (where he was twice announced and each time disappeared mysteriously from the bills) was announced at The Little Theatre in Dean Street, as "a great attraction, for one night only", to play last Monday. An appropriate little dirty rag of a bill, fluttering in the window of an obscure dairy behind the Strand, gave me this intelligence last Saturday. It is like enough that even this striking business did not come off, for I believe the public to have found out the scoundrel, in which lively and sustaining hope this leaves me at present.' This vindictiveness towards a man he had never seen and about whom he, personally, knew nothing, is best explained by one of Dickens' remarks about himself. In a letter to his wife said: 'The intense pursuit of an idea that takes complete possession of me, is one of the qualities that make me different — sometimes for good, sometimes I daresay for evil — from other men.'[5] This quality went to the writing of great novels; it did not lead to the level-headedness and fair judgment possessed by ordinary men who have no genius. He had no personal knowledge of Home but he was positive that Home was a scoundrel, and that any squalid and humiliating detail was appropriate to his image.

Dr. Gully was one of the very few doctors who would have taken Home's condition as a spiritualist into account as an important factor in his physical condition. For the past two years he had been uneasy at the effect on Home's mediumistic powers of the excitement of a brilliant social success. The accusation that he was vain and weak was brought against him several times, but without detailed evidence, except when his foolish arrogance got him expelled from Rome in 1864; but Dr. Gully obviously recognised these traits when he put down his conversation with Severn in his journal without comment. His affection for Home was not weakened by the latter's failings, such as they might be, but he felt obliged to speak about them.

There were several people in Malvern who sat with each other to receive spiritualist messages. Some of them must have possessed psychic faculties, as Dr. Gully did himself to a certain degree; as a boy he had experienced remarkable prophetic dreams; the most endowed member of the group however would appear to have been his great friend Charlotte Dyson. This lady was connected with the families of Dyson and Perrins who had made their fortunes by bottling Malvern water and creating Worcester Sauce. She was forty-five in 1866 and lived with her sister in a comfortable household of housekeeper, cook and maids.[6] Her spacious, early Victorian Gothic house, The Pleasaunce, stood in a road of ample gardens and evergreen trees, between the town and Great Malvern station, but as quiet as if it were remote from either. She and her friend Mrs. Jones and Dr. Gully had had sittings with each other, and with Home when he had been available, over the past two years.

The spirit contact of which Dr. Gully spoke most was that of his child Fanny who had died of croup in 1840 at the age of two. He had never ceased to feel her loss: 'The sadness with which I even now look back to that misery is doubled by the recollection of the suffering which she had to undergo from the treatment, treatment administered by some of the most kind and able practitioners in London.' He had not then investigated hydropathy, with which he would treat the case now, one of the advantages of which was its being able to soothe 'the restlessness, which forms so distressing a feature in this disease, the rather as it falls to the lot of little mortals.'[7] Like the two year old child who returned in a vision to her father, the fourteenth century writer of *Pearl*, Fanny returned to her father, to speak to him with

171

the authority of a knowledge he did not yet possess, and to give him information about the spirit world. When these sittings began, Fanny, it seemed, had spoken to her father on spiritual matters, but over the last months, the sittings with Home had produced only physical phenomena: telekinesis, touches and sounds. Dr. Gully had asked his child what kind of spirits they were who produced physical phenomena only? She had said: 'They are undeveloped spirits.'

Dr. Gully now approached the practical matter of Home's support. He had tried, during the last winter, to see if some of Home's friends would, between them, guarantee a yearly subscription, to provide him with an income, but finding that, in spite of some responses, the sum could not be made up, he had relinquished the scheme. But now he heard that other friends of Home, in London, were trying to arrange subscriptions to give him £150 a year, in return for which he was to undertake to hold a certain number of séances; but Home had altogether declined this suggestion. 'I hear', the doctor wrote, 'that you objected to this because you were not *free*; but who is free, who has to live in the world by the faculties he has? Am I? . . . The plan is every way commendable; by it, your support is ensured without the payment for individual séances and whether you are in power or not, so that no stigma can attach to the exercise of it in consideration of a payment.' He urged the plan, both as a means of spreading interest in spiritualism, and of giving Home the much-needed peace of mind which would come from a sense of security. He himself, Dr. Gully said, would benefit from it very little because he was so seldom in London, but he would willingly be one of the subscribers, and if he could be put in touch with the person who had originated the idea, he would give all his assistance towards getting it organised. 'Meantime, it is plain — and it is reasonable — that people will not aid you materially only that you may have the *freedom* of doing what and going where you please; the world is made of too hard matter for that.'[8]

Dr. Gully thought that if the salary were paid as a separate arrangement, quite unconnected with the individual séances, this arrangement would meet Home's objection to being paid as a medium. Home did not think so. Whatever his shortcomings in any other relation, the one in which he always felt justified, always right, was between the spiritual world and himself. He said that sometimes, when his powers were taken from him, he recognized that this was the result of his having followed an erring course and done what he himself knew to be wrong,[9] but this was a matter between him and his spirit-guides, not one with which human beings had anything to do. When he refused the proposal which even such a perceptive friend as Dr. Gully wanted him to accept, his motives no doubt were mixed, but among them was one which he followed consistently for the whole of his life.

It so happened that in this instance his refusal did not lead to a dismissal of the scheme but to its being remade for him in a more acceptable form. The body of people who were anxious to establish a spiritualists' headquarters went on with their plan. In August 1866, the society was established, under the name of the Spiritual Athenaeum at 22 Sloane Street. The neighbourhood was eligible. At no. 22, the ground floor was occupied by a fashionable milliner, Madame Bellinger; the first and second floors were leased to the Spiritual Athenaeum; the first comprised among its rooms a waiting and a reading room; the second consisted of a drawing room, bedroom and dressing room, and here Home was established as Resident Secretary. His duties were those of a secretary only; he had no concern with the society's finances, and he was under no obligation to hold séances. When he chose to hold them, it was as a private person.

There was great enthusiasm among the founders but some disagreement as to their aims. Some wanted the Spiritual Athenaeum to function as the headquarters of a scientific investigation of spiritualism, others wanted it proclaimed as a society altogether in the interests of promoting the Christian religion, and acting as a bulwark against the materialism of the age. Mrs. S. C. Hall was one of these; she would have liked a Trinitarian test to be administered to everyone who wanted to join, and that no free-thinking material should be allowed among the literature on the tables in the reading-room; the majority of the council, however, were in favour of a more liberal policy. There were fifteen of them; they included Dr. Elliotson, converted to spiritualism by Home three years before, and Dr. Gully, whose usefulness to the scheme was not only that he gave his name to it, but that he had exerted himself to gain members. He wrote to Home: 'I have no doubt we shall keep it going, especially if your health holds out. But the stupid people are so afraid of having their names mentioned in connection with it.' The circular issued by the Spiritual Athenaeum said: 'We ask you to give effect to our plan by agreeing to subscribe five guineas annually, so long as it shall be satisfactory to you to do so . . . We wish to limit the number to one hundred, but we believe that eighty will be sufficient, to meet all requirements.[10]

Mrs. S. C. Hall's eagerness, and that of others who felt as she did, to emphasize the intimate connection of spiritualism with the Christian religion, to claim that spiritualism was one of its aspects, was the direct outcome of the Christian faith's assurance of life beyond the grave, and also of the psychic powers attributed in the Gospels to Jesus Christ. This greatest of all spiritual adepts performed feats which were recognizable as of the same kind as those performed by mediums

173

throughout the ages. The only paranormal act related of Jesus and not, it is said, related of any of them, was walking on the water. The healing of disease, whether the sufferer were present or absent, materialization, the power of becoming invisible, the power to influence the growth of a tree, to control storms, to levitate, to raise the dead, to become illuminated by supernatural light, when told of Jesus, are the more thrilling when they are seen as supreme examples of psychic power, some degree of which had been demonstrated by other adepts, since this invests the figure of Jesus with a reality sometimes difficult to conceive. That the comparison should be made, the connection asserted, struck many people as blasphemous and abhorrent. That psychic powers, producing what were called miracles, should be ascribed to any one else, appeared to them to devalue those ascribed to Jesus. In 1749, Dr. Conyers Middleton, in *A Free Enquiry into the Miraculous Powers which are supposed to have existed in the Christian Church from the Earliest Ages, through several Centuries*, had asserted that miracles ceased with the Apostles and were only performed occasionally, even by them. He concluded: 'To cut off, therefore, all reasonings and inference about them, let it be understood that we deny the facts.' This attitude of summary dismissal has never gone out.

Madame Home said, on the matter of the identity of spirits communicating in Home's séances, 'it is only to those fully convinced of that identity, that spiritualism can ever be spiritualism.' That some people should be convinced of this identity and others should not, is understandable; what poses a question very difficult to answer is why the disbelief should be held with such violence. Disagreements often arouse great heat, but the type and degree of fury aroused by spiritualism in those who object to it is almost unique. It is generally assumed by its opponents to be the result of fraud, but other kinds of fraud, though vigorously condemned, do not inspire this degree of manic fury and vitriolic contempt, such as are scarcely called out by any other subject under dispute. The source of violence is often fear, and the mere fact that spiritualism is concerned with the dead, is apt to inspire a chill, a sensation of repugnance and fear summed up in the term 'spooky'. That the idea of the dead should fill the living with dismay, is perhaps connected with the extremely strong instinct for survival without which the human race would have come to a stop. Anything associated with death can be made terrifying. It is characteristic that in the *Athenaeum*'s notice of Home's lecture in Willis's Rooms, the reporter spoke of Mr. Home's 'ghastly shows'. The term: 'the walking dead', is enough to chill the blood of many people. A skeleton, in itself a beautiful bone-structure, has been turned into a dreadful object by exploitation in this context, rising from a coffin in tattered grave-clothes, with sightless eye sockets and remorseless grin;

and except where embalming or cremation removes it, the idea of corruption adds an unspeakable horror. It has been suggested that a kind of comic nightmare lies in the origin of the circus turn, in which the clown, his face painted white with patches of blue, red and black, pursues someone round the ring and at last jumps on the terrified fugitive's back. It is thought that the turn originally represented the dead body, its face showing the colours of putrefaction, leaping out of the grave and gleefully pursuing its victim.

These impressions would be strenuously denied by some people, as far-fetched or groundless, but those who so ferociously rejected the possibility of spirit-communication, were perhaps, in part, reacting to feelings they did not recognize. The same feelings drove the Christian spiritualists on an opposite course. For them, the shrinking and the dread were charmed away by the spiritualist message: there is no death. The non-spiritualist Christians, though they accepted the belief in immortality, rejected any proof of it on this side of the grave.

The reaction, favourable or unfavourable, found expression far and wide. In *The Water Babies*, published in 1863, Kingsley imagines his son, the four-year-old Grenville, saying, there are no such things as Water Babies, to which he replies: 'My dear little man, till you know a great deal more about Nature than Professor Owen and Professor Huxley put together, don't tell me about what cannot be, or fancy that anything is too wonderful to be true. "We are fearfully and wonderfully made", said old David, and so we are, and so is everything around us, down to the very deal table. Yes, much more fearfully and wonderfully made, already, is the deal table as it stands now, nothing but a piece of dead deal wood, than if, as foxes say, and geese believe, spirits could make it dance, or talk to you by rapping on it.' The passage did not strike Kingsley as self-contradictory. The other two most famous Victorian children's books have what look like references inspired, perhaps unconsciously, by spiritualist phenomena, though of a delightfully light-hearted kind. Published in 1865, *Alice in Wonderland* describes Alice's being elongated, as Home was, in séances with Lord Adare, and in front of J. Hawkins Simpson, though Home's growth was said to be three inches, and Alice elongated till her feet were almost out of sight. This is a single instance, but in *Alice through the Looking Glass*, published in 1872, at Alice's coronation banquet, a cluster of wild effects took place which seem to repeat those of spiritualist phenomena.

The brothers Davenport made no contribution to spiritualism but they were the subjects of physical phenomena as extraordinary as Home's own. Conan Doyle says[11] that on one occasion, 'the children floated up high in the room; once when the family was at breakfast the knives, forks and dishes danced about and the table was raised in the air.' When called upon for a speech, Alice said: 'I rise to return thanks . . . and she really did rise in the air as she spoke, several inches, but she got hold of the edge of the table and managed to pull herself down again . . . Take care of yourself, screamed the White Queen, something is going to happen! The candles all grew up to the ceiling, something like a bed of rushes with fire-works at the top. As for the bottles, they each took a pair of plates, which they hastily fitted on as wings, and so, with forks for legs, went fluttering about . . . Here I am! cried a voice from the soup-tureen and Alice turned again, just in time to see the Queen's broad, good-natured face grinning at her for a moment over the edge of the tureen before she disappeared into the soup . . . the soup ladle was walking up to Alice and signing to her to get out of its way.' Levitation, telekinesis, phenomena affecting lights, the disappearance of a dematerializing figure into the ground till the head only remained above the floor, as was recorded by William Crookes, are all reflected in this enchanting comic version. The Society for Psychical Research was not founded till 1882, but Lewis Carroll was one of its early members.

So many of the references to Home were malicious, angry and scornful, that it is a continual surprise how many people of great distinction were deeply impressed by him. Ruskin, after the fearful experience of his divorce, and, as Madame Home said:[12] 'worn out by his warfare with the spirit of the time', had shown an interest in spiritualism. He was told that, this being so, he must sit with Home. The S. C. Halls were most anxious that he should, but the séance could not be arranged till they themselves were in Ireland. They heard, however, that it had been most successful. 'Only fancy Ruskin's being convinced', wrote Mrs. S. C. Hall. 'Only he doesn't want it talked about.' The effect of Ruskin's sufferings on his temperament made this not surprising. He felt a great liking for Home and when Home had been at Malvern with Dr. Gully in 1865, Ruskin had written to him, apologizing for not having answered the letter Home had written to him from America: 'but it was deep summer time and I was out all day long and came in at night too tired to write, and at last it was too late. But now I hope I may see you soon. Please say I may.'[13]

In 1877, some months after the death of the sixteen year old Rose La Touche whom he had hopelessly loved, his devoted friends, the Cowper Temples, arranged a séance for him with a woman medium at their house, Broadlands. She described to him a spirit beside him, 'young, very tall, graceful and fair, she was stooping down over you, almost speaking into your ear . . . she has not been long in the spirit world, I think, probably not a year.' Ruskin said: 'No, not a year. She died in May.' He said that the séance had left him 'like a flint stone changed suddenly to a firefly'.[14]

Another sitter of whom Madame Home found a record at this time was as widely different from Ruskin as could be imagined. John Bright, fifty years old in 1862, famous as the instigator of the Anti-Corn Law movement and his support for the Reform Bill, had a vigorous intelligence to which his parliamentary career bore striking witness. If anyone could claim to have a clear head and powerful mind, it was he. His brother-in-law, Samuel Lucas, was the editor of the *Morning Star*, who had opened its correspondence columns to letters on spiritualism and had, in 1860, published Dr. Gully's account of the séance in Hyde Park Place. Bright's fellow M.P. Edmond Beale, was a neighbour of the S. C. Halls in Brompton, and got an invitation for Bright, Lucas and himself to a séance. When it was over, Mrs. S. C. Hall asked Bright what he had thought of the manifestations? 'They are wonderful', he said. In 1862, the United States consul, J. M. Peebles, had dined with Bright, who told him that he could attribute them to no cause except the one alleged, that of disembodied spirits. 'But', he added with due caution, 'I do not say that this is so; but if it be true, it is the strongest tangible proof we have of immortality.'[15].

This was the view of Bright, who had sat with Home. Among those who had not, and whose opinion was totally unfavourable, the most eminent was Michael Faraday, the author of the discovery that magnetism produces electricity, who has been called the greatest experimental genius the world has known. When he was in his seventies, between 1860 and 1862, he embarked on an investigation of psychic phenomena; his scientific genius abhorred the idea of superstition and the interest in spiritualism made him fear a revival of it. He began to examine the matter of table-rapping. As Brian Inglis says:[16] 'Of the various possibilities which had been put forward, he had ruled out one in advance: the idea that any super-natural agency could be at work.' Dr. Conyers Middleton himself would have approved of this approach. Faraday developed the theory, in proof of which he devised a movable table-top which registered pressure on a dial, that the movement of the table was caused by 'involuntary muscular action'. As Dr. Inglis says: 'That finger tips pressing down on a movable surface could lead to sideways pressure without the people involved being aware of it, hardly required an instrument to reveal; in any case it could not begin to account for the movements ... of dining room tables so heavy that the groups seated round them found it hard to move them by combined conscious muscular effort.'

Sir Emerson Tennent, an Eastern traveller, a man of letters and an M.P., asked Faraday if he would attend one of Home's séances. Faraday said that he would, provided certain conditions were observed. The séance must take place in the light; to this Home would have made no objection. He preferred a dim light but he never sat in

177

darkness and was a severe critic of any medium who did, and he has often been reported as sitting in rooms brilliantly lit by lamp and candlelight; but Faraday went on to lay down intellectual boundaries within which the investigation must take place. 'Before we proceed to consider any question involving physical principles', he said, 'we should set out with naturally clear ideas of the possible and the impossible.' Did Home consider the phenomena natural or supernatural? If they provided 'glimpses of natural action not yet reduced to law', then it was a duty 'to develop them and aid others in their development.' But if they were ascribable to spirit agency, then Faraday demanded that Home should admit 'the utterly contemptible character of them and their results up to the present time, in respect of yielding either information or instruction, or supplying a force or action of the least value to mankind.' The greater number of Home's recorded séances do not give the actual content of messages received or communications experienced by the sitters, but some of them do. Sophia Cotterell's sitting with her little girl on her lap, saying, Darling, won't you give your hand to Papa? Mrs. Senior's sensations of exquisite comfort in the communications with her husband, Sacha Home's serene happiness in her mother's presence, could all be, no doubt, explained away, but none of them could be described as of 'utterly contemptible character'. Since Home believed that the phenomena were supernatural, he was being called on to say that they were contemptible and ridiculous; the matter, however, was never put to him. Sacha Home was in the last stages of illness and he could not be approached. Sir Emerson Tennent, assuming no doubt that Home would reject a discussion on such terms, did not show him Faraday's letter and the question was not re-opened.

This attitude of mind, surprising to the laity in so great a scientist, that the possible could be pre-determined, was criticised by Gladstone. The most remarkable medium after Home was William Eglinton, with whom Gladstone sat in 1884. After this séance, Gladstone said that scientists 'were too often indisposed to give any attention to matters which seemed to conflict with their established modes of thought. Indeed, they not infrequently attempt to deny that into which they have never inquired.'[17]

In the contest among intelligent people, for and against the claims of spiritualism, Professor De Morgan and his wife were very interesting defenders. Augustus De Morgan was the first holder of the Chair of Mathematics at University College, London; he was also Secretary of the Astronomical Society. His wife Sophia was a patient investigator, a person of great insight and sympathy. In 1863, she had published a book, *From Matter to Spirit*, compiled from her investigations. Her calm, detailed records of psychic phenomena are extremely impressive, and considerable weight is lent by Professor De Morgan's preface, in which he says: 'I write, as will be guessed, for and to those who have been staggered, either by what they have seen, or what they have heard and cannot reject.' The matter appeared to him to demand intensive examination of a very difficult order. He said: 'The physical explanations I have seen are easy, but miserably insufficient; the spirit hypothesis is sufficient but ponderously difficult.' 'What a grand resource is belief in imposture!' he exclaimed feelingly.[18]

Mrs. De Morgan's recorded instances of spirit communication include a passage on a medium's experiences in trance which underline the mystical vision of the writer of 'Pearl', of the heavenly landscape he can image only in terms of jewels. 'She always described herself as passing from one degree to another in a series of ascents.' The first was through lanes, groves and gardens, like those of earth, 'only clearer and brighter and *more real*.' The second stage was through the gold and silver garden. The last and highest degree was through the jewelled garden, 'where all the trees and plants, gloriously clear and delicate, shone with the rich splendour of diamonds and coloured gems'.[19] The passage, like the verses in Ezekiel, casts a light on Home's devotion to the rubies, the diamonds, the great emerald and the great sapphire that princes had given him.

The question of light is intimately connected with spiritualism. Moonlight, whose beauty is almost banished from our cities by the sordid, omnipresent glare of municipal lighting, was still, in the mid-Victorian era, a magical presence, as one can see in Sebastian Pether's 'Moonlight in Trafalgar Square'.

The most accomplished Victorian painter of moonlight was Atkinson Grimshaw. His paintings give indescribable visions of water in moonlight: The Thames by Moonlight, Nightfall down the Thames. These pictures draw the viewer out of ordinary consciousness; they illustrate a frame of mind that seeks communication with another world.

# XXIII

## The Spiritual Athenaeum

Home's position as Resident Secretary of the Spiritual Athenaeum seemed a most fortunate appointment, but it was to prove the one complete disaster of his career. In April 1867, a case was brought against him by Mrs. Jane Lyon: Lyon v. Home, in which she sued him for the return of £60,000 which, she asserted, he had got from her by pretending that the payments had been made in obedience to spirit communications from her dead husband. The case was decided in her favour, but the reasons for his judgement given by the Vice-Chancellor, Sir George Gifford, are usually omitted in hilarious references to Home. Sir George Gifford said he did not find that the Defendant, Home, had demanded the money or had used undue influence in gaining it, while the Plaintiff's evidence contained 'innumerable mis-statements in many important particulars — mis-statements on oath so perversely untrue that they have embarrassed the Court to a great degree and quite discredited the Plaintiff's testimony.' But, he said, the gifts would not have been made to the Defendant unless he had been a medium and as he, the judge, held that spiritualism was 'mischievous nonsense,' he directed that the money must be returned; he added, however, that though in ordinary circumstances, the Defendant would be liable for the whole costs of the action, in this case the Plaintiff must pay her own.

On the face of it, the affair appeared thoroughly disreputable; a medium, receiving from an old woman, first, £24,000, then causing her, it seemed, to draw a will leaving him all the rest of her property, then receiving another £6,000, then a reversionary interest in mortgages to the amount of another £30,000 because, she declared, he had made her believe the spirit of her dead husband wanted her to do this—the mere descriptions of the parties and the staggering nature of the sums involved, have caused many people to judge the matter without enquiring into it. The real nature of the case was widely different from what it appeared.

Mrs. Jane Lyon was an old woman of abounding energy, who, for half a life-time had been burning with resentment and indignation because her well-born husband's relations would not accept her. She had, as is not unusual in primitive types, a touch of psychic capacity, which had led to her taking some interest in spiritualism. She had read Home's 'Incidents of My Life, Vol I', and was aware of his aristocratic, fashionable and distinguished connections. She made her way to the premises of the Spiritual Athenaeum, and there she found the pale and enfeebled but strangely attractive young man who looked as though he would offer little resistance. Within an astonishingly short time from their first meeting, she had insisted on settling a large fortune on him and on his altering his name to hers in sign that he was her adopted son. Since in the most important aspects of the case, Home as Defendant completely contradicted the evidence of Mrs. Lyon as Plaintiff, the readers' opinions will be influenced by their own prejudices and sympathies, but the evidence of some of the forty witnesses called for Home's defence evoke the brightly lit picture of a horrible situation.[1]

In the early years of the century (the date was never established) a wealthy butcher, farmer and cheesemonger named Matthew Gibson, then living on The Sandhill, Newcastle, fathered an illegitimate daughter who got the name of Jane. Gibson seems to have had no concern with her in her early childhood; as a little girl she was found destitute on Newcastle Quay and was afterwards heard of selling sand about the streets for householders to sprinkle on stone floors. By some turn of fortune, her father who had now retired and was living at Bishop Auckland in the neighbouring county of Durham, reclaimed her and brought her up in his household. This was a change indeed, but the house to which she felt the most attachment of any she ever saw, was not her father's rich establishment, but Binchester Hall, a mansion a mile away on the wooded bank of the river Wear.[2]

Her robust vulgarity which a spell at boarding school had not much tamed, was set off by an extraordinary vitality, and this gained her her natural prey, a husband well-born but incompetent and weak. Charles Lyon was a member of the Bowes Lyon family who were offended by his marriage and refused to have anything to do with him and his wife, an insult which had never ceased to rankle in Jane Lyon's mind; but one fulfilment among others came of the marriage: Charles Lyon was the owner of Binchester Hall and their early married life was spent there, but as a result of various misfortunes, family disputes, an adverse Chancery suit, an attempt to mine lead ore which was a failure, Binchester Hall was sold; but a turn of fortune's wheel restored their prosperity; on another of Charles Lyon's properties, coal was found. The marriage was childless but happy, the husband was altogether under the control of his wife and had made over to her almost all his property before his death in 1859. As her father had died leaving her £20,000, she was possessed, in 1866, of £140,000. In money of the day she was a very rich woman.

Nevertheless in the seven years since her husband's death her manner of living had been remarkable. Though she was very conscious of the power that her wealth gave her over other people, she had spent almost nothing. In October 1866 she was living in London, in Westbourne Place, off Westbourne Grove, in rooms over a stationers' shop which was kept by her landlady Mrs. Key with the help of an assistant, Daniel Phillips. She had lived here for two years, and for the previous five years of her widowhood she had occupied premises of an equally humble nature in the house of Mrs. Pepper at 17a Albert Place, Albert Gate, Hyde Park. During the whole of this five years, she said, the only people she had known were Mrs. Sims, the wife of a photographer in Westbourne Grove, and an old woman, Mrs. Pryor, of 2 Parkside opposite Wilton Place, who sold mixed sweets, and with whom it was a comfort to her to sit and chat. Like many of Mrs. Lyon's statements this was not true, for she knew some of her husband's less high-flown connections: the wives of his nephews, Mrs. Tom Fellowes and Mrs. James Fellowes and his niece Mrs. Dennison, to whom, in turn, she held out the prospect of getting some of her husband's money. She had had, besides several protégées, but no relationship of the kind had lasted long. One of them, Fanny Hemming, 'a fine young woman', had been cast off, because when Mrs. Lyon took lodgings with Mrs. Pepper, Mrs. Lyon objected to renting another bedroom for the girl and wanted her to share her own. Mrs. Hemming had declared that this was not good enough and had taken her daughter away. Mrs. Tom Fellowes, known as Plessy because her name was Placentia, saw as much of Mrs. Lyon as any of the family but the position was an abrasive one, Mrs. Lyon thinking all the time that Plessy was after her money. On one occasion she refused to go shopping with her for carpets, thinking that Plessy would try to get her to pay the bill. Plessy did, now and again, get something out of her; once it was a cheque for £50, and Mrs. Lyon never saw the stub in her cheque book without saying, 'I wish I had it back again.' In spite of her wealth, there was neither social, nor emotional satisfaction in her life. She craved such satisfactions, and when she thought she saw the means to gratify the craving, she pursued it with all the vigour and determination of her nature.

She had a portrait of her late husband which she took to Mrs. Sims because she wanted it photographed. In the course of conversation she told Mrs. Sims that at his death, her husband had prophesied that in seven years' time they would be re-united. The seven years had now passed and she thought that 1866 would see her own death. Mrs. Sims assured her this need not be so; if she were a spiritualist, her husband could come to her while she was yet on earth. Mrs. Sims put her in touch with Mr. and Mrs. Burns who kept a shop in Camberwell that sold psychic books, and they told her about the Spiritual Athenaeum. Mrs. Lyon wrote to the Secretary on 30 September, asking for particulars of membership. The Secretary could not reply immediately, since all applications for membership had to be laid before the Committee. Becoming impatient, Mrs. Lyon set out to find the place herself.

Emily Head, the wife of a soldier in the Royal Horse Guards, was employed by Madame Bellinger as a sempstress, and sometimes was called on to admit visitors. Late in the afternoon of 3 October, 1866, she opened the door to an old lady, stout and shabbily dressed, who asked for the premises of the Spiritual Athenaeum. She said she had been hunting up and down for them all the afternoon and was glad to have found them at last. Emily Head directed her to the staircase; at its foot was a counter of Madame Bellinger's displaying artificial flowers. The old lady found some difficulty into getting round it. She said: 'Them that put that counter there did not calculate on stout people having to get through.' Home said of this first visit from Mrs. Lyon:[3] that she told him she had read his book; she added, surprisingly, but in a characteristic strain of paranoia, that she was a much more wonderful medium than he was; but, he said, she appeared to be less interested in spiritualism than in his knowing 'them high folks'. She asked if they were still his friends? He said, they were. She said she would like to see his private rooms, and with the inability to withstand her onslaughts which was to be typical of their relationship, he led her to his drawing room on the second floor. Here, photograph albums and richly bound books were lying on the table; on the wall was the photograph of the Grand Duchess Constantine and her children. Mrs. Lyon asked him how he came by that? He told her and she exclaimed: 'Did she really give it to you with her own hands? Well, you *are* a celebrity! It is only a pity you should be so poor.' Home said that he did not mind poverty, and that he should be very comfortable when his affairs in Russia were settled. She said: 'You may be comfortable before that!' She asked him to call on her next day; he said he could not until two days afterwards. She proposed calling on him again meantime and he said it would be better to wait. She departed, saying: 'Well, I had expected to find you proud and stuck-up from knowing so many fine folks, but I like you very much and I hope you will like me.'

Home said: 'From her dress and manner, and the apparent relish she had for my aristocratic connections, I thought she might be a kind-hearted house-keeper, but it never crossed my mind she could be rich.'

On 4 October, he called, and found her in her indifferent lodgings over the stationer's shop. She told him that though she was rich, she preferred to live as she did. She offered him a cheque for £30. Home refused it, but she pressed it on him, explaining that it was a subscription to the Spiritual Athenaeum. She began to question him about his past life, asking him, if he were to marry again, would his wife be received by the great people whom he knew? Home said he would never marry any one who would not be received by them. Mrs. Lyon then came out with a proposal to adopt him as her son. She said: 'I will settle a very handsome fortune upon you. We will take a house and your son will live with us and have his tutor. You will have a handsome house to entertain your friends and we will travel abroad together when we like.' He laughed, and asked her what her relations would say. She then told her story: that owing to their behaviour, her husband had made a will totally excluding his family, settling the whole of his fortune upon her. Next, she related his prophecy of their re-union seven years after his death; she now believed that it meant, not her own death but her meeting with and adoption of Home, which would create a spiritual re-union. She said Home would have not only an adoptive mother but should speak of her late husband as his spiritual adoptive father. Having sketched the situation which was to unite them, she then revealed her motivation with startling clearness. She told him how isolated she had been in her London life, without acquaintances except Mrs. Key, Mrs. Pepper, Mrs. Sims, and old Mrs. Pryor who sold the mixed sweets. 'Now', she said, 'you will introduce me to your friends, and two people will be made happy.' The doubt crossed his mind as to whether she were sober or in her right senses; but her reasons were so sound, her manner so affectionate and convincing that he came to the conclusion she must be. However, he said: 'I fear you seek me for the strange gift I possess; as that is not in my control I might lose it.' Mrs. Lyon now made the first of her statements denying that she was influenced by his powers as a medium. 'Have I alluded to that?' she said. 'It is true that it will bring people about you and that is what I want. I always select my lodgings in a place where there is bustle and confusion, for I like it, so I shall like to see your friends.' Then she said, making it clear that no belief in spiritual influence was needed to account for her conduct: 'There is nothing will spite my husband's family more than to see me among great folks. I always swore I would be even with them one day, and now I will.' Home said he did not like this attitude; he had no wish to injure anybody; nor, it might be supposed, did he like the idea of making himself offensive to a noble family, under the aegis of such a person as Mrs. Lyon. Then, he said, 'she threw her arms about me and kissed me, saying: It shall be just as you like, darling. I did think,' Home said, 'that this was rather violent, but her age and the conversation we had just had, seemed to justify her conduct.' He could not say what her age might be, she contradicted herself about it, but she was, he said, extremely vigorous, in mind and body. She told him she had followed the progress of Bishop Colenso's trial, and had determined that if he were deprived of his see, she would give him a fortune. 'It is lucky for you I did not,' she added. As matters turned out, it was lucky also for Bishop Colenso. She had no tolerance for any of her husband's relatives except for his sister, Mrs. Clutterbuck, to whom she did not object. Mrs. Clutterbuck had ten thousand a year, and therefore there was no need to suspect her of being on the cadge. As for the others, 'I will prove to them that I may sit up if I please and pitch my money pound after pound out of the window and no one has a right to interfere. I will show them all,' she cried, 'that *I* can be received as well as they when the fancy takes me, for I shall go out with you and your friends will come to us, and my old age will become a joy instead of a burden.' Home was accustomed to using a caressing, family idiom of speech to people to whom he was attached, and he said: 'Well, I promise you that I shall love you as a mother and will call you Mother if you like, for there are plenty of old ladies whom I address as Mother.' This fashion, as well as being used in certain walks of English life, was fairly prevalent in Russia, where people used family terms to those unconnected with them, from Little Father Czar, downwards; Mrs. Lyon, however, did not appreciate it. She replied hastily: 'Thank you, but the less of that kind of love the better.' Seeing herself, perhaps unconsciously, in the role of a wife, she said: 'I shall love your son with a mother's love and he will be my own darling.' Much attracted as Home was by her proposals, since his chief earthly need was of a settled income, they were not fantastic only: his perceptions must have warned him, if obscurely, that they were also ominous. At all events he did not immediately close with them; Mrs. Lyon asked if he would like to consult his friends on the matter. He replied that there was no hurry. Mrs. Lyon said: 'I am apt to change my mind, so you had better catch me while you can.' She was standing in front of him while she said this; then she went to a chair and sat down. She said: 'I have always had my own way and unless you will promise to do what I wish, you will only make me dislike you.' She went to a tin box and brought out a cheque book; this contained another evidence of Mrs. Tom Fellowes' onslaught: 'Mrs. Fellowes, £5, the last to her for ever', was written on a stub. She kissed him and made out a cheque to him for £50. 'That is only a drop in the bucket', she said. Home said that he felt he had no right to obtain money from the strange gift he possessed. 'Why, you foolish fellow,' said Mrs. Lyon, 'I've seen nothing of your strange gift, as you call it, and though it is through your being celebrated for that, that I first heard of you, I love you for yourself and should not care if you never had anything singular occur to you again.'

This meeting took place on 7 October, and Home said that up till then, there had been no psychic manifestations of any kind between them, but as he got up to go, the sounds known as rappings occurred; by the alphabet he translated them into the message: 'Do not, my darling Jane, say, alas the light of other days forever fled. The light is with you. Charles lives and loves you.'

'Whether these sounds were produced by the Plaintiff who pretends to be a medium,' Home said, 'I cannot say, but they were not produced by me. I was not near the table when they occurred.' But then took place what looks like evidence that the sounds had been the effect of genuine mediumship brought about by Home's presence. Mrs. Lyon went into her bedroom and fetched the tin box, out of which she brought 'a bad watercolour sketch of a house.' On it was written, in Mrs. Lyon's hand, Alas, the light of other days for ever fled, and under this: Binchester. This, she said, had been her husband's favourite house, but owing to family disputes it had been sold by order of the Court of Chancery. In this house, among the trees on the banks of the Wear, she had once seen, coming out of a bookcase in the library, the vision of a young man with fair hair. She declared that she recognized in Home an older version of this young apparition.

Home said he could not have produced these words by fraud. 'I did not know her husband's name was Charles. I knew nothing about her and could have learned nothing.' The only people who could have told him anything were the wife of the photographer, the old woman who sold mixed sweets and a lodging-house keeper, who, as he said. 'were not in the circle of my acquaintance.' 'I did not,' he asserted, 'induce her to believe in spirit communication from her husband. I repeatedly told her that the identity of all spirit communication was most uncertain and that we must always use our own reason in judging them.'

On the next day, 8 October, he tried to give the cheque for £50 back to her. She refused to take it, assuring him in a somewhat threatening manner, that she did as she pleased and would accept nobody's control. That, she said, was why she did not, and could not, live with Mrs. Tom Fellowes. Home relinquished the point, but he got into touch with a member of the Committee, Mr. H. Rudall, a wine merchant who lived in the Grove, Camberwell. He felt the need of somebody's advice, and he asked Mr. Rudall to come with him to the bank when he presented Mrs. Lyon's cheque. He thought it might be refused and if so, he would like Mr. Rudall's support in an awkward moment.

Somewhat to their surprise, the bank made no demur and the money was handed over. When Home come back from the bank, Mrs. Lyon was in Madame Bellinger's shop, waiting for him. She came upstairs with him. In his rooms, she examined his table silver and said she did not like the shape of the forks; he had better sell it. Home explained that the silver was precious to him as it had belonged to his wife.

Mrs. Lyon now repeated her determination to adopt him. There was, he said, no manifestation of spirit guidance whatever. Mrs. Lyon said: 'We will have a nice house and make the money fly, and nothing will spite my husband's family more.' Home, who needed time to compose himself, said that he would not be able to meet her next day, but as she had suggested his consulting his friends, he would ask his friend S. C. Hall to call on her. At this point in the conversation, she said: 'I see you wear a very beautiful ring. Is that a present from some great person?' Home told her that the Emperor of Russia had given it to him as a wedding present. Since she had read *Incidents in my Life*, I, she said, 'And he gave you another jewel when your child was born?' That, Home said, had been for his wife. Had he got it? Mrs. Lyon demanded. Home fetched his small jewel case and showed her the brooch, the sixteen large diamonds with the great emerald in their centre. Also in the case was another ring, set with a beautiful diamond; this Mrs. Lyon had not been able to read of; the Czar had given it to Home when he consented to be Gregoire's godfather. Home declared in his affidavit: 'This was the property of my boy from his godfather. But Mrs. Lyon said: Now I am your mother, I shall take care of these things for you.' On this, the fourth time of her seeing him, she took away with her these two jewels, worth several hundred pounds, (a modern estimate would be many thousands) 'and at this moment she has them still.' Home's preposterous weakness in allowing her to take them was fatally characteristic of their mutual relationship in the whole affair. But this was only the beginning of her depredations. In November she took 'three most valuable bracelets and all the rich and valuable Indian and lace shawls and underclothing belonging to my late wife. She has them still,' Home said and he submitted that she should at least offer to return them, as they belonged to his son, when she came into a court of Equity to demand the restitution of her gifts to Home himself.

Home meanwhile consulted S. C. Hall about this extraordinary state of affairs and asked him to call on Mrs. Lyon in Westbourne Place. S. C. Hall was reluctant, not liking the sound of it, but consented to go, on the pretext of talking to her about the Spiritual Athenaeum, and he came back saying that this situation was the most wonderful thing he had ever seen. Mrs. Lyon had told him she meant to settle £700 a year on Home. He had begged her to consider very carefully what she was about; £300, he said would be ample and very generous. Mrs. Lyon said: 'What is £24,000 to me, in comparison with having a son that I can love and who will be kind to me?' On that day she wrote Home a letter of very great importance:

Oct.10 1866
18 Westbourne Place, Hyde Park
   My dear Mr. Home.
I have a desire to render you independent of the world, and having ample means for the purpose. I have the greatest satisfaction in now presenting you with with, and as an *entirely* Free Gift from me, the sum of £24,000.
   My dear sir, Yours very truly and respectfully,

   Jane Lyon.

This letter, making no reference whatever to Home's spiritual faculties, to his services as a medium or to her intention of adopting him, describing the money as 'an entirely free gift', cannot be made to square with Mrs. Lyon's presentation of her case. In his summing-up[4], Sir George Gifford, though finding for the Plaintiff, admitted that this letter, in the context of what he assumed to be the facts of the case, was unaccountable.

Mrs. Lyon arranged to transfer £24,000 of securities to Home's account and on 11 October, they drove together in a cab to the Bank of England, Home said: 'She sat very near me with my hands in hers under her shawl. When we were going down Holborn Hill, she said: 'This, my darling boy, is one of the happy days of my life. I never expected to be so happy again.' At the Bank of England, the transaction was effected; the securities were not made over to him but the dividends from them were to be invested in his name.

Home never seems to have been at ease under this fabulous cascade of wealth; the personality and conduct of Mrs. Lyon, her vigorous vulgarity, her domineering intrusiveness, made this impossible, but the sense of security, that his financial position was now assured, was comforting. His kind friend Mr. Cox of Cox's Hotel had died in 1864, and the widowed Mrs. Cox had retired to her country house at Fleetpond. The hotel at 55 Jermyn Street was now managed by Mr. and Mrs. Maureguy and by 1867 when Trollope was publishing 'Phineas Phinn', it was already known by their name: Lord Chiltern when in London put up 'at Maureguy's'. Besides the hotel, the Maureguys had also taken over the Coxs' protective friendship for Home. Sophia Maureguy was one of the first people to whom he gave his news: 'Dear friend, Thank God all is arranged and I have no longer to think of the future. Yours Faithfully, Dan.'

Some of the people most concerned were Dr. Gully and his family at Malvern. It is clear, from his brief note to Mrs. Maureguy, that Home was incapable of writing the long letter needed to explain everything. He asked his kind old friend Lady Dunsany to send a full relation to The Priory at Malvern. Dr. Gully's sister Ellen wrote on 14 October, 1866:-

'My dear Dan, I never *did*! Why, how wonderful and delightful! I do rejoice with you heartily but it is all so sudden that I can't realize it . . . Lady Dunsany kindly wrote me all the details and it was very kind of you, old fellow, to think of us in your time of happiness . . . Doctor has once or twice (spoken of) asking you to come and see us . . . I do hope that he may do so, and then we shall hear from yourself all about this wonderful gift.' Home was going to Brighton to recuperate and she gave him the address of a mutual friend he wanted. 'Mrs. Nichols' address is Eaton Place, Brighton. I don't know the number, anybody there will tell you. . . . Shall you go on at the Athenaeum? I am distracted to know about many things, which you have not yet settled, I daresay. Now *do* be calm and go to sleep and eat sensible dinners and try to get strong again. Your sympathizing and sincere friend, Nell.'

Lady Dunsany herself wrote to Home on 12 October, telling him she had called on Mrs. Lyon, of whom she had formed a very favourable opinion, as a sensible and amiable lady and she congratulated him most heartily, on this event 'so truly wonderful, even in your wonderful life.'[5] Lady Shelley was another, who, at a distance, saw nothing to fear in this miraculous shower of gold. She wrote at once: 'Nelly's letter with an announcement of your good fortune has indeed delighted me, more than I can tell you . . . My husband begs me to give you his warmest congratulations and good wishes.'[6] Home went to Malvern where he was welcomed at The Priory by an affectionate household. Dr. Gully took the opportunity of examining him and found that the upper half of his right lung was 'seriously congested.' Rest was very necessary, but it was to prove not easily come by.

The Gully family were anxious to meet Mrs. Lyon. Ellen Gully wrote to her on behalf of the doctor, her sister Anne and herself, a warm invitation; but Mrs. Lyon replied that she hoped to have the pleasure another time. She added, in her usual character of a know-all, that she was quite familiar with the neighbourhood, from her father's having taken her on an extended tour of that part of England.

While Home was staying with the Gully family, Mrs. Lyon sent him a cheque for £20. Her story afterwards was that he had asked her for the money; she suppressed the fact that she had urged him to accept some. Home's version of the affair was that she had given him a purse and said afterwards that she would have put some money into it, but his departure for Malvern had been so hasty. She wrote: 'Let me know how I can send you some.' Home then, he said, asked her for £20, 'which I did not need.' He said he felt that if he did not accept her offer, it would give offence. That he should, from every point of view, have withstood the offer, scarcely needs saying. The clue to his foolishness is found in the recollections of him, in a letter from Louise Kennedy to Andrew Lang:[7] 'It seemed (to him) the most natural thing in the world that he should be cared for, cosseted and made the centre of things. He was always contentedly expectant to be carried smoothly and luxuriously along the road ... his share in the adjustment of things was to be delightfully entertaining and gay, or sympathetic and sentimental, or worldly and sarcastic ... but always genuine while the moment lasted ... he appeared to regard unbelief in himself, or dislike, as a mysterious dispensation he could not try to account for.' This estimate shows all too plainly how easily he glided into the relationship with the determined old woman of grateful beneficiary. The evanescent nature of her benefits, however, was very soon foreshadowed. In December she insisted on giving him her husband's watch; as her adopted son, she wanted him, she said, to have something with the Lyon arms on it. Home did not want the watch, he had three of his own, but he accepted it and since it was not going, he had it repaired. Two days after the watch-maker had returned it, Mrs. Lyon asked for it back; Home gave it to her. Meanwhile, he being still at Malvern, Mrs. Lyon sent him affectionate letters, addressing him as 'My dear son' and 'My darling boy', signing herself 'Your affectionate Mother.' In one letter she spoke of her late husband as 'the best of men, your spiritual father, Charles Lyon.'[8] On 1 November, Home came back to 22 Sloane Street.

Mrs. Lyon now asked him if he had a man of business and he named his friend William Martin Wilkinson. On 9th November, she wrote to Mr. Wilkinson at his office, 44 Lincoln's Inn Fields, instructing him to draw a will making Daniel Dunglas Home her residuary legatee. Home was to take the name of Daniel Lyon and the arms of the Lyon family, quartered with those of the Gibsons. It was strange hearing that the Gibsons had arms, but even though they had found some, Mrs. Lyon, as Wilkinson later pointed out, would have had no right to bear them, except with a bend sinister.[9] He said he would have preferred to know the amount of the benefaction and whether there were not some of her husband's relatives to whom she wished to leave legacies? When he called by appointment at Westbourne Place on the evening of 12 November, it was, imprimis, to satisfy himself that she was competent to make a will. He said, he found her memory excellent, and 'her whole manner and conversation giving evidence of a very strong-minded woman.' Wilkinson was a believer in spiritualism; he was also a competent and honest lawyer. He asked her, he said, 'in the most pointed way, if what she was doing was in consequence of any spiritual control or orders and she said it was not, but was her own unbiased wish and determination. She had always been a believer in spiritualism, but she assured me that in what she was doing she was not influenced by any such reasons, but she had taken the greatest liking to Mr. Home . . . and it was a delight to her to make such good use of her money.' He strongly advised her to be cautious, and since he was an intimate friend of Home, he recommended her to instruct another solicitor, 'but', he said, 'she was so energetic and determined that I could make no impression on her.'

On this evening, he found Home with Mrs. Lyon and also Dr. Hawkesley and Mr. Rudall. Mrs. Lyon had extracted the addresses of the two latter from Home without telling him her object, and had asked them to come and witness her will. She now told Home to wait in her bedroom. She explained to Dr. Hawkesley that she had particularly wanted him to act as witness, so that if any discussion arose later, he could testify to her having been of sound mind when she signed the will. He and Mr. Rudall, as well as Mr. Wilkinson and S. C. Hall, all formed the opinion that she was not sane only, but extremely shrewd. The will, which was now signed, attested by two respectable witnesses, one of whom was an eminent physician, seemed to them and to the attending solicitor, a melodramatic but genuine, *coup* of good fortune. This view would have been modified by the knowledge, had any of the three possessed it, that Mrs. Lyon had already made wills in favour of five other beneficiaries and destroyed them all in turn.

Home felt himself to be extremely fortunate, but he knew — also, that he was very ill. He went to Malvern again in the second half of November, such a visit as always did him good, with reviving air, beautiful scenery, tranquillity, sympathy and knowledgable care. This time, however, the visit was not to pass in serene quiet. Dr. Gully's relation[10] of what had passed in his house on the night of 28 November, 1866, is not only interesting in itself, but as yet another evidence of the strength of Home's psychic powers. His presence in The Priory was responsible for one of the most varied and extraordinary psychic demonstrations which even his abnormal faculties produced.

Dr. Gully said that on the night of 28 November, he had sat up after everyone else had gone to bed. He himself went upstairs at twelve o'clock. As he went along the corridor outside the bedrooms, he felt that unseen beings were coming with him; but after all, something of that kind was often felt when Home was under his roof. When he was in his bedroom, an orchestra of raps began. He recognized them as the individual sounds produced by his father, his brothers, his child, all except one, which he had never heard before; even the ones with which he was familiar, came 'with a rapidity, strength and multiplication' he had never known before. Two thundering blows on the left side of his bed's head made him call out for Home who was sleeping next door. Home appeared in a few minutes, and similar blows were now heard on the right side of the bed's head. Home identified the spirits who had produced them as the Guardians of Strength. Every human being had one; their office was to protect you from illness and disease. The four feet of Dr. Gully's bed were standing in thick glass salt-cellars, which had been put there on the advice of other spirits, to strengthen electricity in his body. The dark bedroom was full of presences and atmospheric agitation. Suddenly Home said in a frightened way: 'My wife's spirit has just said to me; there is danger.' They could now hear that objects were being thrown about the room. There was a rustling of the bed curtains and of the silk covered down quilt on the bed. The room was in thick darkness except for a wall of luminous matter at the right side of the bed. They spoke to the spirits by their names and Dr. Gully asked the name of the one whose sounds he had not been able to recognize. The answer was: 'Margaret L—.' He explained in his relation that when he and she were both eighteen, he and Margaret L— had been in love. Her parents forbade the match. She became ill and as he was about to leave for Edinburgh to read for his medical degree, he was allowed to come to her bedside to say goodbye. The slight illness took a turn for the worse and within three weeks he heard that she was dead. He said: 'I have never forgotten the love and the distress of that time.' He found refuge in work, taking his degree in less than the usual period. When he visited her tomb he saw above it her portrait in bas-relief. He had it copied in a marble medallion and this had hung at his bed's head ever since.

'What! Is that Margaret?' he said.

'Yes. I love you always.'

'All these thirty-nine years?'

'Yes, and I must come now.' Then he felt his child's hand lovingly stroke his face. He lit a candle and saw the disorder of the room: the towel horse had been pushed out of its place, the towels thrown about, his slippers and boots scattered over the carpet, the down quilt was lying on the floor. On the wall, the marble medallion hung askew. Still, he said, where was the danger? It was then transmitted to them that the glass cups must be removed. The two from the bed's foot were withdrawn easily; the one under the right upper post was also pulled away without difficulty, it was broken in three pieces; the one under the left hand post they could not shift, that side of the bedstead stood so near the chest of drawers. Both of them now saw a large, luminous mass in a corner of the room. Home exclaimed: 'We can't get near enough to lift the bed and remove it.' Without a touch from either of them, the bed's head was raised, and Home drew out the glass cup; it was in four pieces and partly pulverized. They then lay down on the bed, exhausted. The atmosphere of the room, from being stifling and exciting like that of an approaching thunderstorm, was now calm. 'Our physical sensations changed from tension to placidity.' Home now went back to his own room. Dr. Gully picked up the quilt, spread it over the bed and sank into sleep. In a short while he awoke, again feverish. In waking, he had tossed the quilt off his bed once more. 'A shower of approving raps' told him he had done the right thing. Communication spelt out with the spirits of his family told him that if he had gone to sleep with the electricity of his body isolated by the glass cups, and the silk-covered down-quilt above him, he would have had a seizure. The emergency was so great, it had required the intervention of the Guardians of Strength. The enigma remained as to why spiritis had recommended the glass cups in the first place? Some nights afterwards, Home said suddenly: 'Those glass cups. They say the whole thing was contrived for your good, to impress upon you.' 'Most assuredly it did', said Dr. Gully. Such a night would indeed have impressed upon anybody. He tried to discover to himself why a misleading direction should have been given to him in the first place. He felt that he could not refuse belief in an intelligent, extra-corporeal agent's having been at work. 'Of the existence of such agency I had long ceased to have any doubt, but I may have speculated and spun theories to account for spiritual manifestations in some other way, and it may have been to put a stop to these that this marvellous night was contrived, for strongly impressing me with the reality of the interference.'

In 1866, Dr. Gully was at the height of his practice and such a night as this must have taken a serious toll of his energies; for Home also, in weak health as he was, it must have been extremely taxing; but whether he were right in his interpretation, whether Dr. Gully were right, the significant aspect of the affair was the proof it gave of Home's extraordinary powers, by their involuntary exercise, at a time when he was about to be accused of being nothing but a fraud and a mountebank.

# XXIV

## The Imperious Mrs. Lyon

Home now found himself in an increasing intimacy with Mrs. Lyon which, in spite of the advantages it held out, became more and more embarrasing and painful. She tried to insist that as her adopted son, he should change his name for that of Lyon. When he said he could not relinquish the now famous name of Home, a compromise was reached by which he was to become Daniel Home Lyon. A deed poll was executed in December 1866. This was briefly announced in *The Times* and Mrs. Lyon was disappointed and annoyed that it was not published by other papers.

Home's birthday was in March, but Mrs. Lyon's imperious will over-rode the calendar. On 10 December she said she had a birthday present for him; this was another £6,000, making up her gifts to £30,000. The transfer was effected by Messrs. Croker, Fox, Taylor and Backhouse of 5 Token House Yard, and Mr. John Taylor said afterwards in evidence: 'Mr. D. D. Home and Mrs. Lyon called at our office on 10 December. I accompanied her to the Bank of England where she transferred £6,798.17.4 Consols into the name of the Defendant. She took the stock receipt and handed it to Mr. Home, and said: 'Isn't that a pretty present?' Nothing, either on this, or on the previous, or on any occasion, indicated anything like undue, in fact, any influence on the part of Mr. Home.[1]

Of Home's friends to whom he introduced Mrs. Lyon, one was the barrister H. D. Jencken, who provided another instance of a legal mind which accepted the claims of spiritualism. Mr. Jencken did not now practise at the bar, but he was the Hon. General Secretary to the Association for the Reform and Codification of the Law of Nations. He lived with his old mother at Kilmorey House, Thicket Road. This was a turning off Anerly Road, the long hill that led up to the summit of Sydenham Hill where the Crystal Palace stood. The unassuming, substantial houses in the tree-shaded road were characteristic of the early London suburbs. Through Home, Jencken had become a friend of Dr. Gully and had experienced séances at the doctor's house in

Malvern. One of his neighbours in Thicket Road was Mrs. Hennings, who lived at Sunninghill House. She had become a believer in spiritualism, from the extraordinary séances at Kilmorey House, in which messages from her father and her nephew, both dead, referred to family matters of which, Mrs. Hennings said, no one knew anything but herself. On 2 December, the day before the executing of the deed poll, Home took Mrs. Lyon to call at Kilmorey House. True to her practice of excluding Home from any business discussion (Home said she always laughed at his incompetence and his ignorance of business), Mrs. Lyon asked Mr. Jencken to come apart with her into another room. Here she sought his advice as to how she could settle her money on Home irrevocably so that it should be out of the power of her relations in law, even after her death. Mr. Jencken first asked her if spiritualism had anything to do with these arrangements? No, she said. All she wanted was a son; she had found him in Home, and her only fear was that he might marry again. Jencken's advice was that she should consult a doctor who would confirm that when she made the gift, she was of sound mind. She said that she had done this already, referring no doubt to her care to have Dr. Hawkesley as one of the witnesses of her will. In that case, Mr. Jencken said, he advised her to execute a deed confirming her gift.[2] On 30 December, 1866, Mrs. Hennings gave a small dinner party for Home and Mrs. Lyon. On this occasion, Home said, Mrs. Lyon's behaviour to him was 'so absurdly affectionate' and she talked so much of her fear that Home would leave her, that Mrs. Hennings decided she could not ask her to the house again, 'as even the servants made remarks on her conduct.' The night was one of unleashed forces; the Crystal Palace had caught fire and the blaze was destroying the larger part of the Northern Wing, including the Assyrian Court and the Tropical Department. The flames were still raging, and their terrible splendour, heightened by the winter darkness, was visible from the houses down below in Thicket Road. Mrs. Lyon found that one of the windows of Sunninghill House commanded an excellent view; although this was in a room without a fire, her appetite for the spectacle was so keen that she insisted on staying in the cold till she contracted a severe chill.

In the first week of January 1867, Mrs. Lyon told Wilkinson that she had £30,000 out on mortgages and she wanted this sum converted into a trust for Home; the income from it was to be paid to her during her life time and the capital was to go to him on her death. Wilkinson was to be the trustee. Wilkinson had, several times during these transactions, suggested to her that as he was a friend of Home, it would be better if she instructed another solicitor. Every time Mrs. Lyon had refused the suggestion, repeating that she was perfectly satisfied that he should act for her. He now prepared a deed of gift according to her instructions and on 19 January, 1867, the son of the firm, Mr. W. J. Wilkinson, and their clerk Mr. Hartley brought it to her lodgings. Home was present and when the lawyers came in, he thought he could consult Mrs. Lyon's usual wishes when business was to be discussed, by leaving the room; but he said,[3] 'She called me to her and kicking a footstool from under the table, pointed for me to kneel on it. I did so, close to her and she put her left arm round my neck and fondled my cheek while they were reading the parchment.' He was ashamed and tried to draw away, but Mrs. Lyon held him there. This deed was the last of Mrs. Lyon's great benefactions; and enormous as they were, it began to be felt in Home's immediate circle, that they had been too dearly bought. Home himself was coming to the same view.

He said that from the time of his return from Malvern in November 1866, Mrs. Lyon came to his rooms daily, and he frequently dined or breakfasted at hers. He was beginning to be 'most wonderfully disappointed' in her behaviour which was selfish and often bad-tempered. At Christmas, 1866, the Maureguys gave a children's party. Home was naturally invited and he brought Mrs. Lyon. At about 10 o'clock she wanted to go home. Home who, with his delight in children's amusements must have been in his element, wanted to stay longer, but, Mrs. Maureguy said: 'She did not seem to heed his wish in the least, but went and took him with her, and led him off by the arm. We laughed', she said, 'and made the remark that he had been led off.' They might laugh, but they noticed that his whole manner was changed, 'less cheerful than formerly'. Mrs. Cox, though living down at Fleetpond, spent some time in London and Home and Mrs. Lyon came to dinner with her on Christmas Day. She said of Mrs. Lyon: 'Her manner on this, as on every occasion, was so very affectionate to Mr. Home that some friends, who were present, remarked upon it.' Mrs. Cox said that Home had told her a little before this, that Mrs. Lyon ought to have some more respectable lodging than Mrs. Key's rooms in Westbourne Place. She went with him there to call on Mrs. Lyon and was astonished; neither from Mrs. Lyon's appearance or dress or manners could it be supposed that she was a woman of wealth. Mrs. Lyon did, in fact, decide to leave Mrs. Key's lodgings, but to Home's surprise and disappointment, she chose to return to Mrs. Pepper in Albert Place; in his view this lodging was even more unsuitable than the other but he was never able to make his views and wishes prevail with Mrs. Lyon and she was re-established at 17a Albert Place in November 1866.

Obliged to spend much of his time in these close quarters with a stout, domineering and overpowering woman, the frail young man had much to endure. The carrying away of his Russian jewels had been a serious injury but it was not so painful as Mrs. Lyon's appropriation of Sacha's elegant clothes. Mrs. Pepper had a servant, Eliza Clymow; on several occasions Mrs. Lyon showed her 'the beautiful embroidered chemises trimmed with Valenciennes lace,' and other garments belonging to the late Mrs. Home. She had engaged a workwoman to alter them to suit her figure. One morning when she was dressing she had called Eliza into her room, to let her see how one of the chemises fitted her. Mrs. S. C. Hall could not bear the sight of her in Sacha's things. She said:[4] 'I saw that Mrs. Lyon frequently wore the Indian shawls, the jewels and the laces which I knew had belonged to Mr. Home's dear wife, whom I had loved so well that it pained me to see them.'

A member of the executive committee of the Spiritual Athenaeum, Mr. H. W. Spratt was an architect with offices in Walbrook Buildings. His private house was in South Villas, Greenwich, where he and his wife had Home and Mrs. Lyon to dinner three or four times. If, by a slip of the tongue, Home were called by his proper name, Mrs. Lyon would say in offended tones: 'His name is not Home now, it is Lyon.' On the occasion of these dinner parties, she would talk a great deal about his presents from Royalty and distinguished persons. Home, feeling, naturally, that generosity became him, had given her a brooch, containing a miniature of himself, set in pearls and diamonds taken from his store. Mrs. Lyon showed it to Mr. Spratt exultantly. She told him she had possession of Home's wife's laces and shawls. Home was putting on her shawl for her after a dinner party when she turned round to the host and said 'boastingly' that it had been one of his wife's.

Eliza Clymow saw a great deal of Mrs. Lyon, for though the latter had parted in anger from Mrs. Pepper and gone to Mrs. Key, now that she had returned, she could not keep out of the kitchen. She used to talk to Eliza about her affairs. She would bring the letters which she had written to Lady Dunsany and others of Home's friends down to the kitchen and read them aloud to the landlady and her servant. She never read any business letters aloud to them though. Eliza said, 'she used to call out the names of the persons to whom they were addressed, before she gave them to me to post.'

Eliza Clymow had more to say of the domestic interior of Albert Place. Mrs. Lyon had taken up her quarters there on 24 November and in December, Eliza saw Mrs. Pepper in tears because Mrs. Lyon would not give her £200 to help her son Joe, who had been posted at Tattersalls. Since the Gaming Act of 1845, it had not been possible to enforce legally the payment of gambling debts, and the bookmakers protected themselves by posting a list of defaulters in the betting room at Tattersall's, which meant that no one would accept their bets; this fate threatened Joe Pepper unless he could find £200 to discharge his obligations. Mrs. Pepper in grief and indignation had exclaimed that it was disgusting, the way that old woman went on about that fellow Home. If *he* wanted £200, Mrs. Lyon would have given it to him, and she added: 'But I will ruin him as sure as my name is Pepper.'

Miss Elizabeth Fuller, the needlewoman Mrs. Lyon employed, was once in the kitchen when Mrs. Pepper said she would ruin Mr. Home.

Elizabeth Fuller, of 1 Chapel Place, Brompton Road, said that when she was sewing for Mrs. Lyon in January 1867, she worked in Mrs. Lyon's sitting room and was not required to leave it even when visitors came. One day she was cutting some valuable laces to trim a black satin dress for Mrs. Lyon. Home stood there, watching. He told her the laces had belonged to his wife. Elizabeth Fuller was astonished at the way Mrs. Lyon treated him. 'She kept his cheque book in a locked box, and always asked him what he wanted it for. She took his letters out of his hand and read them.' Mr. Home, Elizabeth Fuller said, was a very kind gentleman. 'He was exceedingly embarrassed when Mrs. Lyon used to be affectionate to him. She used to have the bodices of her dresses tried on in his presence and would not allow him to leave the room though he offered to. Elizabeth Clymow bore this out. She said that when Mrs. Lyon was dressing to go out for dinner in Home's company, 'I have seen her come out of her bedroom in her chemise into the sitting room where Mr. Home was, and Mr. Home used to look very much ashamed that she should do so.'

Home had been dismayed at the sight of 17a Albert Place and of Mrs. Pepper, but worse was to come than the mere sight of Mrs. Pepper in her own premises. Very shortly after Mrs. Lyon's return, Mrs. Pepper called at 22 Sloane Street and demanded, with great freedom, if the old lady had done what she had done in a legal way? Otherwise she would be sure to change her mind. 'She is always changing her will,' Mrs. Pepper said. Once she had put Mrs. Pepper's daughter Louisa into her will, but Louisa had died. Mrs. Pepper had then suggested that as Joe was Louisa's favourite brother, why should not Mrs. Lyon put him into her will in Louisa's place? 'But, law, sir, she was in such a rage with me!'

This visitation was trying enough, but a few mornings later, Mrs. Pepper arrived in Sloane Street before he was out of bed, asking for a loan of £200. Home refused this. Mrs. Pepper called many times again, each time reducing her demand till she brought it down to £15. Home in desperation told her to go back to Mrs. Lyon and show her the letter from Tattershall's, then he himself would try to persuade her to produce the money. Some days afterwards when he had been breakfasting with Mrs. Lyon, Mrs. Pepper came into the room to clear away and burst into tears, adjuring Mrs. Lyon to save Joe. She left the letter from Tattersall's on the table. Home tried to say a few words on the young man's behalf. Mrs. Lyon scolded him sharply, saying she had never allowed anyone, not even her father or her husband, to interfere with her in matters of business, which she always arranged for both of them. She refused either to help Joe Pepper or to allow Home to help him, and from that day, Home said, 'Mrs. Pepper became my enemy.' The state of things between Mrs. Pepper and Mrs. Lyon themselves, was what most people would have called enmity. Though Mrs. Lyon was always going downstairs into the kitchen, she spoke of her landlady as 'that beast, Pepper.' She said that though Mrs. Pepper looked as though she drank, she believed that drunkenness was the one vice Mrs. Pepper did not possess. Eliza Clymow said that Mrs. Pepper owned another establishment next door, 16 Albert Place, which was a house of ill-fame. As she was the servant at 17 Albert Place, she was to her annoyance, on one occasion ordered to go next door, 'to prepare a meat breakfast for a bad woman.'

The wide circle of Home's friends, otherwise in a mist of anonymity, rose to give evidence on his behalf, like points of illumination on this distressing scene. Mrs. Cromwell Varley, of Fleetwood House, Beckenham, the wife of the electrical engineer who had helped in the laying of the Atlantic cable, said that Home had told her that very early in her visits to Sloane Street, Mrs. Lyon had gone to his drawers and looked over his clothes. One of the most interesting of Home's friends was Mr. Ion Perdicaris, the son of a naturalized Greek father. Rich, cultivated and a talented amateur actor, he was a friend of Cora Mowatt Ritchie, with whom he had played a season in Florence with success. He had met Home in Switzerland and been deeply impressed by his powers. When Home returned from St. Petersburg, there were several demonstrations of phenomena in Perdicaris' lodgings, 68 Newman Street, Oxford Street. One evening, all the chairs moved across the floor to the hearth. 'As we reached the marble curb, Home doubled up his knees to his chin, when he was lifted out of his chair and hoisted towards the ceiling by some invisible power.' Perdicaris who had not seen the phenomena before, lost his head; he started forward to seize Home round the waist. Home fell back heavily into the armchair. In most unusual anger he scolded Perdicaris, saying he might well have broken a leg by his precipitous fall.[5] Perdicaris not only regarded his psychic powers with admiration and wonder, he had an affectionate sympathy for him. He said that Home's qualities were 'impulsive and unreflective, easily influenced by the associates of the hour.' He was completely truthful in his own utterance but as a result of these qualities, 'he has once or twice allowed Mrs. Lyon in my presence to make untrue statements, without charging her with them.' He was destitute, Perdicaris said, 'of business knowledge, habits or aptitudes, careless to a fault.' He was easily moved to charity. This last was a serious failing, in Mrs. Lyon's view. Once, when he had subscribed £2 to help a poor old woman, he begged Perdicaris not to mention it to Mrs. Lyon: it would make her angry. Perdicaris was shocked and indignant at her mean tyranny. 'She objected to his spending the most trifling sums on cab-hire, saying he ought to limit himself to omnibuses whenever this was possible.' Perdicaris was astounded by her treatment of Home's letters. 'I was even more astonished when . . . she read me private letters addressed to Home, which she opened in his absence without his authority.'

Gerald Massey was a literary man of some contemporary success. He became deeply interested in spiritualism. His book *Concerning Spiritualism*, published in 1874, shows how the impact of the belief had affected him. He said:[6] it had meant 'such a transformation of *faith* into *facts*', as he could only compare to voyaging, a prisoner, battened under hatches living by the dim light of one candle, and then suddenly, on some splendid starry night, allowed to go on deck for the first time, to see the splendid mechanism of the starry heavens . . . 'and drink in a new life with every breath of that wondrous liberty, which makes you dilate almost large enough to fill the immensity that you see around you.' While the ideas that led to these emotions were awakening, Massey met Home at the S. C. Halls'. Mrs. Lyon was with him. Massey's impression of the pair was such, as he told the court, 'that the charge of Mr. Home's power and ascendancy over Mrs. Lyon is the grossest fiction and impudently absurd. Mrs. Lyon would agree with nothing she did not like or that did not suit her view.' Before Massey's repugnance became too strong to be concealed, he had one or two private conversations with her. In one of these[7] she said: 'She knew Mr. Home as the son of her adoption the moment she set eyes on him. She was very open in speaking of what she had done for him and what she intended yet to do.' Massey asked if she had acted from anything said or done at any of Mr. Home's séances. 'She assured me most emphatically that she had not, and that nothing of the sort had taken place at their early interviews beyond her personal liking.' As one who admired and respected Home, Massey, like Perdicaris, was indignant at the servile condition to which he had been reduced. 'She made him do pretty much as she pleased, even to the going on errands for her and carrying home trivial articles for her . . . I saw him do very humiliating things and put up with very strong displays of Mrs. Lyon's will. I once remarked to him I could not stand that for £30,000 a year. Home had answered: 'Oh, you do not know Mother. She likes to have her own way, but she is kindness itself.' An occasion now and again made it understandable that he thought so. Massey said: 'He was speaking of some hardship he had undergone in early life, when Mrs. Lyon embraced him, wept over him real tears and said how glad she was to be the means of preventing anything of that kind from ever again occurring.' Indeed, she was at times excessively affectionate. 'A more cynical onlooker might have surmised something too fond and fervent.' The chief cause of Massey's dismay however was not the humiliation and indignity which his friend was suffering but the real injury to his health. 'So potent was Mrs. Lyon's power and ascendancy over Mr. Home that I foresaw in all likelihood it would be fatal to one so frail in health.' Massey saw that he had great difficulty in gaining even a little personal freedom. She was very jealous of his going anywhere without her. 'Mrs. Lyon was very ambitious of meeting with and being recognized by . . . persons of title and members of the aristocracy. Mr. Home's acquaintance with such is large, and I found that Mrs. Lyon was irrepressibly anxious to meet with Lady — or go to the house of Lord —. She was greatly gratified with any notice of her by a titled lady . . . and proportionately disappointed if Mr. Home were invited where she could not go.'

When Madame Home was working on her husband's biography she had several thousand letters before her, sent to him from America, from Europe, from Russia, for he kept them all. By 1866, the collection was already formidable and he needed someone to arrange them for him. In November 1866, he engaged the services of Mr. Philip Blair Phillips, who, since he lived at 35, Priory Road, Kilburn, may have been recommended to him by Mr. Wilkinson. Blair Phillips worked on the letters and papers at 22 Sloane Street, where he saw, needless to say, a great deal of Mrs. Lyon. He saw, as Perdicaris and Massey saw, that Home's health was suffering from her treatment of him. 'I would not have changed places with him for five times the money, and I have said so repeatedly,' he said. 'Home', he went on, 'lived in constant dread of Mrs. Lyon's vile and ungovernable temper.' He sometimes came back from her lodgings to Sloane Street, 'so ill and faint,' Blair Phillips said, 'that I pitied him.' Though she often made demonstrations of affection, she was at all times most exacting and tyrannical.' Her temper was absurdly variable. 'I have known her change her mind half a dozen times in one day. She has given various articles to Mr. Home, which she had asked for again within a week.' An instance of this, particularly annoying to a secretary, concerned 'an old portmanteau which she had given to him for my use to put papers in.'

Mrs. Lyon was constantly asking after this, until 'she pressed me one day to promise to return it to her immediately, which I did.' When Mrs. Lyon was composing the case she intended to bring against Home, for having, as she said, made her believe that her husband's spirit was dictating that her fortune should be made over to him, Blair

Phillips said in evidence that she came to 22 Sloane Street in Home's absence and removed several of the letters she had written to him.

# XXV

## Imprisoned for Debt

Mrs. Lyon had made it known to her three nieces-in-law, Mrs. Tom Fellowes, Mrs. James Fellowes and Mrs. Dennison, that she had bestowed £30,000 in securities on Home, given him a reversionary interest in another £30,000 and made him the sole beneficiary under her will. They were, naturally, roused to indignation; they felt some genuine alarm for her as well as envy and resentment on their own behalf, and were, for every reason, on the alert to disparage Home whenever they could. The accusation against him was, that he had fraudulently persuaded her that she was acting in accordance with commands from her husband's spirit, that when S. C. Hall was sent for to advise Home, it was in response to messages spelt out that he was to be summoned, and that when W. M. Wilkinson was instructed to make her will in Home's favour, this was also in obedience to spirit commands relayed by Home. The accusations concerning S. C. Hall and W. M. Wilkinson were disproved on trial, but there remained the testimony of Mrs. James Fellowes and Mrs. Tom Fellowes; the evidence of the latter was supported by Mrs. Key, who, while Mrs. Lyon was still her lodger, before 24 November, 1866, was found by Home on one occasion, kneeling on the floor outside Mrs. Lyon's sitting room, looking through the key-hole. Mrs. James Fellowes also produced evidence of what she had heard while Home and Mrs. Lyon were inside the room. She denied that she had *listened* at the door, it was just that when she was there, she could not help hearing. When asked how long she had just happened to be at the door, she said 'perhaps a few minutes'. She had not been able to help hearing Mrs. Lyon scream out: 'Oh, my darling!' Then a man's voice said: 'Don't interrupt me, or I can't proceed.' She was told by the stationer's assistant, Daniel Phillips, that 'Mrs. Lyon was with Mr. Home, the spirit rapper.'

Mrs. Tom Fellowes was extremely anxious to be present at a séance. She once tried to sit with Home and Mrs. Lyon but nothing occurred, as was not seldom the case with Home. Mrs. Lyon told her, on 8

November, 1866, of Home's wonderful powers and of his having put her in touch with her husband; therefore she had adopted him and transferred her property to him. As regards the reliability of what Mrs. Lyon told Mrs. Tom Fellowes — one evening at dinner when Mrs. Tom Fellowes was there, Mrs. Lyon exclaimed that she felt a spirit by her chair; afterwards she had laughed, and told Home that she had made it up to astonish her niece.[1] Mrs. Lyon went on: 'Plessey does all she can to put me against you, but she will not succeed. Why, she even said, it would make people talk if we lived in the same house together'. Home said, then they would be bad-minded people. Mrs. Tom Fellowes, in evidence, said Mrs. Key had told her that she listened at the door, and Mrs. Tom Fellowes had asked her to go on doing it; Mrs. Tom Fellowes told Mrs. Lyon that if she and Home were to live in the same house, Home would get every farthing she possessed.

The discontent of the nieces had naturally arisen as soon as they saw the situation and heard of Mrs. Lyon's enormous dispositions of her money; but there were signs at the end of 1868 that Mrs. Lyon also was feeling the oncomings of dissatisfaction, as any one who knew the history of her past fits of benevolence and their subsiding might have expected. Mrs. Pepper in fact had already warned Home of the possibility that the benefactions would be cancelled. Mrs. Lyon had at first shown herself affectionate towards Gricha. The boy was now seven, and as his father, though he loved him, was incapable of setting up a home for him, he was cared for by two of Home's friends in succession. One was Cora Mowatt Ritchie, who took him to live with her at 3 Gloucester Terrace, Campden Hill. At first, Mrs. Lyon had wished to establish some sort of claim on him. She had told Mrs. Ritchie that she intended to take a large house, in which Mrs. Ritchie should have a suite to herself and live there with the child. She was avidly anxious that Gricha should develop mediumistic powers. The suggestion shocked Mrs. Ritchie, who told her that no signs of this had yet appeared and it would be most harmful to try to encourage any. Gricha's affidavit was taken on 27 March, 1868, and he spoke of having seen the deed which Mrs. Lyon had executed on 12 December, 1866, which stated her intention to transfer the £24,000 and the £6,000 worth of stocks to Home 'for his absolute benefit', and that she made the deed 'to remove all doubts, suspicions and controversies', and 'to declare irrevocably that the gift was made of her own free will and pleasure and without influence or control.' The child said, 'I remember going with my father, not very long before Christmas', (i.e. in December, 1866) 'to where Mrs. Lyon lived. When we went in, Mr. Wilkinson was there and Mrs. Lyon told me to go into her bedroom with my father as she was going to transact business. In a little while she called me out . . . she drew me close to her and kissed me and pointed to a very big sheet of funny-looking paper, and there was a great deal of writing on it and some red lines and a seal. Mrs. Lyon said: This is your fortune when your father is dead. I remembered the words because I did not want my father to die. I had to go away before dinner was quite done, because it was my dancing-lesson night . . . My father put me into a cab and I went home alone . . . I remember that time because she was going to give me some money but she only took it out of her purse and put it back again.' He had some recollections, though, of Mrs. Lyon's good humour. 'She used to let me fight with her when we were in a cab. She used to laugh when her bonnet fell off.' But presently Mrs. Lyon began to turn against him. On one occasion, Mrs. Ritchie, thinking he would be welcome, sent him to Albert Place, but Gricha was sent back in disgrace. Mrs. Pepper's modest apartments must have contained a piano for Gricha had refused to play a little piece he had played at a concert; he said he couldn't play without his notes and would not even try. He had been very rude and squirted orange-juice over the table cloth. In evidence, Mrs. Lyon declared him to be 'a rude, impertinent contradictious boy.'

The winter of 1866–7 was a severe one and Home suffered very much. He described the pain in his lung as 'neuralgia in the chest'. Dr. Gully wished to examine him and in January 1867, he came to 17a Albert Place; as Home spent so much of his time there, it was a convenient place for the appointment. He brought with him, to introduce to Mrs. Lyon, the Gullys' friend Mrs. Lucy Nichols, for whose address at Brighton Home had asked Ellen Gully. Mrs. Nichols lodged at 25 Eaton Place, Brighton, but she and her husband John Gough Nichols had a house in Malvern, on the hillside, overlooking the town, called Aldwyn Tower. Unlike the graceful Regency and early Victorian Malvern houses, it was a red and white Italianate building, modern and garish; it became famous because in 1878 its garden was the scene, in the presence of William Eglinton, of some of the most extraordinary full-figure materializations ever recorded. Mrs. Nichols in her affidavit said that when she and Dr. Gully arrived at 17a Albert Place, Mrs. Lyon at the window 'beckoned her to come in.' Dr. Gully took Home into the bedroom and Mrs. Nichols, in conversation with Mrs. Lyon, happened to speak of Home by his original name. Mrs. Lyon said, 'in rather an offensive manner, Mr. *Lyon*, if you please, my dear. Do you not know that he has taken my name?' It was the first time of her meeting Mrs. Nichols, but she detailed to the latter the settlements she had made on Home. Lucy Nichols exclaimed: 'All this money because of his wonderful gifts!'

'Not in the least', said Mrs. Lyon, 'spiritualism and his gifts had nothing to do with it.'

Dr. Gully found Home in such a state that he advised his going abroad at once; Home said he could not leave the country unless Mrs. Lyon agreed to come with him. As she had refused to go with him to Malvern, it was inevitable that she should refuse to go out of England. One of the chief pleasures of her connection with Home, was that she knew at least some of his friends: Lady Dunsany, Mrs. Parkes, the S. C. Halls, and many of his acquaintances. She meant to stay in England and enjoy to the full such social opportunities as were now available to her. In November 1866, Home had introduced her to Lady Shelley. Mrs. Lyon was agog with eagerness. Lady Shelley's maiden name had been Gibson, and Mrs. Lyon had determined that their fathers had been second or third cousins. She wrote of her to Home as 'dear cousin Lady Shelley,' and in a moment of excitement during one of her numerous fallings-out with him, threatened to make a new will in the Shelleys' favour. Since Home could not be persuaded to go abroad, Dr. Gully urged him to try the south coast immediately. Home agreed and on 26 January, he went to Hastings. He came back to London for a fortnight in February and then went away again to Torquay and Plymouth.

Behind his back, an ominous situation was developing. He had felt obliged to say that he would not go abroad without Mrs. Lyon, but he took no care to guard his position with her at home; indeed, it was stated at the trial that out of an acquaintance of thirty four weeks, Home had been absent from her for seventeen. He was now away for the greater part of three months, and during this time, the vultures gathered. Home said that during his absence, his friends no longer visited her, and she felt resentful and defrauded; but meantime, the one member of the committee of the Spiritual Athenaeum who was unreliable, began to press his attendance on her. Mr. Henry Gould Gibson, who had her family name but was not claimed as a relation, was a merchant with offices at 33 Mark Lane by the Tower, and a house in Mecklenburg Square. He began to visit Mrs. Lyon every day, and brought her presents of Hungarian bread and sardines and vinegar. Elizabeth Fuller, still at work sewing for Mrs. Lyon, said that one day Mr. Gibson brought 'a Singing Jinny,' a rich currant cake baked on a griddle, of the kind given to singers on New Year's Eve. She heard him tell Mrs. Lyon that it was a pity she had ever adopted Home. Meanwhile, according to Mrs. Lyon herself, he borrowed £30 from her, then £400, then £100, then £80. These sums, she explained in court, were loans only; she had his notes of hand for them, but she had grown sick of his repeated borrowings. Gibson however was now a member of the coterie at 17a Albert Place. Mrs.

206

Lyon had said that during the first five years of her widowhood, she had known no one in London except Mrs. Sims, Mrs. Pryor and Mrs. Pepper; in fact, among others, she had had a friend of twenty-one years' standing; this was Mrs. Berry who lived in St. George's Terrace. Mrs. Berry said that she was not a 'rapping medium' but the channel through which spirit forces produced drawings and paintings; her niece Emma, aged eleven, was a gifted medium, however; then there was the young man Fred Kent; he was a very wonderful medium too, and they all sat at 17a Albert Place. At one of these séances, Mrs. Lyon was assured that Home had deceived her and she was advised to go to law for the return of her money. 'Go to law and be firm', the spirits said. As Mrs. Lyon had declared to W. M. Wilkinson that she had every confidence in him and wanted no other legal adviser, the firm of Messrs W. M. and M. Wilkinson, in February 1867, were still her solicitors, but Mr. Gibson now introduced her to Messrs. Druce and Jackson.

Two pieces of evidence were produced, as of this time, so significant that it seems remarkable that more was not made of them at the trial. In the domestic situation at 17a Albert Place, Mrs. Lyon was often quarrelsome and abusive, but she paid no attention to distinction of class. She was always in and out of Mrs. Pepper's kitchen and the motto: 'Not in front of the servants' was unknown there. Elizabeth Clymow, the maid of all work, and Elizabeth Fuller, the working dress-maker, were able to state what Mrs. Lyon had said on the most private matters. While Home was at Torquay, Elizabeth Clymow had several times heard Mrs. Lyon say that she could easily take back what she had given him by saying that the spirits had made her do it, and she would say so, 'and I have heard her say that she was a fool to tie herself to a dying man.' Faced with this statement in court, Mrs. Lyon had declared that 'Eliza was a very bad slut and a story-teller.' But Elizabeth Fuller had much graver evidence to give. She said that Mrs. Lyon had asked her to say that Home had cheated her and made her write all her letters of business as he wanted them. 'Then', Elizabeth Fuller said: 'she would do something handsome for me.' Elizabeth Fuller refused the request, and Mrs. Lyon passed the matter off, saying: 'she had only proposed it to see if I were honest.' Mrs. Lyon's comment on this was that she had never asked Elizabeth Fuller to say anything, that her affidavit was 'abominable stuff' and that lawyers made out affidavits to say what they wanted to have said. When Mrs. Lyon made the accusation that her letters to stockbrokers and to W. M. Wilkinson about the drawing of her will were either dictated to her by Home, or copied by her from drafts of his which he then destroyed, the evidence produced on her behalf was that of Mrs. Key, who said that, when she was listening at Mrs. Lyon's door on the evening of 8 November, 1866, she heard Home say: 'Write what I tell you', and something about a will, and taking the Lyon family arms. Mrs. Lyon had failed in her attempt on Elizabeth Fuller; with Mrs. Key, she appears to have been more successful.

Mrs. Lyon's *volte face* seemed to come with complete suddenness but the reasons for it had been in force for some time. Her disappointment that Home's social circle was only partly open to her; her growing vindictive anger against Gricha, who, like most boys of seven, if he felt annoyed and fractious, saw no reason for concealing it, and her personal anger against him reinforced by the passionate value she set upon her own wealth. Ion Perdicaris now shared with Mrs. Ritchie the care of the boy, and Mrs. Lyon had told him that she hated the child, that she would rather be in a lunatic asylum than that any of her money should go to him. This was perhaps an echo of a fear that she might be judged of unsound mind, the fear that had made her take care to secure Dr. Hawkesley as one of the witnesses to her will. The idea that if Home's health continued to deteriorate and he should die, Gricha, as affairs then stood, would be her heir, increased her eagerness to break the connection. She had been accustomed to sign herself in letters to Home, as his loving mother. The letter she wrote on 19 March, 1867, was the last time she did so.

Home's health was becoming alarmingly worse. Dr. Gully examined him again on 29 April, 1867. He found that the patient's 'respiration was weakened', with the danger of 'fatal disease to the lungs, a malady to which there is a constant recurring tendency in Mr. Home.' Dr. Gully told him he must be extremely careful of himself and wanted to take him to Malvern. Home was, Dr. Gully said, too much frightened to put the suggestion to Mrs. Lyon, but when Dr. Gully made it himself, she agreed with unexpected readiness.

Mrs. Lyon still wrote to him affectionately, but there had been another of those outbursts of ill-temper Home was getting absolutely to dread. Monsieur Eugène Rimmel, the perfumer whose enchanting shop at 96 The Strand sold not scent only, but scented gloves, scented artificial flowers, little aromatic fountains and crackers for parties with tiny phials of scent inside them, was one of the attractive, good-natured people whom Home collected round him. He and Home sat on the committee of the French Hospital. Mrs. Lyon had promised to subscribe a guinea and after a good deal of delay, during which Monsieur Rimmel said he had been promised a guinea but had never had it, Mrs. Lyon in one of her letters asked Home to send it for her. When she heard that Home himself had subscribed ten guineas, she said angrily that he was very lavish with other people's money.

In May, Home being in Malvern, Mrs. Lyon consulted Mr. Jencken once more. Before, she had wanted guidance as to how she could make her gifts firm and irrevocable; now she wanted to be advised how she should cancel the trust deed, making Home after her death the beneficiary of the £30,000 worth of mortgages. She said that she did not want to withdraw the £24,000 and the £6,000 worth of securities, but she felt that she had been too generous as to the second £30,000. Had this been all she did, no one could have criticized her decision, but it appeared afterwards, that without ever asking Home to return the deeds to her, she had, from 6 May onwards, been taking steps to file a suit in Chancery against him, for the return of all her moneys.

Dr. Gully, whose leading professional interest was hydropathy, had heard interesting accounts of the German baths, particularly of Bad Kissingen, with its salt mud. He thought that Home would benefit physically from the treatment and that the mental benefit would be considerable in being right away from Mrs. Lyon. This time he was more successful in persuading the patient to go abroad; Home was by now so much the more ill. He agreed to put in hand the necessary arrangements and Dr. Gully was to make the final decision as to when he was fit to travel. Meanwhile Home came to London, to collect his clothes and to pack up his treasures in Sloane Street so that they should be safe during his absence. He wrote to Mrs. Lyon, telling her that Dr. Gully very urgently recommended his visiting the German baths, and asking her yet again if she would not come with him? He received an affectionate reply, not indeed agreeing to take the journey with him, but saying: 'I perfectly approve of your determination. I think it will do you good . . . and I wish you every enjoyment, that of health in particular.' The letter ended by asking him to come and see her. Entirely unsuspecting he went to 17a Albert Place at 8 o'clock on the evening of 11 June.

He saw that she was very pale; she did not return his greeting, and without a moment's warning her batteries were unmasked. She said: 'Now Daniel, I wish you to return me that trust deed, as I wish to have it.' This referred to the £30,000 worth of mortgages. Home said: 'Certainly, mother. You know I never asked you for it.' She exclaimed: 'It is just as well for you to do so quietly, as I have made up my mind to expose the whole swindle. You first sought me out', she said, ignoring that afternoon of the last October, when she described herself as having hunted up and down to find the Spiritual Athenaeum; 'then', she asserted, 'you surrounded me with a set of people whom I now find to be a pack of well-known swindlers. I have written to Wilkinson, to bring that deed and I will burn it before his eyes. You may come with him and I will tell you both what I think of you. And you may bring all your friends and I will tell them the same.'

Home was in a state of shock. He said afterwards that he would have returned every document in his possession, but for 'the vile charges' she had made against him and his friends.

On 17 June, he wrote to her, reminding her that she had given him the mortgage deed, unasked, of her own free will. Since she had now changed her mind and wanted it back, nothing was more natural and he would return it, on the following conditions:—

'You will write a kind letter in which you will acknowledge my personal honesty and that of my friends who have been introduced to you. You will give me your written permission to resume my name of Home without that of Lyon. You will return all my valuable jewels, laces etc. with the exception of the two brooches I had made for you. I will return the two rings you gave me and anything else I may have of that kind. You will leave me and mine in undisputed possession of the £30,000 you in your noble generosity and kindness of heart gave me.' He now mentioned the transaction by which Mrs. Lyon had withdrawn some thousands of pounds from the securities given him in the first assignment of £24,000, to complete another purchase. 'I would like to have you refund the sum you borrowed last winter, but leave that quite for you to decide.' He concluded: 'I must act with decision in a case like this. My name in every country where I have been stands high for honesty and I could not allow a taint of that kind to attach itself to me now, when, God knows, I deserve it so little.'

On the very day this was written, Mrs. Lyon procured a writ against him to prevent Home from leaving the country. She suppressed all mention of the fact that he had asked her to come with him and that she had written to him saying she approved of his going. This fact appeared to Home and his friends as all of a piece with Mrs. Lyon's odious conduct, but her solicitors must have advised her that if Home went abroad, he would be out of the jurisdiction of the Court of Chancery and there would be no hope of recovering her money unless and until he returned to England. As he was about to leave for the German baths, the obvious course was to apply immediately for a writ of Ne Exeat Regno. On the morning of June 18, the Sheriff's Officers took him into custody and he was lodged in Whitecross Prison. This was one of the four debtors' prisons, the others being the Queen's Bench, the Fleet and the Marshalsea. Whitecross Prison, off Old Street in the City, belonged to the Sheriffs of London. Imprisonment for debt was abolished in 1869, and Whitecross was pulled down in 1870, but in 1867 it was still one of the most formidable jails, though its conditions may have improved since 1837, when Mr. Perker said to Mr. Pickwick: 'You can't go to Whitecross Street, my dear Sir. Impossible! There are sixty beds in one ward and the bolt's on sixteen hours out of the twenty-four!'

The shock Home suffered, in his then state of health, had a very serious effect. What saved him from a nervous breakdown was the constant care of two new friends, Lord Adare and the Master of Lindsay. The former was the son of Lord Dunraven, who had stood on the steps of the Athenaeum, determining to investigate the claims of spiritualism as he listened to Sir David Brewster. Lord Adare, now twenty-six, was a Lieutenant in The First Life Guards. He was slight, hardy and athletic, devoted to racing, yachting and hunting. In 1867 he had returned from reporting the Abyssinian War for the *Daily Telegraph*. He had met Home in Paris, and renewed the acquaintance at Malvern while he himself was undergoing Dr. Gully's treatment for rheumatism. Lord Dunraven, hearing of the meeting, asked his son to attend as many séances with Home as possible and to write down a meticuluous account of each. The result was the work: *Experiences in Spiritualism with D. D. Home*, privately printed in 1869. Lord Lindsay, whose father had provided the brilliant report on the séances at the Villa Colombaia, was Adare's constant colleague and they were often helped by Adare's cousin Captain Charles Wynne and their friend Captain Gerard Smith. The investigations were not begun till the autumn of 1867, but by the previous summer the bonds of Adare and Wynne with Home were very close. Madame Home says[2] that when Home was arrested on the morning of 18 June, the young men went with him to the prison (which the arrangements governing a debtors' prison allowed them to do) and 'never left him' till his release twenty-four hours later. This was obtained by his depositing in the Court of Chancery all the documents covering the gifts of £60,000 which Mrs. Lyon had insisted on bestowing on him. Dr. Alfred Armstrong signed a certificate on 2 August, saying that Home required at least two months' complete rest before undertaking any business, if a complete nervous collapse were to be avoided. Dr. Gully then got him to Malvern, where, with his partner Dr. Fernie, he again examined him; they, like Dr. Armstrong, forbade all attention to business for the time being; they had found him on the verge of an acute nervous breakdown.

Mrs. Lyon's attack, delivered with the suddenness of a thunderclap, caused Home's friends not indignation only but utter astonishment. Ion Perdicaris had called at Albert Place on the evening of 17 June itself. Mrs. Pepper had attempted to deny him entrance but he got himself past her and went up to Mrs. Lyon's room. She was sitting in twilight, the only light coming from a lighted gas lamp outside the window. This was the occasion on which he had had the conversation with her about her hatred of Gricha. Her violent language about the child was startling, but, he said, 'she gave me not the slightest indication that she had already instituted proceedings against the Defendant Home. At that very time a warrant for his arrest was out, and the next morning he was in Whitecross Prison.' Dr. Gully wrote to Mrs. Lyon, asking what had driven her to behave in so cruel and unjust a fashion, but Mrs. Lyon felt herself on a mental plane superior to Dr. Gully's. The previous year when Home was at Malvern, undergoing some treatment at the doctor's hands, Mrs. Lyon had said in a letter to him, that she herself was 'half a doctor' and she advised Dr. Gully to alter the method he was applying. She now wrote: 'My dear Dr. Gully, you have your eyes shut by the medium of falsehood, mine have been opened by the medium of truth.' She said that talking was better than writing, and she would be glad to see him when he was next in London; but when he wrote, later in August, suggesting an interview, she replied that her solicitors had forbidden her to see any of the Defendant's friends.

Mrs. Varley was another friend who could not credit that Mrs. Lyon should have begun a Chancery action against Home. She also went to Albert Place. 'A big, red-faced woman came to the door and said Mrs. Lyon was engaged.' But as she went away, Mrs. Varley saw Mrs. Lyon looking out of the window.

The question was now, whether or not Home should fight the case Mrs. Lyon was preparing to bring. He could have avoided all trouble, all expense, all publicity, by relinquishing his claim to the documents he had already given up, but his friends appear to have been divided in their advice. Those who encouraged him to fight the action were not only anxious on his behalf that he should be allowed to keep some, at least, of the money which had been forcibly bestowed on him; they were afraid that if he resigned it, his action would be tantamount to a confession of fraud. With hindsight, it is easy to see that to give the money up would have been the wiser course; it could be said at the same time that it would have been far wiser never to have allowed Mrs. Lyon to have anything to do with him.

Home was still too ill to be able to instruct solicitors or prepare an affidavit; the case, in fact, was not heard till April of the next year; but by the middle of July 1867, the matter was being discussed. On 19 July, 1867, Browning, in London, wrote about it to Isa Blagden. He had been dining with Dr. Stanley the Dean of Westminster, where another guest had been Dr. Liddell, the Dean of Christchurch and father of Lewis Carroll's Alice. Dr. Liddell's mother had been Charlotte Lyon, Charles Lyon's sister, and Liddell was therefore Mrs. Lyon's nephew by marriage. The Lyon family might not accept Mrs. Lyon on terms of family intimacy, but they could not but be interested in the outcome of an affair in which so much of what had once been their family money was at stake, and Dr. Liddell had had some conversation with Mr. W. M. James, Q.C., who was already briefed to lead for Mrs. Lyon. Browning wrote of Liddell, that he was 'a near relation of Mrs. Lyon, I think he said her brother-in-law.' This was a minor mistake, but he then went on to a characteristic inaccuracy – that Home had been arrested by the Sherriff's officers 'at a snug evening party', when as Perdicaris said, the arrest had taken place in the morning. Browning said Dr. Liddell had told him 'all the rascality of Home, and how his own stupidity as well as greediness wrought his downfall in the foolish old soul's estimation.' Home, Browning had heard, would be exposed by the evidence of 'an old servant', who listened at the keyhole, thinking, 'with commendable sagacity' that he could be up to no good with her mistress, neither he nor 'his respectable associates, S. C. Hall and Wilkinson, who have both got pretty pickings out of the plunder.' The accusations against the two latter were in Browning's best vein. Wilkinson was exonerated by the judge from any charge of improper conduct, and had stated in his affidavit that he had never received a penny from Mrs. Lyon, or from Home, for legal work that he had done for either of them. S. C. Hall in November 1866, had been given a gold snuff box by Mrs. Lyon, 'worth three or four pounds' and a silver pencil. She had afterwards demanded the return of the snuff box, and S. C. Hall, when sending it back, had sent the silver pencil with it. He had given Mrs. Lyon some valuable books to which she had taken a fancy. These she had not felt it necessary to return.

Browning finished his letter by saying that Home had at first wanted to marry Mrs. Lyon, adding:— 'There's a misfortune for ... Mrs. Milner Gibson and such-like vermin!'[3]

# XXVI

# Verdict for the Plaintiff

To anyone interested in psychic phenomena and convinced of Home's extraordinary powers, one question stands out in the case: Lyon v. Home, which is not decisively answered by the evidence: what was the nature and extent of the psychic communication received by Home on Mrs. Lyon's behalf? That she lied when she said spirit powers demanded the summoning of S. C. Hall as Home's collaborator, that they dictated the benefactions of £24,000, £6,000 and £30,000, and the instructions to W. M. Wilkinson to draw her will, seems reasonably evident to people who accept Home as an honest and sympathetic character, and to have been by no means unsuspected by the Vice-Chancellor, whose opinion of Mrs. Lyon as a witness, expressed throughout the trial, was such that his verdict came as a surprise to many. But there was obviously some communication; where this rests solely on Mrs. Lyon's word it is altogether unreliable, since Elizabeth Clymow and Elizabeth Fuller had both heard her declare that she would get everything back from Home by saying that he had pretended that her husband's spirit had commanded her to make the gifts; but in two instances, Home's own evidence was to the effect that spirit communication had been received. The first was on the occasion of his calling on her on 7 October, 1866, when a message was received that Charles Lyon was in touch with her, that he loved her as ever, and told her not to believe that the light of other days was fled. This had caused Mrs. Lyon to bring out the water-colour daub of Binchester Hall, under which she had written those words. This not only sounds like a real manifestation, but Home himself said it had occurred. The other piece of genuine information, supplied by Home, was that in a letter to Mrs. Lyon, quoted at the trial, written from Malvern but with the date not given, a message to himself was written down signed M. G., which Home said were the initials of Mrs. Lyon's father, Mathew Gibson. The message said: 'Dear Daniel, be patient and hopeful; you are recovering and, with care, will have many years of usefulness on earth. Your mother, my darling Jane, is well and we are near her at all times.' Home said he could not remember how this message was imparted to him. 'I was at that time exceedingly ill, almost dying.'[1]

Mrs. Lyon was unacceptable in her manners and behaviour which, in a stout and common old woman made her personally repulsive; but it is not for other human beings to say that spirit communication is reserved for those who are honest, attractive and well-bred. The psychic faculty is often found in people of low moral standards. That Mrs. Lyon had some small but authentic touch of it seems likely. She was as little spiritually minded as could well be imagined and her very kindness to Home had been inspired almost entirely by a demand for affection and a lust for power; but in spite of her domineering, egotistical nature, she and her weak husband had, it seemed, been happy in their marriage of thirty-six years, and to accept the possibility of spirit communication is to accept that Mrs. Lyon may have received it from her husband and her father through such a highly powered medium as Home. The latter, however, had always said, and repeated it at the trial, that there were evil spirits as well as good; that a declaration of identity was no proof of identity, and that sitters must use their own God-given reason before they accepted a communication as genuine. Mrs. Lyon was a shocking example of the type that brings spiritualism into public contempt. Her vulgarity and deceitfulness, her bumptious attitude to her own psychic capacity, whatever it may have been, which allowed her to tell Home that she was a much greater medium than he was, the fraudulent and squalid atmosphere she created below stairs in Mrs. Pepper's kitchen, her acts of exaggerated generosity which her meanness then led her to cancel, all combined to form the picture of an ill-balanced mind and a disreputable character, for which the blame was laid on spiritualism.

Another passage of evidence brought up at the trial, as to Home's producing false communication from the spirit of Charles Lyon, was quoted from one of two manuscript books, referred to as B and A. Book B contained conversations, in Home's handwriting, supposedly between Mrs. Lyon and her husband's spirit and one of them ran: 'It stands to reason Daniel is the best medium on earth; we have chosen him for you. What we have to say and what we have to do, we can both say and do through him.' Home said that Mrs. Lyon had concocted these to gain *éclat* as someone highly gifted with mediumistic power. Elizabeth Fuller said that she saw 'scraps of writing' which Mrs. Lyon told her were spirit communications, and that she had heard Mrs. Lyon dictating to Home. It may be asked: first, what satisfaction could Mrs. Lyon gain from writings which she knew to be untrue, and secondly, why should Home have lent himself to this absurd charade? Answers to both queries may be found in Mrs. Lyon's bizarre mentality. For seven years she had been starved of emotional stimulus, and she now longed to attract fascinated attention. That she had no conscience about the fraudulent representation of phenomena was shown when she played the vulgar practical joke on Mrs. Tom Fellowes at the dinner table. Her standard of truthfulness in ordinary affairs was low, and this was combined with a voracious demand for emotional satisfaction, for affection, for social excitement, all the enjoyments of that society from which she had been shut out. Her romancing in Book B is more easily understood when viewed in the perspective of her lying in the witness box. As the Vice-Chancellor said: 'She said almost anything which occurred to her from time to time as seeming likely to make her of importance to those with whom she was conversing.'[2]

Why Home consented to write down her forgeries is at least partly explained by a passage from his affidavit, of which nothing was made at the trial. Mrs. Lyon had two fears of what he might do; one was that he would marry again, some woman other than herself, the other than he would go to Russia for an indefinite time, to prosecute his claim to his wife's estate. He said that in April 1867, she began a conversation by telling him that Mrs. Pepper had said Gricha was looking forward to her death, so that he might be rich. Home, sick at heart, said nothing but in his silence he noticed that Mrs. Lyon's watch on the chimney-piece stood at quarter past twelve. In a few moments she said: 'Are you awake, dear?' She then told him that he had been in a trance for half an hour, and knowing that he retained no memory of what he had said while he was in this state, she told him he had said that he had no property in Russia, or claims to any; but while she was saying this, Home saw that the watch said seventeen minutes past twelve only. It was too much; he got up exclaiming that he would leave her altogether; whereupon Mrs. Lyon burst into a frightening rage. She cried: 'I have always warned you not to turn my love to hate, for I will hunt you to death, there is no insult I will not heap on you. I will say it was all by undue influence that you got what you have from me. When the woman who gave me birth was on her deathbed and wanted to see me, I said she might die like a dog by the wayside before I lifted a finger to save her. So beware.' Home said: 'My mouth filled with blood. I must have fainted.' When he came to, Mrs. Lyon was beside him; she seemed much frightened; she kissed him and begged him to forgive her.

She told him that Mrs. Pepper had put her up to all this, and explained her bad temper by saying that she had been annoyed by H. G. Gibson's pestering her for money. This was in the period when she was making Home write down her 'inspired' sayings in Book B. Ion Perdicaris had said that though Home was thoroughly truthful in himself, he sometimes allowed Mrs. Lyon to utter falsehoods in his presence without checking her. Of these writings in Book B, he said: 'I was so weak and ill that for the sake of peace I used to write down what she wished.' From that time, he said: 'I grew afraid of the Plaintiff and shrank from being alone with her, for she would taunt me one moment and be too loving the next ... she used to swear at me when I was so ill I scarcely knew what I was doing, or where I was, but I felt that I was bound to her and that I had not the moral courage to free myself.'

The other manuscript book, spoken of as Book A, conveyed a significant suggestion. Here, Home had written his own account of his meeting and subsequent dealings with Mrs. Lyon; she had torn out a good deal of this; she said it was untrue and had annoyed her.

A mutual accusation between the Plaintiff and Defendant at the trial was that each had wanted to marry the other, and each had rejected the suggestion with indignation and distaste. Home said he ascribed the beginnings of Mrs. Lyon's enmity towards him to his having rejected her advances. Mrs. Lyon did not say in so many words that Home had proposed to her, only that she foresaw he was going to, and she showed him by her manner that she would not listen to anything of the sort. Home had said in his affidavit, quoted at the trial, that 'the Plaintiff had, in a laughing way, suggested that they should marry and expressed a hope that they might become nearer related, to which he replied: "That can never be while God gives me reason." ' That Mrs. Lyon had made this approach is mentioned in Dr. Gully's affidavit — 'I can readily believe that the said Mrs. Lyon made the proposition to Mr. Home which he told me she had done.' That some scene of this sort actually took place seems probable from the extreme violence with which Mrs. Lyon repudiated the notion. Mrs. Maureguy, Elizabeth Clymow, Mr. Massey, Mr. William Spratt, had all testified to her demonstrative affection for Home, while Mrs. Hennings had found it so embarrassing as carried on in front of the servants that she had decided she could not have Mrs. Lyon in the house again; but in court Mrs. Lyon declared: 'I disliked him, I hated him, he made me angry, I did not like his love.'

'Do you mean to say that you were not attached to the Defendant?'

'Certainly not. Never. I deliberately state that I was not attached to him.'

'Did you not love him?'

'No, I never loved him.'

'What did you mean by subscribing yourself, your loving mother, in your letter to him?'

'I am sure I don't know why I should have written in such a foolish way, it must have been under the influence of this fellow . . . it is so very extraordinary, I could not have been in my right senses.'

'You say,' said Mr. Mathews, 'I have a knowledge that you have not.'

'I don't know what it means. I don't know what I meant when I wrote it.'

One of her most preposterous denials was that she did not know when Home changed his name to Lyon. Blair Phillips said that Mrs. Lyon was most anxious to keep several copies of *The Times* which carried the announcement and had asked him to try to get her three or four as a memento.

'In fact,' said the Vice-Chancellor, 'it comes to this: she contradicts everything.'

These words must have filled Home and his supporters with hopes of a favourable verdict, but they were not fulfilled.


Before the 1870s, when the present Law Courts were erected in the Strand, the courts of Chancery sat in Westminster Hall, some of whose enormous area was partitioned off for them. Here the case of Lyon v. Home had opened before Vice-Chancellor Sir George Gifford on the morning of 1 April, 1868.

The news of the action resulted in a crowded court even on the first day, but on the second day the court was so full that long before the Vice-Chancellor took his seat, it was almost impossible to gain entrance. By four in the afternoon when the court rose, the crowd collected about the door was so great that the court officials took Home into the Vice-Chancellor's private room to wait for police escort. When the police arrived, they got him out through a window and he 'drove off, unobserved, in a cab.'

On the third day, the court was again crowded to suffocation, and now the *Daily Telegraph* reported: 'Ladies were in privileged seats.' 1868 was the era of small hats balanced over chignons in hair nets, of modified crinolines, short enough to show ankles in bright stockings. The crowd was as intensely concentrated in its attention as the audience at an exciting play. They laughed when Mrs. Lyon made her rumbustious replies to cross-examination. The loudest laughter broke out when this stout, rough-looking old party (as sketched for the *Police News*), her large, strong-featured face framed in a crepe veil, first indignantly denied ever kissing Mr. Home, and then said she had on two occasions at his own request; on one of these he was lying ill on a sofa and it was thought he would die. 'The tone in which Mrs. Lyon mimicked Home's entreaties that she would kiss him, seemed to cause great amusement,' the *Police News* said. Mrs. Lyon consistently tried to make it appear that the setting-up of an affectionate relationship had been Home's doing and not hers. Mr. Mathews for Home said: 'Where is this letter in which the Defendant makes the sentimental request, asking you to sign yourself, Dear Mother, and Affectionate Mother?' Witness said, she did not know where it was. 'I will take it,' said Mr. Mathews, 'that there is no such letter?' Learned Counsel for the Plaintiff said, if the letter could be found, it should be produced. Mrs. Lyon said: 'I did not think it worth keeping.'

The sight of Home himself in the witness box was the highest point of interest. The *Daily Telegraph* reported: 'The Defendant is about thirty-five years of age, of gentlemanly bearing. About middle height, of rather fair complexion, light hair and moustache. He has a somewhat effeminate appearance.' The Vice-Chancellor in his summing up was presently to make a more perceptive comment.

The explanation of how spirit communication was spelt out by letters indicated by knocks as the alphabet was recited, was given by the Defendant in reply to cross-examination, but Mr. James, Q.C. had not grasped the point, though Home had already made it, that he himself was unable to summon spirits: that he was used merely as an instrument if spirits were there and wished to speak. Mr. James said: 'Give me a knock, please.' The *Telegraph* reported: 'There was instantly a dead silence in the court to hear it.' Home said: 'I cannot do so.' The reporter said: 'There was an expression in court as of disappointment, particularly on the part of the ladies, who had eagerly leaned forward.'

Thursday 24 April was the fourth day of the trial, and on that evening a strange incident occurred, an attack on Home similar to the one of which he had been a victim in Florence. The Spiritual Athenaeum had closed very soon after Home's resigning the secretaryship and with it his tenancy of the rooms at 22 Sloane Street. He was, for the period of the trial at least, living at Maureguy's Hotel, late Cox's. On the evening of Thursday 24 April, the *Daily Telegraph* reported that as he was returning from dining with some friends, going up Duke Street on the way to his hotel in Jermyn Street, he came abreast of several men grouped on the opposite side of the street. One of them left the gang and darted across the road to Home, making an attempt to stab him. Home threw up his arm and received the wound on the back of his hand. It bled a good deal but it did not prevent his appearing in court next day. The news had reached Dr. Gully by 29 April, who wrote to him saying that as he had seen (in the newspaper reports) that Home had been well enough to stand up to cross-examination, he hoped that 'all the shock of last Thursday' was over. He added: 'It seems to me that the shock of the *case* is over too; for the old woman is nowhere.' So it might well have seemed; but meanwhile Mr. Mathews had warned Home of an adverse verdict, and Sir William Bovill, Chief Justice of the Court of Common Pleas, had been heard to remark: 'The precedents are against Home, though the evidence is for him.'[3] Dr. Gully was one of those who took an optimistic view of the outcome, expecting that Home would be ordered to resign the £30,000 mortgage deed but allowed to keep the first £30,000. Even so, he ended his letter by saying: 'You will need some Malvern air and water when it is over.'

The trial continued through six more days of unabated public interest. On 1 May, the Vice-Chancellor said he reserved judgment. This he delivered three weeks later on May 22. Neither the Plaintiff nor the Defendant was in court but as soon as the doors were opened, the *Telegraph* reporter said: 'there was an ugly rush for seating accommodation.' On this occasion, 'a considerable number of young and fashionably dressed ladies were favoured by earlier admittance.'

The Vice-Chancellor's judgment thoroughly destroyed anything that was left of Mrs. Lyon's credibility as a witness. He would not, his Lordship said, go through the Plaintiff's affidavits or her cross-examination, 'because I think no one could have read those affidavits, contrasted them with the evidence adduced on the part of the Defendant and heard that cross-examination without coming to the conclusion that reliance cannot be placed on her testimony, and it would not be just to found on it a decree against any man, save insofar as what she has sworn to may be corroborated by written documents or unimpeached witnesses or incontestable facts.' Nevertheless, the Vice-Chancellor went on, 'Much as I distrust all the Plaintiff has said, and much as I suspect what she has done, in contemplation of this suit,' he disbelieved the Defendant's assertion that the Plaintiff had turned against him originally because of his rejection of her advances. He founded his judgment that the money must be given back, on the evidence of Mrs. Dennison, Mrs. James Fellowes and Mrs. Tom Fellowes. This evidence had been absolutely contradicted by the Plaintiff and these witnesses were, as Madame Home did not fail to point out in her comments on the case[4], 'the very people most deeply concerned in seeing her gifts revoked,' but the Vice-Chancellor said that he was satisfied that both Mrs. James Fellowes and Mrs. Tom Fellowes (he did not again mention Mrs. Dennison) were witnesses of truth and of reliable memory. They had both said that Mrs. Lyon told them that in making these gifts she was obeying her husband's commands. Mrs. Tom Fellowes had said that, in Home's presence, Mrs. Lyon had explained to her the disposition of her property, and that the Defendant had continually checked her, saying it was not necessary to go into these minute particulars, but the Plaintiff had said she wanted 'Plessy, meaning myself,' said Mrs. Tom Fellowes, 'to know exactly what she had done, as she had only obeyed her husband's commands as communicated by his spirit through the mediumship of the Defendant.' But, said the witness, the Defendant then denied that he had had anything to do with the matter. The Vice-Chancellor said he could not accept this denial as meaning more than that the communications from the Plaintiff's husband were not caused by any act or volition of his; but from whatever source they came, it would still be a most improper reason for allowing the gifts to stand. He had formed the conclusion that when Mrs. Lyon told so many people, as his Lordship admitted that she did, that her gifts were not influenced by spiritualism but only by personal affection for Home, she said this because she was afraid that otherwise the gifts would be considered as evidence of unsound mind. He said, he believed that 'much more occurred on Sunday 7 October, 1866, in the shape of manifestations and communications than the Defendant admits.'

His Lordship said so much against Mrs. Lyon that she was deprived of all claims to public respect and though he found against Home, he did not impair Home's credibility to anything like the same degree. In the course of his judgment the Vice-Chancellor made one of those rare comments which, coming from people who actually saw Home, are of so much interest: 'When it was said that the Defendant was under her influence and not she under his, I disagree entirely . . . the Defendant's appearance here in court, the antecedents of both parties, and the statements in the Defendant's answer of what occurred when and after he and the Plaintiff quarrelled, lead irresistibly to a widely different conclusion.' Home had been described by the reporter as somewhat effeminate in appearance. The Judge's keener insight, comparing him even with the robust and violent Mrs. Lyon, decided that Home's was the stronger personality. It is possible to think that the Vice-Chancellor was mistaken in the deduction he made from his impression: that his perception of some strange element in Home's *persona* led him to misconstrue what the relationship had been, in spite of the accumulated evidence of Home's witnesses as to what, in fact, it was; but this vision of a highly trained observer, brief and undefined as it was, is extremely interesting.

The Vice-Chancellor said, finally, that the onus was on the Defendant of proving that the Plaintiff's gifts were entirely voluntary and made while she was in her rational mind: reversing the usual practice of English criminal law, which assumes that the accused is innocent until he is proved guilty; but in his references to other cases involving disputed gifts, he made clear what Sir William Bovill had meant when he made his sinister prophecy that the evidence being in Home's favour would be of no avail while the precedents were against him. Among the precedents quoted by the Vice-Chancellor, was Lord Eldon's judgment in Hatch v. Hatch: 'The Court cannot permit [the gift] unless quite satisfied that it is an act of . . . a rational consideration, an act of pure volition uninfluenced, and that enquiry is so easily baffled in a Court of Justice . . . that if the court does not watch these transactions with a jealousy almost invincible, in a great majority of cases it will lend its assistance to fraud.' He concluded by saying (though he carefully refrained from any suggestion that Home had produced phenomena by fraud) that if the Defendant had not been a medium he could not have gained this influence over the Plaintiff; and that 'the system, as presented by the evidence, is mischievous nonsense.' He therefore directed that the £60,000 must be returned to her.

When he had ordered Home to pay his costs and Mrs. Lyon to pay hers and Mr. Wilkinson's, Mr. Mathews asked for an order against Mrs. Lyon to return the jewels and laces she had taken from Home. The Vice-Chancellor said that was a matter in which he could not interfere. Mrs. Lyon refused to make restitution until Home lodged a notice of appeal against her. She then, at long last, returned at least some of the property.* In a letter to the *Evening Standard* of November 12, 1876, Home said that he withdrew his notice of appeal 'when Mrs. Lyon restored to me the jewels and laces of my late wife which she had had in her possession and which she intended to retain.' But Madame Home, writing in 1888, said that 'some of the most valuable objects were never restored.'

*Mrs. Lyon died on 5 January, 1872. Her will left bequests to a great number of charities, £2,000 to her landlady Mrs. Sarah Pepper and the bulk of her fortune to her husband's nephew and nieces.

# XXVII

## From Reciting to Fire-handling

The adverse verdict was not, as hostile writers assert, a catastrophe to
Home, although that part of the press which was viciously untruthful
about him did, of course, not desist. On 29 April 1868, while the Lyon
v. Home case was still on, a passage from '*Echoes from the Clubs*',
quoted by Home[1] said under the heading: A *Home* Thrust, that two
years ago a young gentleman was sitting in his club when he was
addressed by 'a dark-complexioned stranger . . . with curly and oily-
looking black hair and a nose which seemed to vouch for a purely
Caucasian descent.' The stranger began to boast of his illustrious
acquaintances; 'This', he said extending a hand on which sparkled
two splendid rings, and indicating a magnificent diamond, 'was the
gift of Louis Napoleon for a service I rendered him . . . and this
sapphire was a present from the Czar.' The young gentleman smiled
so broadly that the stranger observed in a reproachful tone: 'I suppose,
then, you think that I am a humbug?' 'Think', was the cutting reply,
'I don't think you're one, I know you're one.' It was not till many
months afterwards, said the article, 'that he was pointed out to his
unappreciative companion as the celebrated Mr. Home.' On 29 April
it would still have been possible for the journalist who created the
scene between Home and the hypothetical young gentleman, to gain
entrance to the Vice-Chancellor's court and to see for himself what
Home really looked like; it is clear from his description that he had
not taken the opportunity.

At the end of May, 1868, immediately after the Vice-Chancellor
had delivered his judgment, the *Daily News* said: 'Mrs. Lyon proposed
to be Mr. Home's mother . . . she insisted on his acceptance of £30,000
as a free and absolute gift, and of an equal sum in reversion, subject
to her life interest . . . Mr. Home had the necessary deeds prepared
with no undue haste and with reasonable caution.' This fair recapi-
tulation, made at the time, was drastically revised in the same paper's
reference to the trial in June 1886, the month of Home's death. This

said, speaking of the rappings Mrs. Lyon declared had been heard: 'Mr. Home explained the meaning of this utterance from another world to be that £24,000 of stock should be invested for him in the Bank of England. Soon afterwards he declared it to be the spirit's will that Mrs. Lyon should leave him everything she possessed.' Madame Home ascribed this discrepancy to the fact that as Home was now dead he could not sue the newspaper for libel; no doubt this consideration bore weight, but even more potent was the hidden force beneath the current of public comment which, utterly regardless of evidence, official or private, spread like a morbid growth which could not be put down.

'You are of course pained, my dear Daniel', wrote Mrs. S. C. Hall, 'that the Vice-Chancellor did not clear you by a few words from suspicion of fraud as a spiritualist, but how would you have felt if he had blasted your character, as he has that of Mrs. Lyon, by being the first to accuse her of perjury?'[2] Home could always rely on the affectionate tender-hearted friendship of Mrs. S. C. Hall; he also had friends of a sterner kind. Sir William Gomm had fought in the Peninsular War and had been on Wellington's staff at Quatre Bras and Waterloo, ultimately receiving the appointment of Commander-in-Chief in India. He had been created Field Marshal in January 1868, and was now living in retirement with his wife in Brighton at 33 Brunswick Terrace. Sir William had been very popular in the army because his high military capacity went with great good nature and his wife's charming friendliness contributed to his social success. Home had known them for some time and they had both sat with him. On 12 June 1868, three weeks after the Vice-Chancellor had given his judgment, Lady Gomm wrote to Home: 'I hope most sincerely that each year may see you a stronger man, but I fear the life of excitement which seems ordained for you, must take a great deal of strength from your system. Yet to be the means of doing so much good to fellow mortals must bring its own reward and blessing. Sir William and I dwell constantly, in conversation with each other, on those evenings in New Street. Sir William desires me to give you his most kind regards.'[3]

But since Home was now thrown on his own resources once more, (the Spiritual Athenaeum had foundered since his leaving it, and the income from his wife's estate was still withheld from him) it was imperative that he should find some immediate means of making money. He had not only to support himself (though his son was provided for among his father's friends) but he had also to pay by instalments his legal costs in Lyon v. Home. The success he had already gained in America and England as a public reader decided him to take to this career in earnest. Engagements for a tour of fifty cities were made for him and the press notices which recorded it show that though not equal to the stupendous success of Dickens in the same sphere, his own was great. Home seems to have had an extremely versatile talent. Audiences, without the opportunity of cinema or television, relying for entertainment on gifted but untrained performers, found him enthralling in tragical and comic numbers. In August 1869, the *Court Circular* spoke of him as: 'Mr. D. D. Home, who is now established as one of our best readers.' When he was booked to appear among other artists, his encores were liable to disrupt the programmes. On one occasion, in the north of England, he gave Tennyson's poem: 'The Grandmother' and when an encore was vociferously demanded he pleaded with the audience that a great deal of the programme was yet to come: A voice from the back seats shouted: 'Programme be . . .! Cut out all the rest of it and give us the old lady again!'[4] It is interesting that this poem was so successful with a rough audience. It is not one of Tennyson's comic soliloquies in a Lincolnshire dialect. Jowett had given him the idea, telling him of an old woman who said, very simply, 'The spirits of my children always seem to hover about me'. Tennyson's grandmother, who has outlived husband and children, says:—

> They come and sit by my chair, they hover about my bed,
> I am not always certain if they be alive or dead.

But it was in Poe's poetry that Home made his greatest effects, in 'The Raven' with its harrowing, haunted misery, and 'The Bells', in which he displayed an amazing variety of expression, of gaiety and passion, terror and power.

As he went up and down the country on these engagements he was eagerly welcomed by people who already knew him or were anxious to meet him. Lady Caithness had first married a Spanish nobleman, the Condé de Medina Pomar. After his death she married, in 1872, James, fourteenth Earl of Caithness, but in 1879, Pope Leo XIII created her Duchesse de Pomar and her young son Duc de Pomar. Often spoken of in séances with Home she is referred to by both titles. Home came to her house in Brighton to a small tea party; he had come directly from a reading at Brighton Pavilion and in the clothes he had worn on the platform, so that he had had no time to conceal, in special garments, the machinery which people who had not sat with him sometimes accused him of using. Present at the séance were two ladies who were very anxious about the safety of a friend who was coming from Canada. This was one of the occasions when a great volume of sound was produced in Home's presence. The powerful noise of a steamship threshing its way through waters filled the

225

Brighton drawing room. One of the ladies asked whether their friend was safe? The answer was spelt out: Yes, William watches over her. The message moved them greatly. William was their friend's son who had lately died.

Home was giving another reading at the Pavilion next evening. Lady Caithness called for him in her carriage and conveyed him from the Pavilion to the Gomms' house. The eighty-four year old Field Marshal was in bed but the rest of the party experienced a séance with a startling manifestation of light. Lady Caithness wrote: 'In answer to some conversation of our own, the following message was rapped out:- It brings Light, and Light is Love. Almost immediately, a bright, clear, pale light shone over the table, lighting us all up, clear and white as moonlight. We all saw it ... strange to say, it seemed to shine out through Mr. Home; at all events he was very much illumined.'[5]

Some of the most remarkable séances of this period were given while Home was in Scotland on reading engagements. He was invited in Edinburgh to the house of old Dr. Doun, an army doctor, who had till this time been wholly sceptical of spiritualist phenomena. A séance was arranged and Dr. Doun invited another sceptic, the Edinburgh man of letters, Mr. Patrick Alexander who, in turn, asked to be allowed to bring with him Dr. Findlater of the Chambers publishing company, who completed the triumvirate of unbelievers. The phenomena of telekinesis, of music played by invisible hands, of messages to those present from the dead, astounded the party but the most interesting result was the publication of Alexander's work, *Spiritualism: a Narrative*, in which he attested his own astonishment at seeing the manifestations occur in a brightly-lit room, in a house in which Home was a total stranger. One of the guests of Dr. Doun's party, General Boldero, invited Home to visit him at Coupar, in Fife. At so many of Home's séances the phenomena were not recorded that it can hardly be said that those experienced at a particular séance were unique, but at least those at the séance in the Bolderos' house do not appear to have been described as occurring elsewhere. Mrs. Boldero, standing by her piano, did not see a hand touching the keys, but she saw the keys depressed as beautiful chords sounded. The voices of a man and a child appeared to be talking to each other from opposite corners of the ceiling. The company strained to catch the words but to their distress, Home kept up a stream of conversation. When they complained, he said that he did this so that he might not be suspected of ventriloquism. Mrs. Boldero said: 'During the whole of this séance, the whole room seemed to be *alive* with something; and I remember thinking that no manifestation would surprise me, feeling that the power present could produce anything.'[6]

Following the course of his tour to Aberdeen, Home was asked there to give an interview to a body of reporters, and he invited them to supper at the Northern Hotel. General Boldero was present and gave an account of what happened. The waiters were frightened by a loud rap on the side-board and then by several on the corners of the ceiling. The table quivered violently and the plates rattled and moved so much that the General could not get on with his supper. A large armchair near the fire-place rushed across the room and placed itself near one of the reporters, at a distance from Home. This manifestation was felt to be extraordinary beyond words, as Home had not entered the coffee room until the party assembled there for supper, and if he had, no apparatus of strings, such as Mrs. Lynn Linton's fertile imagination had assumed, could have moved the chair 'with the precision and velocity with which it left its place and joined them at the table.'[7]

But these occurrences, though amazing to the people who saw them, were not the outstanding events of Home's life for the years 1868 and 1869. These events were fully and carefully recorded by Lord Adare in a work privately printed in July 1869, under the title *Experiences in Spiritualism with D. D. Home*. The writing was instigated by Adare's father, Lord Dunraven. When the latter could be present at the séances he was, when he could not, he received accounts of them, transmitted by his son; the whole body of experiences, some with Lord Dunraven and some without, was covered in descriptions of eighty séances. The work: 'Printed for Private Circulation', by Thomas Scott, of Warwick Court, Holborn, is a richly bound little volume, the violet cloth covers ornamented in gilt, the title in gilt on the front cover and the spine, with thickly gilt edges to the leaves. Copies of the original edition are very scarce, two of them being in the Harry Price Library of Magical Literature, in the Library of the University of London; but it was published fifty-five years later by Lord Adare, then Lord Dunraven (Robert Maclehose, 1924).

Lord Dunraven, who was a Catholic, had written an introduction to the edition of 1869, of great interest since it explains the objections of some Catholics to the practice of spiritualism (pp. 33 et seq, Edition of 1929). He lists the objections as follows: The Atonement is never mentioned in séances; eternal punishment is denied; miracles are ascribed to natural laws; whereas in the New Testament submission and child-like obedience are inculcated, spiritualism brings everything to the test of reason. Spiritualism is indeed ethical, but all reference to Our Lord's office and work as the sole passport to Heaven is omitted. Our Lord seems to form but a small part of the thoughts or teaching of the spirits who speak to us from beyond the grave. These spirits describe the next world as one of continued progression, not as a state fixed eternally at the hour of death. Lord Dunraven put his finger on

227

the chief difficulty which confronts spiritualists who have eliminated the possibility of fraud: this is to be assured of the identity of the spirit communicating. He said that the work was circulated 'to enable honest enquirers to decide whether this subject is one which they can with propriety pursue, or one which they feel themselves bound, as sincere followers of Christ, and for the safety of their souls, to abandon.'

Lord Dunraven's remark to Home showed how capable he was of making investigations. He wrote to Home on 8 August 1868, 'I have taken the greatest pains to contradict the idea that you called up spirits; and always say that I looked on you as a mere "physical" machine, such as a battery and wire are, *through* which, not *by* which, communications are made — who by, being *the* question, which does not more concern you than any of us.'[8]

In his introduction to the edition of 1924, Lord Adare gave some interesting details of himself, and Home. He said: 'I had no inclination to investigate the nature of these forces. Study of the occult was not congenial to me ... séances for physical manifestations were very exhausting to me. I was only twenty-four; I loved sport and an active, out-door life.' He, like his father, showed an attitude of mind which made his work very valuable. 'It must be borne in mind', he said, 'that an actual record of facts, and not the adoption or refutation of any particular theory is the main object in view.' The question of identity he explained could not always be fully proved: 'Even in the original letters to my father, I was obliged to omit a few circumstances of great interest, their having reference to persons who did not wish those circumstances to be mentioned.' He said that when he and his father had both been present at a séance, each wrote a record and compared it with the other's, and records were sent to other sitters, inviting their confirmation, which was given in every case.

Lord Adare added two details about Home; he had 'an irresistible charm of manner, coupled with his joyous nature and kindliness of heart.' He also said: 'Home was proud of his gift but not happy with it.'

During these eighty recorded séances, the most remarkable manifestations were: the materialisation of complete spirit forms, the levitation of Home, and two phenomena which though mentioned before, were much more fully attested in these sittings: Home's power to hold burning substances; red hot coals or ardently heated lamp-chimneys in his hands without being burnt, and to convey the same immunity to other sitters provided he saw that they had faith, and his astounding and inexplicable capacity for physical elongation.

The places in which the séances were held were varied: they included three houses in Sydenham: Mr. Jencken's Kilmorey House and Mrs. Hennings' Sunninghill House, in Anerley Road, and Mr. Enmore

Jones' Enmore Place, of which the site is now recalled by Enmore Road in South Norwood; the S. C. Halls' house in Essex Villas and the one to which they afterwards removed, 15 Ashley Place; Lord Dunraven's town house, 5 Buckingham Gate, and the apartments Lord Adare occupied in Ashley House.

The loose manner in which nineteenth-century writers and indeed *Kelly's Directory*, sometimes identified addresses is often a source of confusion now. Albert Place was sometimes called Albert Terrace, Essex Villas was said to be on Campden Hill, from which it is far enough; Kilburn was called Hampstead and the Milner Gibsons' address is sometimes given not as Hyde Park Place, but Hyde Park Terrace, a non-existent locality. The very important scene of Lord Adare's rooms, known variously as Ashley House and Ashley Place, was defined once for all by Mr. Trevor Hall, in his book: *New Light on Old Ghosts*,[9] Ashley Place is a small street joining Carlisle Street and the large thoroughfare of Victoria Street. Mr. Hall discovered that the houses, nos 1–10 Ashley Place, were called Ashley House. The block was separated into sets of chambers. Lord Adare's rooms may have been at any of the numbers 1–10, except no 9 which, according to *Kelly's Directory*, was occupied by a Mrs. Mainwaring. Lord Adare said his rooms were on the third floor. Lord Lindsay said, first, that the windows were about eighty-five feet from the ground, and in a second account that the distance was about seventy feet; Mr. Hall deduced that the height was thirty-five to forty feet.*

The first of the recorded séances was not in London but in Dr. Gully's house at Malvern, in November 1867, when Home was Dr. Gully's guest and Lord Adare the doctor's patient, undergoing the hydropathic treatment for rheumatism. Dr. Gully had two houses for the accommodation of patients; these stood side by side on the Wells Road, above the town and under the lee of the steep, wooded hill-side. Of early Victorian Gothic, delicate and fantastic, decorated with Gothic plaster mouldings and coloured glass, they were called Tudor House and Holyrood House. Lord Adare was lodged in the former. The séance included Mrs. Thayer, an American lady living in Malvern, who up till that time had had no belief in psychic phenomena. The demonstration that impressed her most was the playing of music by an accordion, in a part of the room entirely out of Home's reach. After this arresting evening, Lord Adare says he went back to Tudor House. The beautiful Malvern scene, in the quiet of a November night must have been favourable to his thoughts. His friendship with Home became a close one; after the commotion of the Lyon v. Home case,

* The houses in this block have been re-built since the publication of Trevor Hall's book in 1965.

for over a year, Home spent a considerable time as his guest, either at 5 Buckingham Gate which, as Adare said, was his parents' town house in which, during their absence, he and Home slept merely, and had their meals out, and Adare's own rooms in Ashley House, also in the cottage at Garinish, on Lord Dunraven's Irish estate on the coast of Kerry. Lord Lindsay, who had rooms at 9 Grosvenor Square, was constantly with them and so was Adare's cousin, Captain Charles Wynne. Lord Adare, in the Life Guards, Lord Lindsay in the Grenadier Guards and Captain Wynne, a serving officer stationed at the Tower, were an unusual trio to find undergoing psychic experiences. The young soldiers were obviously, by Adare's account, very deeply under Home's influence; but to maintain as Mr. Hall does that Home hypnotized them into thinking that they saw him perform phenomenal feats which he did not perform, would not explain those of his feats which were seen by so many other people in widely differing localities. As Dr. John Beloff has said, if Home had such powers as these, 'they would have had to be absolute . . . and this is tantamount to crediting him with another kind of paranormal power, one for which there is no parallel.'

Much of Home's social life remains undocumented, and the details that casually appear have, often, a surprising interest for this reason. Describing a séance of August 1868, Adare says that he and Home had known the American actress Ada Menken; they had called on her at her hotel the previous year. They now saw her death announced in the papers. Ada Menken had produced one of the most exciting theatrical turns of the century. She was a brilliant horsewoman, and she made her *coup de théâtre* from the story of 'Mazeppa'. This Polish nobleman had been made the victim of a savage penalty. Bound, naked, on the back of a wild horse which was then lashed into frenzy, he was borne by it through forests and over plains, till the animal fell dead of exhaustion and peasants rescued him at the point of death. Astley's, the theatre used for exhibitions that needed horses and elephants, stood at the end of Westminster Bridge. Its interior alone was a thrilling spectacle. The auditorium contained four thousand seats, rising in tiers around the oval arena, forty feet in diameter which was called the Royal Amphitheatre. There was a stage, but the amphitheatre, strewn with white sand, was the scene of the characteristic productions; and the troupes of mounted performers entered it from openings on each side of the orchestra pit. Ada Menken, in an era when even ballet dancers' legs were not seen above the knee, on her back and wearing flesh-coloured tights, lay flat on a horse's back and went careering round and round the ring, under the blaze of enormous cut-glass chandeliers, evoking in the audience an atmosphere intoxicating to the verge of madness. The young guardsman naturally called on her at her hotel and he took Home with him. The following year, Ada Menken died at Montparnasse and was buried under a white marble monument on which were inscribed lines from Swinburne's poem, 'Ilicet', 'Thou knowest.' On a night of August 1868[10] Adare said: 'I perceived Home was in a trance and that Menken was speaking through him. He walked slowly over to my bed and knelt down beside it, took both my hands in his and began speaking. I shall never forget the awfully thrilling way in which she spoke ... I was, to all intents and purposes, actually conversing with the dead ... listening, talking, receiving answers from Menken ... She spoke of the intense desire of the spirit, sometimes to communicate with, and do good to, those on earth. At last she said: 'I must go now, I must not make too much use of Dan.' Home then got up and walked slowly away, turning round twice and raising his hands above his head in an attitude of prayer and blessing. As he went away from me, his clothes became slightly luminous.' In séance 22, raps began signalling Ada Menken's approach, but they died away without any manifestation. 'Just as I was going to sleep', Adare said, 'Home turned in his bed and said: I have been trying and I cannot ... I said, never mind, which awoke him and he asked me if he had been talking in his sleep.'

The materialization of spirits of the dead was the most awe-inspiring feature of Home's mediumship, and it was most unfortunate that it should ever have occurred in the presence of anyone who could not endure it. In October, 1868,[11] with Mr. and Mrs. S. C. Hall and several other people, the young Duc de Pomar was among the sitters. They saw, presently, a form standing behind Home and another form at the opposite side of the room. The boy was so much frightened that the sitting had to be abandoned.[12] Among the materializations which gave great comfort to the bereaved, a most remarkable one, recalling that given to Sophia Cotterell, but much more complete, occurred in October 1868. On 11 October, the widowed Mrs. Cox lost her seven year old son, Daniel. The child was killed by falling out of a swing in the garden of Stockton House. The accounts of the séance at Stockton House are given both by Lord Adare and Ion Perdicaris. The latter said:[13] that the child's body was brought to 55 Jermyn Street, where it would seem that Mrs. Cox retained rooms. The body was laid on a bed, and Perdicaris found Home in the room, talking about Danny's death to Gricha. There were raps on the door, but when it was opened there was no one outside. Home, saying he was worn out, asked Perdicaris to interpret the raps, since he was now able to do so easily, and the message said that the child's father wanted him to be buried in the little cemetery near Stockton House. Mrs. Cox therefore asked Perdicaris to arrange with the undertakers and to see to the transport of the coffin. Lord Adare went down to Hampshire with Mrs. Cox and Home while Perdicaris arrived at Waterloo with the undertaker's men, only just in time to jump into the guard's van with the coffin. When he arrived at Stockton House, he found the rest of the party had disappeared upstairs with Mrs. Cox. He therefore made the arrangements in her absence. He had the coffin laid on a table in the drawing room and covered with a white sheet. From the conservatory opening out of the far end of the room, he collected flowers and ferns and as the coffin lid was not screwed down, he put some flowers in the child's hands. The drawing room had three tall windows with Argand lamps standing between them. Home then came in, carrying a wreath, and asked to have the lamps lowered. From that moment the manifestations were astounding. Perdicaris said there were raps on the glass roof of the conservatory, and from its interior a little ball of electric light came bounding into the room and played about the ceiling. Other balls of light appeared and flowers and leaves floated into the room from between the conservatory's glass doors. Mrs. Cox stood by the coffin, and the form of a child's head and shoulders covered by the sheet, 'pushed forward from the end of the table and rested on its mother's shoulder.' Lord Adare[14] confirmed his journey down to Hampshire with Mrs. Cox and Home. When he went into the conservatory, he said he heard the child rapping on the glass. They had supper at ten o'clock and afterwards Home led Mrs. Cox back into the drawing room. She heard something rustle near the coffin and felt a little hand touch hers. Then in her hand she found a sprig of laurestinus.

Later, when they were all in bed Home, in trance, came to Adare's bedside in the darkness and led him downstairs to the drawing room. There were no lights, but Home said: 'I require no light to guide my footsteps', and led Adare across the dark drawing room to the side of the coffin. Adare said: 'I felt a little soft hand touch mine and a flower was given to me.' Then, he said, 'I felt a strong tremor run through Home's hands and he spoke as little Danny and said: You must get into bed quickly; Dan is going to awake; if you would like very much to see what you have got, you can make an excuse to light a candle presently. Accordingly, after Home had awoke, I lit a candle and found I had been given a purple and white petunia that had been placed in one of the little hands in the coffin.'

Lord Adare said in his preface of 1924 that he found the strains of physical manifestations very great. The experiences read sometimes as if they must have been almost unbearable.

The phenomenon of fire-handling, though not so interesting as levitation and spirit materialization, provides the evidence most readily accepted by people who did not see it, as it offers no possibility of hallucination or mistake. Mrs. Honywood, who provided the detail that Home always took off his rings before a sitting, 'lest inadvertently they might make a sound', was present when Home proved the heat of a glass lamp-chimney by getting some one to touch it with a lucifer match on which the match burst into flame, and then reminding the audience that the lips and tongue are the parts most sensitive to heat, took the top of the chimney into his mouth. Home was not only, when in a trance, impervious to heat himself but could convey the insensitivity to another person. Lord Adare asked Mrs. S. C. Hall to write down for him the extraordinary scene that took place in their new house, 15 Ashley Place. He had accompanied Home on a first visit here, and Home had prayed at the threshold, the hearth, the dining table and at Mr. Hall's writing table. The scene of fire-handling occurred in the summer of 1869. Mrs. S. C. Hall said that the party were seated in the small back drawing room; one lamp was burning on the table, but a very large fire was blazing in the front drawing room on to which the folding doors opened. 'I know', she said, 'that there was plenty of light.' After a lapse of about an hour, Home went into a trance. 'He got up, walked about the room in his usual manner, went to the fire-place, half knelt on the fender-stool, took up the poker and stirred the fire which was like a red-hot furnace, so as to increase the heat, held his hands over the fire for some time and finally drew out of the fire with his hand a huge lump of live, burning coal, so large that he held it in both hands as he came from the fire-place in the large room into the smaller room, where seated round the table, we were all watching his movements.' Her husband was sitting opposite her, and after Home had stood behind his chair for half a minute, she saw Home deposit the glowing coal on his head. 'I have often since wondered that I was not frightened', she said, 'but I was not; I had perfect faith that he would not be injured.' One of the party exclaimed: 'Is it not hot?' S. C. Hall said: 'Warm, but not hot.' Home then drew up S. C. Hall's long, white hair over the red coal; the hair looked like silver thread. After four or five minutes, Home took the coal away and speaking in 'the peculiar, low voice' which Mrs. S. C. Hall said he always spoke in, during trance, he asked one of the ladies if she would hold it? She shrank back and he murmured: 'Ah, little faith, little faith!' Two or three other sitters attempted to touch it but drew back with burned fingers. Mrs. S. C. Hall then said: 'Daniel, bring it to me. I am not afraid to take it.' The coal was not now red all over as it had been when it was balanced on her husband's head but it still glowed red in parts. Home came and knelt beside her and she put out her right hand. He murmured: Not that, the other hand. She put out her left hand and he laid the coal in it. She held it for half a minute. Instead of being unbearably hot, it was warm, merely; but when she bent her head to examine it, her face felt the heat so much she was obliged to raise it again. That night her husband, when brushing his hair, found a quantity of cinder dust in it.[15]

Another of the fire-handling scenes recorded both by Lord Adare and Mr. Jencken took place at Sydenham in the winter of 1868, in Mrs. Hennings' house, where Mrs. Lyon's behaviour had caused such embarrassment. Home, in trance, with his naked hand stirred the red embers of the fire into flame. 'Then', Lord Adare said, 'kneeling down he placed his face right among the burning coals, moving it about as though bathing it in water.' Mr. Jencken said: 'He placed his hands and his face in the flames and on the burning coals.' Adare said that Home took from the fire a burning ember about twice the size of an orange. He carried this round to the sitters; he held it within four or five inches of the hands of two of them, but they could not endure the heat. Then he brought it to Lord Adare, saying: 'Now, if you are not afraid, hold out your hand.' 'I did so', Adare said, 'and having made two rapid passes over my hand, he placed the coal in it. I must have held it for half a minute, long enough to have burned my hand fearfully; the coal felt scarcely warm. Home then took it away, laughed and seemed much pleased.'[16]

Horace Wyndham, in *Mr. Sludge the Medium*[17] quotes Home as saying: 'The spirits have the power of abstracting heat.' Mr. Wyndham says 'he might have added that a sprinkling of lemon juice would have a similar power.' Would Mr. Wyndham, it may be asked, have consented to pick up a red hot coal if his palm had been bathed in lemon juice? On p. 232, he says: 'there is also the possibility that the red hot coal was really a small lump of spongy platinum, which could have been palmed, together with a bulb of hydrogen. This, when pressed on, would release a jet and make platinum irridescent. But perhaps the simplest methods are best, and after all, a glow-worm hidden in a box of red glass would have answered the purpose.' Mrs. Lynn Linton and Mr. Wyndham were of course entitled to their views as to whether the phenomena produced by Home were genuine; but the folly they ascribe to people who accepted them as such is nothing to the absurdity of their own suggestions as to how Home might have produced them by fraud.

# XXVIII

## Elongation and Levitation

Home's capacity to receive spirit communication was accompanied by extraordinary physical attributes; independence of the laws of gravity, immunity from the effects of burning heat, and he displayed a third peculiarity: his height could be extended up to eleven inches or reduced by six or eight inches. This last is the least interesting of his traits; it is claimed that conjurors and contortionists are able to achieve much the same effects, since the muscles and ligaments of the human frame have an elasticity which is normally unsuspected and the effects themselves are grotesque rather than interesting from an imaginative point of view; but since they were part of his abnormal constitution, Lord Adare noticed and recorded ten instances of them. Home on one occasion stationed him and Lord Lindsay at the posts of folding doors and lay on the floor between them, touching one with his head, the other with his feet. As he elongated, he pushed each of them back, his arms and hands remaining motionless at his sides. The most remarkable evidence in this connection was given by Hawkins Simpson, the electrical engineer, who had made an affidavit on Home's behalf in the Lyon v. Home case, that 'the physical effects in Mr. Home's case are produced without aid from electricity, ferro-magnetism or apparatus of any kind.' He stated also that he had, with Lord Lindsay, investigated an elongation of Home's when alterations occurred not only in the length of the body, but the size of the face. 'The changes Mr. Home's face underwent, first larger, then smaller, then normal size, were extraordinary. First the face seemed to be gradually enlarged at all points, then it gradually became smaller in features and deeply wrinkled and puckered.'[1]

The event, recorded by Lord Adare, Lord Lindsay and Captain Charles Wynne, which has become famous beyond any other recorded by any of them, has been often denied out of hand or painstakingly investigated with a view to rejecting it. It was described by Lord Adare[2] in séance 41, as follows: on the night of 16 December, 1868 (he afterwards corrected the date to 13 December), Adare, Lindsay,

Wynne and Home were holding a séance in Ashley House. The scene was identified by Mr. Hall (op. cit); Lord Adare having originally caused some confusion by apparently heading the account as that of a séance at 5 Buckingham Gate, but it turned out that 5 Buckingham Gate was merely the address from which he had written the account for Lord Dunraven. Lord Adare said, in this, that the room in which they sat was unlighted except by the window, but they could distinguish each other and the furniture. The window of this room and of the room next door were side by side on the façade of the house and were seven feet four inches apart. Outside each window was a small balcony nineteen inches deep, surrounded by a balustrade eighteen inches high; these ledges were meant for holding plants. The only connection between the windows on the outside wall, was a string-course four inches wide at the base of the balustrade, and one three inches wide at the top. Lord Adare said the rooms were on the third floor, and Mr. Hall calculated that the drop to the street level was between thirty-five and forty feet.

Lord Adare said that in the course of the séance, Home rose into the air, and was elongated. Presently he went into trance, walked about the room and then left them for the room next door; then Lord Lindsay said: 'Oh, good heavens, I know what he is going to do, it is too fearful . . . he is going out of the window in the other room and coming in at this window.' When asked how he had known this, Lindsay afterward said that it was a spirit communication; he had not heard the words but they had been impressed on his mind. They now heard Home in the next room throw up the sash; presently he appeared, standing outside their window. Then Adare said, he opened that window and walked in, 'quite coolly.' Home said they had behaved well in not trying to prevent him in what he was about. Captain Wynne said: 'What are you laughing at?' Home said in the plural as he usually did in trance: 'We are thinking that if a policeman had been passing and had looked up and seen a man turning round and round along the wall in the air, he would have been much astonished.' Then he said: 'Adare, shut the window in the next room.' Lord Adare went to do this, and found the sash open only about a foot. Coming back he said, how could Home have got out through such a narrow opening?

What happened next is the proof offered that Home had not merely jumped across the seven odd feet between one balustraded ledge and another, or crawled along a four inch wide string-course, above a drop of thirty-five feet, but had in fact performed genuine levitation. At Adare's words of wonder, Home said: 'Come and see.' They went into the next room and Home told him to open the window again, as far as it had been opened before. 'I did so; he told me to stand a little distance off; then he went through the open space, head first, quite rapidly, his body being nearly horizontal and apparently rigid. He came in again feet foremost.' It was too dark for Adare to see how Home was supported outside, but: 'He did not appear to grasp or rest upon the balustrade, but rather to be swung in and out.'[3]

As the small balcony outside was only nineteen inches wide, it could not have supported Home in a horizontal position and rigid, nor, if it had, would this have explained how he propelled himself inside again, in the same position, feet first. The evidence for the levitation along the outside wall is therefore in two parts: that Home shot out of and in again at the window next door, and that he appeared outside the window of the séance room, standing on the little ledge.

The arguments used by those who deny that Home's passage from the window could have been paranormal is founded on the fact that the evidence of Lord Adare and Lord Lindsay contain discrepancies on minor points. Lord Adare's was given in his book,[4] Lord Lindsay's was given in the same year before the Committee of the Dialectical Society, and in 1871, in a letter to *The Spiritualist*. The latter said before the Dialectical Society that the height of the windows above the ground was some eighty-five feet; in *The Spiritualist* he estimated it at seventy; these miscalculations were not very important; what was very injurious to his credibility was his saying that on this evening the moon was shining brightly into the room, whereas it has now been proved that on 13 December of 1868, the moon was new and did not rise till 1.30 am. It is unexpected and disappointing that Lindsay should have made this mistake; ten years later, in 1878, he was President of the Astronomical Society; this, with Adare's vagueness about the date and the scene of the séance, are thought by some people to show that the sitters were in a state of mental confusion which makes it impossible to accept their evidence. Horace Wyndham adds[5] that as the séance took place after dinner, it is allowable to suppose that the witnesses were fuddled. Dr. Zorab has pointed out that this suggestion is refuted by Lord Adare's having written a detailed report for his father three days after the séance 'showing an excellent and accurate memory' quite incompatible with a tipsy condition. Wyndham offers, as other possible solutions, that Home lowered himself from the parapet above by a rope, or, that having the run of the house, he had fixed clamps into the wall beforehand, removing them afterwards.

A very valuable tribute to Home's honesty came from the third sitter, Captain Wynne. A fanatical opponent of Home, equalling even Sir David Brewster in irresponsibility, was Dr. W. B. Carpenter, Vice-President of the Royal Society. Lord Adare had stated that Captain Wynne was present but had not ascribed to him any comment on the actual levitation. Dr. Carpenter, seizing on this point with great adroitness, published an article in *The Contemporary Review* of January 1876, in which he said: 'A whole party of believers will affirm that they saw Mr. Home float out of one window and in at another, while a single honest sceptic declares that Mr. Home was sitting in his chair all the time . . . during this prevalence of an epidemic delusion, the honest testimony of any number of individuals on one side, if given under a prepossession, is of no more weight than that of a single, adverse witness, — if so much.' Carpenter's implication was obvious, and it was picked up in 1876 by an American author, Dr. Hammond, who in his work: *Spiritualism and Nervous Derangement*, stated on the authority of Dr. Carpenter that the 'honest sceptic' was Lord Adare's cousin. Home in January 1877 wrote to Captain Wynne from Nice, asking him to say whether the accounts of Lord Adare and Lord Lindsay were, or were not, 'a simple and concise statement of the facts, just as they took place?' Captain Wynne replied: 'I don't think anyone who knows me would for a moment say that I was a victim to hallucination . . . the fact of your having gone out of the window and in at the other I can swear to . . . I don't care a straw whether Dr. Carpenter or Mr. Hammond believe me or not . . . it does not prevent the fact having occurred . . . Ever yours, C. Wynne. P.S. *Honest* but not a *sceptic*.[6]

Man had always longed to fly, and before he could, there were people to whom the spectacle of Home's levitations (of which, according to Sir William Crookes alone, there were over a hundred), was the most exciting of all his phenomena, but to others who yearned, as Tennyson did, for some confirmation that those who had been lost to them by death, were not lost eternally, his being visited in the presence of onlookers by completely materialized spirit forms, was his crowning achievement. Of the period when Lord Dunraven, Lord Adare and Lord Lindsay were collaborating with him, the most absorbing events were the full-form materializations of his wife Sacha.

Lord Lindsay in his report to the Committee of the Dialectical Society of July 1869, said that Home introduced him to Mr. Jencken, who asked him to dinner at Kilmorey House where Home was then staying. Lord Lindsay missed the last train from the Crystal Palace station back into London and so he was given a shake-down on a sofa in Home's bedroom. He was falling asleep when he was roused by feeling that the pillow under his head was being pulled away. 'Then', he said, 'I saw at the foot of my sofa, a woman in profile to me, and asked Home if he saw anything?' Home answered: A woman, looking at me. 'Our beds,' Lindsay said, 'were at right angles to each other and about twelve feet apart. I saw the features perfectly and impressed them on my memory. She seemed to be dressed in a long wrap, going down from the shoulders and not going in at the waist. Home then said: It is my wife; she often comes to me. And then she seemed to fade away.' Shortly after this, Lindsay saw a flame about nine inches high alight on his knee. He put his hand through it but the flame burned on. 'Home turned in his bed; I looked at him and saw his eyes were glowing with light. The appearance was frightening.' The flame which had been flitting about Lindsay, now crossed the room about four feet from the ground and reached the curtains of Home's bed. 'The light went right through them and settled on his head, and then went out, and then we went to sleep.' Lindsay had made a mistake about light from the moon on 13 December the previous year; but the visual image on this night at Kilmorey House was so vivid, it seems hardly possible he could have been mistaken this time. He said: 'There were no shutters, blinds or curtains over the window, and there was snow on the ground and a bright moon. It was as lovely a night as I ever saw.' Next morning, before going back to London, he was looking at a photograph album with Mr. Jencken's old mother. He recognized a photograph as the young woman he had seen the night before. Mrs. Jencken told him it was Home's wife.[7]

On 9 February, 1869, a séance was held in Adare's rooms in Ashley House, the other sitters being Captain Gerard Smith and Dr. Gully. The room was lighted only by the window. Home got up and stood in front of it.

Although it is suggested by Mr. Hall that Lord Adare was so deeply under Home's influence that he was suffering in his health and his wits, he was, in fact, looking forward to being married in two months' time to Lady Florence Kerr, the daughter of Lord Charles Lennox Kerr. On this evening, he said that Sacha, speaking through Home, 'addressed a few most touching and appropriate words to me on the subject of marriage. Home then said: Sacha will try to make herself visible to you. Her form gradually became apparent to us; she moved close to Home and kissed him. She stood beside him against the window, intercepting the light as a solid body and appeared fully as material as Home himself, no one could have told which was the mortal body and which the spirit. It was too dark to distinguish the features. I could see that she had her full face turned towards us, and that either her hair was parted in the middle and flowed down over her shoulders,or that she had on what appeared to be a veil.'

Lord Adare got Captain Gerard Smith to write his account of the apparition; the latter said: '(Home) rose and stood at the window with his right arm extended, and the spirit seemed to sweep down until it rested both hands on his outstretched arm, looking up into his face. From where I sat; the profile of the face was perfectly visible to me, and when the two faces approached each other to kiss, there was no apparent difference in the density of the two figures.'[8] These materializations seem the climax of the whole spiritualist movement. What would not Tennyson have given for such an experience.

In the following month, March 1869, Lord Dunraven and Lord Adare took Home to Ireland. Adare Manor, on the coast of Kerry, was partly a ruin, but the party stayed in a small house of Lord Dunraven's, Garinish. The phenomena that occurred here were vivid, but the most thrilling one took place out of doors. At ten o'clock on the night of 4 March, Lord Dunraven and Lord Adare with Captain Wynne and Home walked down to the half ruined Abbey church. Lord Adare said: 'The night was perfectly still, but the birds were in a singularly disturbed state; owls were flitting about and some other birds flew round the church, screaming harshly.' Before they left the Abbey, the light of the moon, just about to rise, enabled them to see what was before them; 'the sky, too, had become clear and the stars shone out.' Home, Adare said, left the church by the choir door and crossed a low, broken wall, saying he saw a figure standing against part of the ruins. 'I saw a dark shadow against the wall, and I saw a light flash from it as distinctly as if someone had struck a match there; Charlie Wynne said he saw the light flash at the same moment I did; my father saw the light also, but faintly.' Home went out of their sight but when he returned, 'somebody or something was with him.' They could clearly see some indefinable substance moving beside him as he walked. It disappeared, and Home came up to them, not walking on the ground but raised above it. He floated past the three watchers at a height that carried him over the base of a broken wall about two feet high. 'The distance that we saw him carried must have been at least ten or twelve yards.'[9] The spectacle recalls the description in Book XII of 'Paradise Lost', of the cherubim advancing over the ground, just above it:

> Gliding meteorous as evening mist
> Ris'n from a river, o'er the marish glides.

Another instance is recorded of Home's making this progress that Milton imagined. It was given by Mr. Enmore Jones' daughter to the Committee of the Dialectical Society. Miss Alice Jones had been staying at Stockton House where Mrs. Cox had a house party. About 8 pm one evening, Home who felt oppressed and ill, went on to the verandah and walked up and down. They saw a bright light in a conical shape issuing upwards from him, about half his own length; it looked like phosphorous, Alice Jones said. The room was filled with scent but each person recognized a different one; she herself smelt eau-de-cologne. It was a rainy evening; Home went on to the grass, and was 'carried' across the lawn, over a hundred feet, to a rhododendron bed. When he reached it, he returned. When he was in the room again 'Everyone saw a light down by the rhododendron bed; Home said: "Yes, it is a spirit I have left there." ' Though it was raining, there was no rain on his coat and his feet were not wet.

Cox's Hotel, still sometimes so-called, though it was now Maureguy's, played such a part in Home's London life that it is interesting to gain a glimpse of its interior. Home was going once more to Russia at the end of 1870; Lord and Lady Adare, who had been married the previous year, were present at a dinner party for him given at Cox's before he set off. Ion Perdicaris was one of the guests and in describing some phenomena which occurred during dinner he also described the room. It had two sash windows, with a mirror between them over a marble-topped table loaded with flowers. Tall lamps stood on the dinner table, which heaved itself up without displacing them; one of the bunches of flowers from the table under the mirror, travelled through the air and presented itself to Perdicaris.

Lord Adare's happiness in his marriage was not marred by Lady Adare's being a frightened or unwilling participant in séances. Mrs. Honywood described one held at Ashley House on 23 December, 1870 at which Lady Adare was asked to examine the accordion which Home held by one strap; she saw the keys being played by an unseen player. She asked for the instrument to play 'The Last Rose of Summer', and the plaintive air was given exquisitely. Home then went into trance and approached the fireplace. Mrs. Honywood had a double view of his movements, for, she said: 'looking before me his form was visible against the bright firelight, and looking sideways I saw it reflected in a mirror on the side wall.' Home plunged his hands among the burning coals and drew out one, red underneath and flaming on top. He asked Lady Adare if she could hold it without fear? She held her hand out and he placed it on her palm. After some moments, he took it away and laid it on the outstretched hand of Mrs. S. C. Hall; she endured it equally and then Mrs. Honywood asked to be allowed to hold it. Home now chose another coal, straight from the heart of the fire. Mrs. Honywood did not feel it even hot. Home said, let everyone look. Lord Adare and another sitter held a doubled piece of cartridge paper between them. With his forefinger Home pushed the coal from Mrs. Honywood's palm on to the paper, which at once caught fire and was burned into a hole.[10]

Lord Adare's friendship for Home never wavered. He said: 'My belief in the phenomena remained unshaken and my friendship with Mr. Home did not diminish or change.' But he, like Dr. Garth Wilkinson, like Nathaniel Hawthorne, having satisfied himself that the phenomena were the result of some force, distinct from human agency, was content to abandon the matter.

Home went to Russia where he met Julie de Gloumeline who was to be his second wife; but he returned to England meantime, in March 1871, to collaborate with William Crookes in a series of experiments designed by this distinguished scientist to prove the nature of the phenomena he produced.

# XXIX

## Remarriage

Trevor Hall noted[1] that the privately produced edition of Lord Adare's *Experiences in Spiritualism* was in print at the end of July 1869; this was proved by the date of the inscription in the copy Lord Dunraven had given to his daughter; but the last séance recorded in the book was dated as late as 7 July, 1869; Mr. Hall believed that this was unusually rapid printing, and a sign that Home had used his influence with the family to get the book in printed form at the first possible moment, so that its distribution might act as a countercheck to the damaging effect of the verdict in Lyon v. Home. It would seem, however, that Mr. Hall, accustomed to the slowness of modern printing, attaches too much importance to the production of a small work, even ornately bound as this one was, by Messrs. Thomas Scott in three weeks. *Jane Eyre*, a novel in three volumes, was sent to Messrs. Smith, Elder on 24 August, 1847, and was published by them on 16 October, seven weeks after their receiving it from the author. At the same time, if Lord Dunraven and Lord Adare thought they could do Home a service in distributing the book as soon as possible, they were no doubt glad to do it. An event which seems directly traceable to the Lyon v. Home case however, was the action of the London Dialectical Society. This was a rationalist debating society, with a distinguished membership. Early in 1869, the Society decided to make an investigation into the claims of spiritualism. Part of this was to consist of spoken and written evidence before a committee appointed by the Society, and part by tests carried out by six sub-committees to see whether psychic phenomena could be produced in circumstances that absolutely excluded all possibility of deception. Of those who were to give evidence, the most distinguished was Home. The meetings began in February 1869 and were finished by the following December.[2] Of the six sub-committees, two had nothing that was felt to be worth reporting, a third, the one which sat with Home, reported that after four séances held in a brightly lit room, nothing was received except a few raps and movements of a table. Home was very ill at the time, and since he never undertook that phenomena would occur in his presence, the failure was, though disappointing, of little account. In spite of it, the sub-committee reported that they had been impressed by Home's readiness to 'afford them every facility for examination.' The remaining three sub-committees, sitting with mediums, experienced phenomena which convinced them that a force existed 'sufficient to set in motion heavy substances, without contact or material connection between such substances and the body of any person present.' The witnesses before the committee testified to levitations, telekinesis, musical instruments playing of themselves, red hot coals held without pain, the receiving of information unknown to anyone present which afterwards proved to be true, prophecies of future events which were correct, apports of flowers and fruit brought into closed rooms. Among the opinions printed by the Committee, a characteristic one was that of Edwin Arnold, leader-writer and afterwards editor of *The Daily Telegraph*. Arnold, who had spent much time in India (he was President of the Deccan College in Bombay from 1856 to 1861), was presently to write a long poem which had an enormous contemporary success, dealing with the life of Gautama Buddha, which he called *The Light of Asia*. His opinion, given to the Committee, reflects not only a rational acceptance of spiritualism but a suggestion of the oriental view of psychic powers. 'I regard many of the manifestations as genuine, undeniable, inexplicable by any human law, or any collusion, arrangement or deception of the senses.' He accepted the phenomena 'not as being in any way supernatural but rather as initiatory demonstrations of mental and vital power not yet comprehended or regularly exercised.' Among the rubbish of ignorance, folly and fraud, he felt that there was 'a body of well established facts, beyond denial, which facts promise to open a new world of human enquiry and experience, are in the highest degree interesting, and tend to elevate ideas of the continuity of life, and to reconcile, perhaps, the materialist and metaphysician.'

The most interesting part of the Report is the evidence given by people of Home's circle: the paper submitted by H. D. Jencken with details of (inter alia): instances of Home's elongation, Alice Jones' evidence as to his floating over the lawn in the rainy evening at Stockton House, Lord Lindsay's evidence as to the levitation outside the windows of Ashley House and to the apparition of Sacha Home in Home's bedroom at Kilmorey House. Particularly important was Home's own evidence in answer to questions about his experience of mediumship and his sensations during them: 'Can you state the conditions under which manifestations take place?' 'You never can tell. I have frequently sat with persons and no phenomena have occurred, but when not expecting it, when in another room, or even sleeping in the house, the manifestations took place ... I try to forget all about these things, for the mind would become partly diseased if it were suffered to dwell on them. I therefore go to theatres and concerts for change of attention.' 'What are your sensations when in trance?' 'I feel for two or three minutes in a dreamy state, then I become quite dizzy and then I lose all consciousness. When I awake I find my feet and limbs cold and it is difficult to restore the circulation. When I am told what has taken place during the trance, it is quite unpleasant to me and I ask those present not to tell me at once when I awake.' (This is a remarkable description of the boundary between the two states.) 'I have no knowledge on my own part of what occurs during the trance.' Manifestations, Home said, came at all times: 'during a thunder-storm, when I am feverish or ill, or even suffering from a haemmorrhage of the lungs.' When the law-suit with Mrs. Lyon was pending, he said: 'I had congestion of the brain, I was paralysed, my memory left me.' This was the time when Dr. Armstrong and Dr. Gully had pronounced, independently, that Home was incapable of attending to any business, but he said that the spirits then had told him that he would get well again and he had done so.

On the question of spirit communication, Home said: 'In trance I see spirits connected with persons present. Those spirits take possession of me.' His voice, he said, became like theirs (an explanation of the now extremely rare 'direct voice' communication). He went on: 'I have a particularly mobile face as you may see, and I sometimes take a sort of identity with the spirits who are in communication with me. I attribute the mobility of my face, which is not natural, to the spirits.' Lord Dunraven had said that Home acted merely as a means of communication, like a telegraph wire. Home's own description of himself as an agent so passive that his face and voice were taken over by the communicating spirits bears out the simile. He said also, of himself, what any reader of the account of his treatment of, for instance, the boy Emile de Cardonne would recognize: 'I cannot mesmerize but I have an exceedingly soothing power, an exceedingly gentle way of approaching anyone, whether well or ill, and they like to have me near them.' He then threw in a detail: 'I may say that I am exceedingly sick after elongations.'

When the Report was completed, the London Dialectical Society thanked the committee warmly for the trouble they had taken in compiling it, but decided that the Society would not publish it; the committee thereupon published it themselves; it appeared as *Report on Spiritualism of the Committee of the London Dialectical Society, together with the Evidence, Oral and Written and a selection from the Correspondence.* This was published by Longman's, in 1870. In 1873, a cheap edition was brought out, which omitted fifty six pages of the original as these contained only 'personal opinions of individual members of the committee'.

A collection of press notices in the latter edition shows a wide difference of attitude. The *Pall Mall Gazette* said it was difficult to speak or think 'with anything but contemptuous pain of proceedings such as those described in this Report.' The *Daily Telegraph* which seems always to have shown outstanding good sense, said: 'We may be asked how we can explain all these things and we simply reply that we cannot, that it is not our business to do so . . . (but) the fact that some men, respectable in intellect and conversant with science have testified their faith in the reality of the phenomena makes it worth our while to investigate the matter with keener eyes than if the believers were all impulsive and unscientific observers.' The *Morning Post* said, 'The *Report* which has been published is entirely worthless', the *Saturday Review* said it was a good thing that the *Report* should have been brought out, as it would lead to the still further discrediting of this 'unequivocally degrading superstition.' The *Medical Times and Gazette* and the *London Medical Journal* received it favourably, and the *Standard* said that people made a mistake when they said vaguely of spiritualism, there may be something in it. 'If there is anything whatever in it beyond imposture and imbecility, there is the whole of another world in it.' The most invigorating comment of all was made by the *Sporting Times* whose writer said: 'If I had my way, a few of the leading professional spiritualists should be sent as rogues and vagabonds to the treadmill for a few weeks. It would do them good.'

In the spring of 1870, the expansion of Germany under Bismarck was seen as a prospect threatening to France. Napoleon III declared, however, that it was no matter for French concern since the French army was equipped to the last button on the last private's uniform. The Germans speedily blasted this fallacious confidence. In July 1870 the Franco-Prussian War began and the French army sustained a crushing defeat at the battle of Sedan. Home received an assignment from some American newspapers including the *San Francisco Chronicle* to cover the war, and as Lord Adare had received one from the *Daily Telegraph*, they were together at the front. After Sedan, the French army retreated on Versailles and the great palace was turned into a hospital for the wounded. Home wrote of the 'long line of beds with the poor wounded forms writhing on them.' He said the medical attention was very good, but the soldiers' sufferings were terrible to witness. 'Could you have gone there as I have done in the stillness of the night and seen those long and lofty rooms lighted by some three or four hundred candles (enclosed in a kind of wire frame-work, to be carried about by doctors or nurses) could you have heard the groans of men who groaned only in their sleep but were uncomplaining when awake!'

Home had told the Committee of the Dialectical Society that there was something soothing in his presence which made people, ill or well, glad to have him near them. This was proved over and over again in his caring for the wounded. One night when he was on his way to visit another patient, he passed the bed of a desperately wounded young Polish soldier, who asked Home to lift him up a little in his bed. His hands were so cold, Home asked him if he were feeling worse?' 'I am better, much better', the boy said, 'but I want the light to see you by.' Home brought one of the lights in its wire frame; as he did so, a smile came over the boy's face, 'and the light of a never-ending day dawned on him. In the palace, all was silent as the tomb.' Above the bed was a large picture of one of the early victories of Napoleon I. Indignation and a loathing of the insensate horrors of war overcame Home. He said he could almost have torn the picture down and trampled on it.[3] Home's ambivalent position between the French and German powers was marked by the graciousness towards him of King William of Prussia, the father-in-law of Queen Victoria's daughter. The King received Home at his headquarters and reminded him of the remarkable séances Home had conducted for him at Baden-Baden in 1857, séances of which, Dr. Zorab says, no records appear to have been made.

On 5 January, 1871, the Germans made their first attack on Paris itself; the siege lasted till 28 January, with the enemy's shells exploding in the streets, fighting on the barricades, the destruction of the Tuileries, the perishing by wounds and hunger of great numbers within the city. At the capitulation of the capital, Napoleon III and Eugénie sought refuge in England, where they took a lease of Camden House, a graceful, late eighteenth-century mansion at Chislehurst in Kent. It belonged to Mr. Strode, the guardian of Miss Howard, who had been one of the Emperor's mistresses. Napoleon III died there two years later.

Home had shown considerable courage as a non-combatant by remaining in Paris during the siege. He now was glad to accept the invitation to Russia of his old friend, Baron Mayendorff. This visit was to prove one of the outstandingly important events of his life.

At the University of St. Petersburg, the chair of Chemistry was held by Professor Boutlerow who was deeply interested in psychic phenomena. This interest was shared by the Imperial Councillor, Alexander Aksakoff, and the two men were also connected by another link. Mademoiselle Julie de Gloumeline was the daughter of another Imperial Councillor, now dead; but she was also the cousin of Aksakoff and the sister-in-law of Boutlerow. That she and Home should be introduced to each other on his arrival at St. Petersburg was not only natural it was, it seemed, pre-ordained. The first time she saw Home, in February 1871, a voice said within her: 'Here is your husband.' A similar message was given to Home. So definite were the tidings to each, they afterwards discovered that there was no room for hesitation or even for surprise. Numerous people have left it on record that Home was very charming, but to the two young women who married him, his charm seems to have been overwhelming. In each case, the girl vowed herself to him almost at sight, and none of his obvious disadvantages caused any objection on the part of their families, both of whom were well-established, highly connected and, compared with Home himself, rich. Each marriage was one of delightful, unfailing mutual happiness. Sacha who was not twenty and of fragile constitution, was in a somewhat childish relation to her husband, but Julie was mentally and physically vigorous; she married Home when he was thirty eight and already in an advanced condition of tuberculosis, and her idolizing love was combined with a passionate instinct for protection. Although the betrothal was made, Home felt obliged to depart from Russia for the time being, as he had undertaken to collaborate in experiments in London of a very important nature.

William Crookes was a scientist of great eminence. A Fellow of the Royal Society, he was the discoverer of the metallic chemical element, thallium; he was to be the inventor of Crookes' glass for use in spectacles and by Crookes' Tube to make electricity available for use in domestic lighting. He was, in 1870, the editor of the *Quarterly Journal of Science* and in this he stated: 'I consider it the duty of scientific men who have learnt exact modes of working, to examine phenomena which attract the attention of the public.' He was introduced to Home by Lady Burton, the widow of the Orientalist, Sir Richard Burton, an eccentric, gracious, wild-looking woman with a capacity for deep emotion and a vein of salty common-sense, yet another of the interesting characters who were drawn into Home's circle of sympathetic attraction. As a result of the introduction, Crookes devised a series of experiments with Home of which the two most fully described were directed to proving whether or not an accordion playing in his presence was moved by any action of his, and with testing Home's power to make the pointer of a balance move, indicating the force of a pressure on it, without Home's exerting any physical pressure. To carry out the first of these tests, Crookes made a circular wire cage, inside which the contents were of course visible. The cage was put under a table. A newly-bought accordion which Home had never seen and so could not have tampered with, was put at the bottom of the cage. Home, sitting at the table, had one hand underneath it in which, inside the cage, he held the accordion; his other hand was laid on top of the table. The accordion began to expand and contract as if two hands were playing it; it gave out notes; sometimes it floated up and down inside the cage and while the onlookers could see that no hand was touching the keys, 'it played a well-known, sweet and plaintive melody.' To perform his other experiment Crookes attached a board to a balance in such a way that the pressure of the medium's fingers could not move the pointer; but when Home touched the board, the pointer oscillated and registered a pressure, and Crookes felt justified in saying that these experiments established 'the existence of a new force, in some unknown manner connected with the human organism.'

A collaborator in the experiments had been Mr. Edward Cox, a barrister of the Middle Temple and a Serjeant-at-Law, who added a legal capacity for the evaluation of evidence to Crooke's scientific one. It was Cox who coined the term for this mysterious faculty: psychic force. He and Crookes now conducted an intensive series of experiments with Home, including levitations, of which Crookes said he witnessed more than a hundred. One of the most arresting was a full form materialization, which was only less remarkable than that of Sacha Home at Kilmorey House because it was less substantial. This manifestation was interrupted because Mrs. Crookes' nerves gave way. It occurred in the Crookes' house, 20 Mornington Road (now called Mornington Street) in Camden Town, a fairly large house in an unpretending neighbourhood (the Crookes, by the early 1870's, had ten children). The ground floor had, as usual, two rooms separated by folding doors. The back room, called the back dining room, had a large window which, since the room was on street level, was filled with ground glass. As the window had no blinds or curtains, gas light outside gave enough light, even without inside lighting, to show everything in the room distinctly. Home placed Mrs. Crookes in a chair beside this window, then he went and stood between the two rooms. In a letter to F. W. H. Myers, dated 9 March 1893, 'The accordion', Mrs. Crookes said, 'was immediately taken from his hand by a cloudy appearance which seemed to condense into a distinct human form, clothed in a filmy drapery, standing near Mr. Home . . . The accordion began to play. (I do not remember whether on this occasion there was any recognizable melody) and the figure gradually advanced towards me till it almost touched me, playing continuously. It was semi-transparent and I could see the sitters through it all the time. Mr. Home remained near the sliding doors. As the figure approached, I felt an intense cold, getting stronger as it got nearer, and as it was giving me the accordion. I could not help screaming. The figure immediately seemed to sink into the floor to the waist, leaving only the head and shoulders visible, still playing the accordion which was then about a foot off the floor. Mr. Home and my husband came to me at once and I have no clear recollection of what then occurred, except that the accordion did not cease playing immediately. Serjeant Cox was rather angry at my want of nerves and exclaimed: 'Mrs. Crookes, you have spoiled the finest manifestation we have ever had.'[4]

Beside Serjeant Cox, Crookes had two other collaborators in his experiments: Dr. William Huggins, a Fellow of the Royal Society and an astronomer, and Cromwell Varley, the electrical engineer. Crookes published a report in the Quarterly Journal of Science, naming Huggins and Varley as his witnesses and stating the conclusions of all three as to the existence of what Cox had called psychic force. He drew much abuse, since many scientists had hoped that he would have exposed the manifestations as so much trickery, and so struck a blow in the cause of materialism. The most violent, however, came from Dr. W. B. Carpenter, who, in an article in the *Quarterly Review*: Spiritualism and its Recent Converts, abused Crookes, Huggins and Varley in terms so patently untrue in mere matters of fact, that as Brian Inglis has said[5], he was forgiven only 'because he had erred in orthodoxy's service.' Huggins, Carpenter said, was a brewer and only an amateur astronomer. In fact, Huggins, the son of a wealthy brewer, had been able to set up his own observatory; he was ultimately to become the President of the Royal Society. Of Varley, Carpenter said that his abilities were 'so cheaply estimated by those best qualified to judge of them, that he has never been admitted to the Royal Society, though he has more than once been a candidate for that honour.' When the article appeared, Varley was already a Fellow of the Royal Society, having been admitted some months earlier. Of Crookes himself, Carpenter admitted that he had been made a Fellow after his discovery of thallium, but 'this distinction was conferred on him with considerable hesitation, the ability he displayed in the investigation being purely technical. He was, said Carpenter, totally destitute of any knowledge of Chemical Philosophy and utterly untrustworthy as to any enquiry which requires more than technical knowledge for its successful conduct.' In Dr. Inglis' words[6] 'Of all the British scientists of the era, Crookes was the most catholic in his interests . . . and so far from there having been any hesitation in conferring on him his Fellowship of the Royal Society, he had been elected on first application, at that time an unusual honour for so young a candidate.' In view of the fact that Carpenter himself was a Fellow of the Royal Society, and the Registrar at London University, his conduct appears almost unbelievable. Robert Browning, Sir David Brewster, Dr. W. B. Carpenter— and these were supposed to be men of distinguished intellect, integrity and sense, courageously exposing stupidity and fraud.

Darwin's cousin Francis Galton, the General Secretary of the British Association, attended three séances arranged by Crookes with Home, and he was so much impressed by them that he wrote begging Darwin to join the investigation; he assured his cousin that he would undergo no nervous strain in the process. Darwin had for years suffered painfully from exhaustion. In 1856 he had been Dr. Gully's patient at Malvern: 'My beloved Dr. Gully' as he called him, and then his exhaustion had been such that he had said it tired him even to look at beautiful scenery. He agreed however to fall in with Galton's suggestion and the latter wrote to Home to propose it, but no reply was gained as Home had gone to Paris for his wedding.

Meantime, Professor Boutlerow, in correspondence with Crookes, discovered that the experiments he had conducted with Home in St. Petersburg had led him to the same conclusions which Crookes had reached. When the engagement of Home with Mademoiselle de Gloumeline was announced, Boutlerow wrote to Crookes asking for his confidential opinion of Home as a prospective husband. Crookes replied on 13 April, 1871, that the life's happiness of a young lady was a serious matter, and therefore he was very glad to be able to say of Home: 'I thoroughly believe in his uprightness and honour; I consider him incapable of practising deception or meanness.' He went on to say that he had called on Home at all times of the day and had often seen him in company with other young men but had never heard him say anything which could not be repeated to a lady.[7] Crookes said that Home lived in comfortable apartments in the West End of London, but without saying exactly where these were, which adds to the mystery of where Home lived and how he supported himself. Letters in the Harry Price Library are written from 17 Hanover Square and from Bury Street, St. James's, but with no date. In the library of the College of Psychic Studies is a copy of the second edition of *Incidents of My Life*, Series I. This is inscribed on the fly-leaf to Benjamin Coleman:-

'What with breakfasts, picture hanging and other pleasing INCI-DENTS IN MY LIFE, my dear Ben, I trust not to be forgotten by Ben.'

This is written from 20 North Audley Street and dated 6 June, 1870; Home must therefore have been living at this address immediately before his departure to the scene of the Franco Prussian War. It is not possible to locate his comfortable apartments which Crookes said were in the West End of London, but they must have been in a much more eligible quarter than Crookes' family house in Mornington Road, Camden Town.

It was agreed that the marriage should take place in Paris; in October 1871, it was celebrated, first at the Russian church and afterwards at the English Embassy. When Home had left Russia the previous March, the Czar Alexander II had congratulated him on his approaching marriage and given him another superb ring, this time a magnificent sapphire set in diamonds. The following year saw the conclusion, at last, of Home's suit to be awarded the fortune of his first wife. He became the possessor of £1,500, representing in money of the time a small but comfortable fortune. He wrote of the good news to Mrs. Carter Hall, one of his friends whom he knew would sympathize joyfully. 'This will enable me to pay off the remainder of my Lyon debts. There's good news for you! I can't tell you how sadly put about we have been and how these debts have depressed me. I had determined to sell my jewels.' He asked Mrs. S. C. Hall kindly to tell his 'dear, good friend Mrs. Senior' of his good fortune. 'I know she will be pleased,' he said.

# XXX

## 'Discerning of Spirits'

It has been said, in more than one reference to Home, speaking of his life after the verdict of 1868, that since he had risen high, he had a long way to fall; but where, it might be asked, did he fall? Sections of the press continued to vilify him but this they had always done. George Eliot, writing to Mrs. Beecher Stowe in 1869, told her that spiritualism in Britain was regarded 'either as a degrading folly, imbecile in the estimate of evidence, or else as impudent imposture', and that, as for Home, 'I could not choose to enter a room where he held a séance. He is an object of moral disgust to me, and nothing of late reported by Mr. Crookes, Lord Lindsay and the rest carries conviction to my mind that Mr. Home is not simply an impostor.' George Eliot was entitled to her views, though they meant that she rejected all the evidence of people who had studied the matter while she herself had no personal experience of it, but Home after 1868 not only retained the close personal friends he already had, his fame became so extensive that for the last seventeen years of his life which he spent between Italy, France, Switzerland and Russia, his wife's anxiety was to shield him from the inroads of letters, requests and invitations which poured in on him, so that he should not, in his fragile state of health, become completely exhausted.

Miss Louise Kennedy in a letter to Andrew Lang of 18 July, 1891[1], said that she had known the couple very well, and Home's relations with his wife were 'very charming'. She was proud, elegant and deeply devoted to him. She combined a cynical knowledge of the world with an artless adoration of Home as a 'prophet'. 'Her attitude towards him was tenderly protective . . . with dashes of derision for his simplicity.' The pain he endured for the last few years of his illness was terrible, and 'she was angelic, as he fully realized'. The two books she published about him after his death: *The Life and Mission of D. D. Home*, in 1888, and *The Gift of D. D. Home*, in 1890, besides providing a mass of information, of which she was very careful to give the references, make her defensive affection plain on every page. She was exposing injustice, ingratitude and slander, and her emotion was the keener because Home's own temper was not only without vindictiveness but without even the normal instincts of self-protection. Her books were written in French, and with a French liveliness and scorn which their translation by Home's secretary Veitch only partly masks. The happiness of the marriage was completed the following summer by the birth of a daughter. She was christened Marie and Home said when he wrote of her to Mrs. S. C. Hall that her beauty was wonderful.

In the spring of 1872, Home brought out his second volume of *Incidents of my Life*, Series II. This contained the account of Browning's conduct, with Home's comments on 'Mr. Sludge the Medium', and the affidavits prepared for the Lyon v. Home case by Mrs. Lyon, W. M. Wilkinson and Home himself. Home intended to produce a third volume covering the trial itself, and it is a great disappointment to those interested in the case that he did not, but he abandoned the project for one which he felt to be of wider importance.

In the autumn of that same year the child of the marriage died at a few months old. His grief for little Marie's loss was piercing. His love for children as a whole seemed to have been concentrated in this love and loss. He said that when he came to be buried, let him be interred beside the body in the cemetery of St. Germain.

The outstanding events of his mediumistic career were over but some striking instances of his powers still occurred. Hamilton Aidé, artist, composer, musician and writer of society novels had a mind open to interesting ideas. The Homes were in Nice in 1872 and Hamilton Aidé, with Alphonse Karr the editor of *Le Figaro*, were able to attend a séance, Karr, who was noted for irony and scepticism, announcing that he should soon get to the bottom of the thing. They were shown into a large room, sparsely furnished, the tables, mostly of marble, without cloths, the scene brightly lit by a lamp on the centre table and twenty candles on the chimney piece. The visitors scanned the room narrowly but could detect no trace of apparatus or machinery; but presently a large arm-chair rushed violently towards them across the room, then the central table began to tilt, so that they could see under it as well as over it. As it rose on one of its claws, the lamp and pencils which were on it, slid across the surface but did not fall off. Podmore's suggested explanation of this type of phenomena[2] is:- 'the articles probably, it may be suggested, were held in position by hairs or fine threads, attached to Home's dress'. This ingenious supposition did not present itself to Hamilton Aidé, who was deeply perplexed, or to Karr, who was irritated and nonplussed. Hamilton Aidé demanded: was hypnotism the answer? How else could they explain things which could not possibly have occurred, yet which did occur?[3]

In 1873, the Homes paid one of their last visits to England, which called up recollections of Home's past. In Camden House, the widowed Eugénie was mourning. Princess Caroline Murat was with her, and Eugénie demanded that she should find out where Home was, and tell him to come to her. The Princess was dismayed. She knew that Eugénie was determined to gain a sight of her husband, and she was afraid of the results on a temperament so emotional. However, she felt obliged to send Home the summons.

It was refused. Home, however, consented to a meeting with the Princess. She said: 'When I saw him I thought him looking dreadfully ill.' (How different from his appearance those years ago in Paris, when his presence in the house would set all the lustres tinkling!) They had a long conversation but nothing would persuade him to go to the Empress. 'He knew, as I did, that she wished to see the Emperor.' Home told her that if such a manifestation did occur in his presence, the drain on his strength would be too much. He was immovable. The Princess wrote that the Empress was deeply grieved and disappointed.[4]

It may well have been that Home's decision was partly influenced by a feeling of what he owed to his wife in her anxiety about him. If he had consented to the séance, Madame Home would have been aghast. When he was in Russia in 1871, the experiments which Professor Boutlerow had tried to conduct with him were almost fruitless because of Home's lack of power at that time. Crookes commented on this, that whatever the nature of Mr. Home's power, it was very variable, and at times, as Crookes himself had found, completely absent[5]. Madame Home said that Home would have been willing to return to Russia in the winter after their marriage, to allow the investigators to renew their experiments, 'but,' she said, 'as I did not care at all whether the scientific world was converted or not, and felt very anxious about Home's health, which over frequent séances fatigued, I entreated him not to carry out his intention.' When she recorded the death of their baby,[6] she said, 'From this moment the health of Home became my sole care. A complete repose was necessary to him, and I entreated him that he would hold séances very seldom.'

Change of scene had always done Home good, and they moved frequently between France, Italy and Switzerland. In 1874, they were at Nice, where Madame Home said, 'the blue sky and brilliant sunshine of the Riviera did something to lighten for Home the burden of almost ceaseless physical suffering.' Here too he found the pleasure of meeting friends of the past, unchanged in their affection for him: Count Alexander de Komar and Count Alexis Tolstoy.[7]

In spite of general weakness and attacks of severe pain, Home managed to put together, and to publish in 1877, what he regarded as his most important work: *Lights and Shadows of Spiritualism*.[8] A large section of this consisted in an exposal of the methods of fraud adopted by so-called spiritualists. It is not easy to say how much he was inspired by that jealousy of other mediums with which he had often been credited. ('No other medium had he a good word for, nor any kind of manifestation which he himself had not been favoured with', as Louise Kennedy said.[9]) But his chief motive was undoubtedly the burning desire to expose, to abolish if possible, the vicious frauds from which a certain section of the public were suffering: bringing into total disrepute the belief which he himself held with religious intensity. He did not attack individual tricksters, but he exposed their methods with relentless thoroughness; it was partly owing to the great public interest which his own mediumship had aroused, that a rabble of frauds and hypocrites were now preying on those who longed for spirit communication. Crookes by 1875 had gone through a harassing series of experiences with a young medium, Florence Cook, one of the band of those who combined some considerable degree of psychic power with the mentality of a criminal. The evidence for and against the genuineness of her manifestations is contradictory and confusing, while her subsequent criminal record was such that Crookes, while maintaining the value of the experiments he had originally sponsored, washed his hands of her. He wrote to Home on November 24, 1875:[10] 'I am so disgusted with the whole thing that were it not for the regard we bear to you, I would cut the whole spiritualist connection and never read, speak or think of the subject again.'

Home's most important pronouncement in the work was one against séances held in the dark. 'Light is the single test necessary, and it is a test which can and must be given.'[11] He much regretted that he had ever given séances in anything but full light; the great majority of his were so given, and 'every form of phenomena ever occurring through me at the few dark séances has been repeated over and over again in the light.' He explained what he meant by 'dark'. 'It consisted of extinguishing the lights in the room, and then we used to open the curtains, or, in very many instances have the fire lit, which, if burning, was never extinguished, when we could, with perfect ease, distinguish the outline form of everyone in the room.' Modern systems of heating have, for many people, banished the memory of how much a room is illuminated by a glowing coal fire in an ample grate.

The book aroused fierce animosity in people whose vested interests it attacked and a shower of abusive letters was directed upon Home; even more injurious were the notices in certain papers whose reviewers had not been able to spare the time to read the work, and had quoted Home's descriptions of fraudulent methods as confessions, now published, of what he had been accustomed to do himself. Mrs. S. C. Hall wrote to him that the book had made her very sad. 'So it did me',

Home replied, 'but it was written to expose those falsehoods which are fast obscuring a truth which is all-important to mankind.'

Home had naturally infuriated the evil practitioners of fraud, who, though their names had not been mentioned, felt that their source of income was being threatened; but he had also aroused the anger of a person of psychic gifts as impressive as his own. Helena Petrovna Blavatsky, a woman of immense occult learning and amazing supernormal powers, was committed to the Buddhist doctrine of reincarnation, and the Theosophical Society of which she was the founder, made it their leading tenet. Home, whose whole existence was directed to prove that human personality survived intact after death, rejected, by definition, the theory that it was changed for that of some quite other being, or even for an animal. 'No one', he declared, 'loses their identity in the spirit world.'[12] He wrote vigorous passages in refutation of this, to him, absurd and preposterous theory, and this element in his beliefs was no doubt responsible for the brief but bitter comments on him by Madame Blavatsky. It was said among her followers and adherents that Home would be visited by her anger in some signal fashion, and in April 1876, this almost appeared to have been the case. A French newspaper published a telegram announcing that he had been found dead in a railway carriage travelling between Berlin and St. Petersburg. For the rest of April, Home was able to read a profusion of obituary notices of himself, from all quarters, in a dozen different languages. Angry as she was, Madame Home remarked with some humour that this 'was a class of reading that it has fallen to the lot of few men beside Home to enjoy.' The shock of the announcement, however, killed his aunt Mrs. McNiel Cook. She had driven him out of her house over thirty years before, but one of the first uses he had made of his own money when he thought it was safe to spend it because he had been given Mrs. Lyon's, was to buy his aunt a cottage, where she had lived for the past eight years; the false news had given her a stroke and she died of it.

The links of both Home and his wife with Russia were so strong that they naturally returned there often, to a circle including the Czar himself, that welcomed them warmly. They went there in 1877 after the publication of *Lights and Shadows*, and Home wrote to the S. C. Halls that the scenery of the Volga was wild and waste beyond anything that could be imagined, but that he enjoyed it. 'I seem to have left the world and its cares far away, and the past even seems at times only like a dream wherein clouds and sunshine have been playing at hide and seek with each other.' He asked the Halls to send him cuttings of all the notices of his book which they could find. 'You must not forget that this is Russia, and no newspapers are admitted till they have been read by the censor. Where we are, we have a post once a week and have to go eight miles for that.'[13] The wild, waste landscape had a healing quality that Home needed, and being where the weekly post came no nearer to him than eight miles away, was a special benefit. Madame Home spoke of his being 'oppressed by the burden of an enormous correspondence'. She said, 'it was impossible for him, a constant invalid to reply one half.' Inquirers sent requests for séances or for information and correspondents by the score inflicted on him at merciless length their particular opinions concerning spiritualism. If he had not had such a sweet temper, his wife said, 'he would have lost it almost every time a fresh batch of letters reached us.'

On 20 March, 1883, Home's fiftieth birthday was celebrated at Nice. He had been so ill all the winter that he had gone nowhere, though he had friends to the house as often as he felt equal to it. On his birthday a crowd of the residents in the foreign colony of Nice came to fête him. Home was in pain and could not leave his armchair, but he was surrounded there with heaps of baskets and bouquets of flowers. He welcomed and thanked them all, and when they begged him to, he recited several poems in French and English; one of the latter was Tennyson's 'The Grandmother', the piece with which he had always had a great success. Home was very ill, but his wife said he had never given the poem with more effect.

In this same March, 1883, Home's friend and doctor died. Dr. Gully had retired from practice in Malvern in 1871, among demonstrations, from civic bodies and personal friends, of recognition of how much his presence there for the past thirty years had brought prosperity to Malvern and of his outstanding skill as a doctor. His retirement at only sixty-three was a surprise and a source of keen regret to patients, neighbours and friends, but he had become entangled with a young woman, the beautiful and selfish Florence Ricardo, whose husband was a hopeless alcoholic. When she gained a separation from him, completed shortly afterwards by his death, she and Dr. Gully would have married, but that the doctor's wife from whom he had parted twenty-eight years ago, was still living. In the meantime, they entered on a liaison which came to a natural end when Florence Ricardo wanted to be respectably married and to have a young husband. She accepted the proposal of Charles Bravo; and his agonizing death from a massive dose of antimony, within eighteen months of the marriage, was one of the most famous of Victorian murder mysteries. Dr. Gully had parted with her and never seen her again after her marriage, but at the inquest on Charles Bravo, she and her companion, Mrs. Cox, desperate to make the death appear suicide, declared that this had been due to Charles Bravo's retrospective jealousy of Dr. Gully. Mrs. Cox, to underline the matter, brought out at the inquest that during the liaison with Florence, Dr. Gully had performed an abortion on her. The verdict of the inquest was that the poison had been administered by person or persons unknown, and the matter never came to trial, but the disclosures about his private life were very damaging to Dr. Gully; but just as certain writers have confidently asserted that Home's reputation was destroyed by the case of Lyon v. Home, others have declared with equal groundlessness that Dr. Gully's life was ruined by the publicity of the Bravo inquest. The originator of this mis-statement was the writer of the article on Dr. Gully in the *Dictionary of National Biography*, who said that his name was removed from the learned societies to which he belonged. That this is untrue is confirmed by the Wellcome Medical Historical Library. Dr. Gully's name was removed from the Medical Register — the reason being given that his address was no longer known. As his address on Bedford Hill was by this time known to every newspaper reader in the country, this showed that his profession wished to deal gently with him. More significant still, the Garrick Club did not ask for his resignation; he was a member of it when he died. Patients continued to consult him in his retirement. His burial at Kensal Green was attended by a crowd of mourners, the hearse was loaded with wreaths, and on the day of the funeral, the shops in the neighbourhood of his house at Balham were closed as a mark of respect.[14]

The moonlight paintings of Atkinson Grimshaw have been cited as in mystical sympathy with the longings of the age for spiritualist communion. One of these could be take as an unconscious illustration of the close of Dr. Gully's life. In that year, 1883, the artist painted the scene of a quiet street which he called 'Moonlight After Rain'.

Towards the close of 1884, Home warned his wife that he had been told that his illness was approaching its term and that the end would be long drawn out and painful, though death itself would come without a pang. The prophecy was only too true. With short intermissions, the rending pain in his lungs made him suffer 'long and cruelly'. On 18 June, 1888, the final phase of the illness developed. His wife said: 'The last three days we both knew that all was ended for us on earth.' Home remained fully conscious; his one thought, she said, was to inspire me with strength to survive him, and make me feel that he was but gone a little way before me.' He could see his dead friends round him; he spoke their names and stretched out his hands to them. The moment of death, as he had been told it would be, was painless. In his last letter to Mrs. S. C. Hall, he had said, 'I wait for the shadow that precedes the never-fading light.' His wife said: 'On the face was left a peace neither of sleep nor of death, but of immortality.'

He was buried beside his baby in St. Germain. The white marble cross above was inscribed with words from Corinthians I, 12, v. 10: 'To another, discerning of spirits'.

# NOTES

## Chapter I.   ESCAPE INTO ANOTHER WORLD

1  C. R. Fay, *The Palace of Industry 1851*, C.U.P. 1951, p. 89.
2  *Punch*, XIX, p. 183
3  Charles Kingsley, Letters and Memorials, Vol. II, p. 171.
4  D.N.B.
5  E. Moir, *The Discovery of Britain*, Routledge & Kegan Paul, London, 1964.
6  Ibid.

## Chapter II.   SPIRITUALISM IN AMERICA

1  Brian Inglis, *Natural and Supernatural*, Hodder and Stoughton, London, 1978, p. 200.
2  William Howitt, A History of the Supernatural, Vol. II, 1863, p. 216.

## Chapter III.   A GLORIOUS MISSION

1  Daniel Dunglas Home, *Incidents of My Life*, Series I, 1863, (hereafter referred to as *Incidents*), p. 7.
2  Ibid., pp. 7 and 8.
3  Madame Home, *D. D. Home, His Life and Mission*, 1888 (hereafter referred to as *L & M*), p. 15.
4  Ibid., pp. 19–22.
5  *Incidents* I, p. 38
6  Ibid., p. 39 et seq.
7  *L & M*, pp. 23–25
8  *Incidents* I, pp. 13–15.
9  Ibid., pp. 47–48.
10  Frank Podmore, Modern Spiritualism, Vol II, p. 225. Methuen 1902
11  *L & M*, pp. 31–33.

## Chapter IV.   A SENSATION IN LONDON

1  Madame Home, *The Gift of D. D. Home*, Kegan Paul & Co, London, 1890 (hereafter referred to as *G of D.D.H.*), p. 35.
2  *Incidents* I, p. 66.
3  Ibid., p. 66.

## Chapter V.   SIR DAVID BREWSTER CHANGES HIS TUNE

1  Thomas Adolphus Trollope, *What I Remember*, R. Bentley and Son, London, 1887, Vol. I, p. 376 et seq.
2  *Incidents* I, p. 66.
3  Benjamin Coleman, *Exposition of Spiritualism*, 1862, Letter VIII, p. 59.
4  A. R. Wallace, *The Scientific Aspect of the Supernatural*, London, 1866, p. 18.

Chapter VI.   BROWNING ON THE OFFENSIVE

1  Philip Elliott, *Tennyson and Spiritualism*, Tennyson Research Bulletin, Vol. III, No. 3, 1979.
2  Elizabeth Barrett Browning, *Letters to her Sister*, ed. Leonard Huxley, John Murray, London, 1929.
3  Betty Miller, 'The Séance at Ealing', *Cornhill Magazine*, 1957-58.
4  Elizabeth Barrett Browning, op. cit.
5  *Incidents* II, pp. 105-106.
6  Frank Podmore, op. cit.
7  *Incidents* II, p. 106 et seq.
8  *Journal of the Society for Psychical Research*, II, 1903-1904, pp. 11-16, pp. 76-80.
9  A. Conan Doyle, *History of Spiritualism*, Cassell & Co, London, 1926, Vol. II, p. 101 et seq.
10 Ibid., Vol. I, p. 310.

Chapter VII.   'THERE'S A HEART IN MY CHAIR'

1  Clement J. Wilkinson, *J. J. Garth Wilkinson, Memoir of his Life*, Kegan Paul, 1911, pp. 2-3.
2  John Jones of Peckham, *The Natural and Supernatural: or Man, Physical, Apparitional and Spiritual*, 1861.
3  Ibid., p. 326.

Chapter VIII.   THEODOSIA TROLLOPE HAS DOUBTS

1  *L & M*, p. 58.
2  Elizabeth Barrett Browning, op. cit.
3  Ibid., p. 262.
4  T. A. Trollope, op. cit., Vol. I, p. 378 et seq.
5  Ibid., p. 382.
6  *Incidents* I.
7  *G of D.D.H.*, p. 91.
8  *L & M*, p. 59.
9  A. Conan Doyle, *The Wanderings of a Spiritualist*, Hodder and Stoughton, London, 1921, p. 170 et seq.
10 *Incidents* I, p. 93.
11 Elizabeth Barrett Browning, op. cit. p. 241.
12 Ibid., p. 262.
13 *Incidents* I, p. 93.
14 *L & M*, pp. 48-49.

Chapter IX.   AT THE VILLA COLOMBAIA

1  *Incidents* I, p. 56.
2  *G OF D.D.H.*, p. 105 et seq.
3  *Incidents* I, pp. 87-92.
4  *L & M*, p. 132.
5  British Journal of Psychology, 44, 1953, pp. 61-69.

Chapter X.   SÉANCES WITH NAPOLEON III

1  *Incidents* I, p. 94.
2  Robert Dale Owen, *Footfalls on the Boundary of Another World*, London, 1860.

3 Aldous Huxley, *Heaven and Hell*, Chatto and Windus, 1956, p. 24.
4 *L & M*, p. 66.
5 *Incidents* I, p. 94.
6 Ibid., p. 95.
7 Ibid., p. 95.
8 Jean Burton, *Heyday of a Wizard*, Harrap and Co., London, 1940, p. 100.
9 *L & M*, p. 73.
10 Ibid., p. 73.
11 Eugénie l'Impératrice: *Lettres Familières*, Paris 1935, Vol. I, pp. 136–138.
12 M. Fleury et L. Sonolet, *Société du Second Empire, 1851–1858*, Paris 1911, Vol. I, quoted by Zorab.
13 *L & M*, p. 72.
14 *Incidents* I, p. 100.
15 Ibid., pp. 103–104.
16 Ibid., p. 110.
17 Ibid., p. 114.

Chapter XI.  THE EMPRESS'S CONFIDENCE

1 *Incidents* I, p. 117.
2 Horace Rumbold, *Recollections of a Diplomatist*, Edward Arnold, London, 1902, Vol. II, p. 234.
3 *Incidents* I, p. 117.
4 E. Barthez, *The Empress Eugénie and her Circle*, trans. Bernard Miall, p. 99.
5 *L & M*, p. 78.
6 *Incidents* I, p. 118.
7 E. Osty, 'Le Médium Daniel Home', *Revue Métaphysique*, 1934, pp. 357–76 (quoted by Dr. Zorab).
8 Frank Podmore, op. cit., Vol. II, pp. 240 and 320.

Chapter XII.  MARRIAGE

1 *Incidents* I. p. 124.
2 Quoted by Dr. Zorab.
3 *L & M*, p. 105.
4 Ibid., p. 105.
5 *Incidents* I, p. 107.
6 Elizabeth Barrett Browning, op. cit., April 28, 1858, p. 293.
7 Alexandre Dumas, *De Paris à Astrakhan*, 1860, Vol. I, p. 57.
8 Ibid., p. 74.
9 *L & M*, p. 110.
10 Miriam Kochan, *Life in Russia under Catherine the Great*, 1969, Batsford, pp. 43–45.
11 *L & M*, p. 116.
12 *G of D.D.H.*, p. 350.
13 *Quarterly Journal of Science*, Oct. 1871
14 *G of D.D.H.*, pp. 340–341.
15 George Chapman, *Surgeon from Another World*, 1978, W. H. Allen, pp. 26–31.
16 *Incidents* I, p. 131.

Chapter XIII.  THE SHADE OF CAGLIOSTRO

1 *Incidents* I, pp. 220 et seq.
2 Ibid., p. 210.

3 Ibid., p. 138.
4 Ibid., p. 139.
5 *L & M*, pp. 183–184.
6 Home did not say in what language the communication was received but as Cagliostro spoke French, which both Home and his wife spoke themselves, it may be assumed to have been in French.

Chapter XIV.   THE HYDE PARK PLACE SÉANCES

1 *Incidents* I, pp. 140–141.
2 Maud Rolleston, *Talks with Lady Shelley*, Harrap & Co., London, 1925; Dr. Gully in *The Spiritualist*, March, 1876.
3 Walford, *Old and New London*, 1873, Vol. IV, pp. 121–124.
4 *L & M*, p. 170.
5 Ibid., pp. 162 et seq.
6 Horace Wyndham, *Mr Sludge the Medium*, Geoffrey Bles, London, 1937, p. 102.

Chapter XV.   CONFLICTING EVIDENCE

1 C. R. Weld, *Last Winter in Rome*, London, 1865.
2 G. S. Layard, *Mrs Lynn Linton, Her Life, Letters and Opinions*, Methuen, London, 1901, p. 173.
3 *Incidents* I, p. 142.
4 Ibid., p. 146.
5 G. S. Layard, op. cit., p. 168.
6 *Incidents* I, p. 164.

Chapter XVI.   THE DEATH OF SACHA

1 *Incidents* I, pp. 168–170.
2 *L & M*, p. 178.
3 Ibid., p. 153.
4 Ibid., pp. 150–151.
5 Ibid., p. 190.
6 *G of D.D.H.*, Appendix, p. 176.
7 Brian Inglis, op. cit., p. 237.
8 Charles Osborne, *Independent Review*, 1910, p. 324 et seq.
9 *Incidents* I, p. 179 et seq.
10 Ibid., p. 211.
11 Ibid., pp. 213 et seq.
12 *L & M*, p. 191.
13 Ibid., p. 192.
14 *Incidents* I, p. 219 et seq.
15 *L & M*, p. 196.

Chapter XVII.   'IMPOSSIBLE TO BELIEVE'

1 *L & M*, p. 176.
2 *G of D.D.H.*, p. 357.
3 Princess Pauline Metternich, *The Days that are no More*, pp. 180–185.
4 Ibid., pp. 217–219.
5 Nathaniel Hawthorne, *French and Italian Note Books*, Vol. I, 1858.
6 *Incidents* II, p. 61 et seq.
7 Ibid., p. 165.

8  *G of D.D.H.*, Appendix, p. 376.
9  *Incidents* II, Chapter V, passim.

Chapter XVIII.   EXPELLED FROM ROME

1  *Incidents* II, p. 70 et seq.
2  *L & M.*, p. 207.
3  *Incidents* II, p. 81.
4  C. R. Weld, op. cit., p. 176.

Chapter XIX.   THE BLOT ON BROWNING'S SCUTCHEON

1  *Letters, Elizabeth Barrett Browning*, ed. F. G. Kenyon, Smith Elder, London,
     1897, Vol. II, p. 388.
2  *L & M*, 18 July, 1864, p. 185.
3  *Incidents* II, p. 95.
4  Ibid., pp. 97–98.
5  Edgar Allan Poe.
6  *Incidents* II, p. 98.
7  *Diary of William Allingham*, Macmillan, 1907, p. 101.
8  *L & M*, pp. 56–57.
9  *Journal of the Society for Psychical Research*, July 1889.
10 Andrew Lang, 'The Case of Daniel Dunglas Home', *Cornhill* Magazine 1904,
     and subsequently reprinted in *Historical Mysteries*, Nelson, pp. 226–227.
11 F. Merrifield, 28 November, 1902.
12 Coventry Patmore, 'Magna est Veritas'.

Chapter XX.   TROUBLE AT WILLIS'S ROOMS

1  *L & M*, p. 235.
2  Peter Castle, *Collecting and Valuing Old Photographs*, Garnstone Press, 1973,
     pp. 54 and 121.
3  *G of D.D.H.*, p. 182.
4  *L & M*, p. 243.
5  Ibid., p. 242.
6  *G of D.D.H.*, pp. 153–4.
7  Ibid., p. 129.
8  G. A. Layard, op. cit.
9  *Incidents* II, pp. 123 et seq.
10 *All the Year Round*, 3 March 1866.
11 The *Spiritual Times*, 17 March 1866.

Chapter XXI.   'TRIUMPHAL MUSIC'

1  *Spiritual Magazine*, October 1865.
2  *Evening Citizen*
3  T. A. Trollope, op. cit., Vol. I, p. 389.
4  *The Queen v. Coleman, Opinions of the Press, 1866*, British Library, Dept, of
     Printed Books, 6497–c7.
5  Henrietta Mary Ada Ward, *Memories of Ninety Years*, Hutchinson, 1924.
6  Ibid., p. 162.
7  Brian Inglis, op. cit., p. 265.
8  *L & M*, p. 247.
9  *Incidents*, II, pp. 120–122.

264

Chapter XXII. IN QUEST OF AN OCCUPATION

1 *G of D.D.H.*, p. 189.
2 Harley Granville Barker, *Prefaces to Shakespeare: Hamlet*, Batsford Paperback, 1963.
3 *G of D.D.H.*, p. 189.
4 T. A. Trollope, op. cit.
5 Walter Dorter, *Mr. and Mrs. Charles Dickens*
6 Census return 1871.
7 Unpublished letter of Dr. Gully, Archives of Society for Psychical Research.
8 Society for Psychical Research, *Archives*.
9 *Incidents* I, p. 12.
10 *G of D.D.H.*, pp. 190–191.
11 A. Conan Doyle, *History of Spiritualism*, Vol. I, p. 219.
12 *L & M*, p. 212.
13 Ibid., p. 214.
14 Van Akin Burd, *John Ruskin and Rose La Touche*, Clarendon Press, 1979, pp. 134–135.
15 *L & M*, pp. 218, 219.
16 Brian Inglis, op. cit., p. 216.
17 Ibid., p. 362.
18 Sophia De Morgan, *From Matter to Spirit*, Introduction.
19 Ibid., pp. 302, 303.

Chapter XXIII. THE SPIRITUAL ATHENAEUM

1 Transcript in the Archives of the Society for Psychical Research headed *Cross Examination of Home*.
2 *Newcastle Daily Chronicle*, 27 April, 1868.
3 *Incidents* II, pp. 209 et seq.
4 *Equity Cases*, Vol. II, p. 679.
5 *L & M*, p. 258.
6 *G of D.D.H.*, p. 146.
7 Louise Kennedy, letter to Andrew Lang, *Journal of the Society for Psychical Research*, Jan. 1894.,
8 *Equity Cases*, Vol. VI, p. 658.
9 *Incidents* II, pp. 309 et seq: Affidavit of W. M. W. Wilkinson.
10 *Spiritual Magazine*, March 1867.

Chapter XXIV. THE IMPERIOUS MRS. LYON

1 Archives of S.P.R., Transcript.
2 *Incidents* II, Affidavit of D. D. Home; pp. 209 et seq.
3 Ibid.
4 Archives of S.P.R., Transcript.
5 Ion Perdicaris, *The Hand of Fate*, Holdon & Hardingham, London, 1921, p. 222.
6 Gerald Massey, *Concerning Spiritualism*, 1871, p. 167.
7 *The Great Spiritual Case, Lyon v. Home, Illustrated Police News* office, London, 1868, p. 24.

Chapter XXV. IMPRISONED FOR DEBT

1 *Incidents* II, pp. 209 et seq: Affidavit of D. D. Home.
2 *L & M*, p. 264.
3 Robert Browning, *Letters*, ed. Thurman L. Hood, York University Press, 1933.

Chapter XXVI. VERDICT FOR THE PLAINTIFF

1 *Equity Cases* VI, p. 676.
2 Ibid., p. 679.
3 *L & M*, p. 270.
4 Ibid., p. 270.


Chapter XXVII. FROM RECITING TO FIRE-HANDLING

1 *Incidents* II, pp. 108, 109.
2 *L & M*, p. 252.
3 Ibid., p. 284.
4 Ibid., p. 313.
5 *G of D.D.H.*, pp. 246, 247.
6 Ibid., pp. 242, 243.
7 Ibid., pp. 239–243.
8 Ibid., p. 260.
9 Trevor Henry Hall, *Light on Old Ghosts*, London, 1965, p. 368: 'The D. D. Home Levitations at Ashley House'.
10 Lord Adare (later Lord Dunraven), *Experiences in Spiritualism with D. D. Home*, 1869, republished Robert Maclehose, 1924: Séance 15, pp. 91 et seq.
11 Ibid., Séance 24.
12 *G of D.D.H.*, p. 261.
13 Ion Perdicaris, op. cit., pp. 234 et seq.
14 Lord Adare, op. cit., Séance 26.
15 *L & M*, pp. 284, 285.
16 Ibid., p. 286.
17 Horace Wyndham, op. cit., p. 204.


Chapter XXVIII. ELONGATION AND LEVITATION

1 *G of D.D.H.*, p. 245.
2 Lord Adare, op. cit., Séance 41, pp. 151 et seq.
3 Ibid., pp. 155, 156.
4 Ibid.
5 Horace Wyndham, op. cit., p. 204.
6 *L & M*, p. 304.
7 Evidence to the Dialectical Society, p. 208.
8 Lord Adare, op. cit., pp. 172, 173.
9 Ibid., pp. 198 et seq.
10 *G of D.D.H.*, p. 304.


Chapter XXIX. REMARRIAGE

1 Trevor Henry Hall, op. cit.
2 London Dialectical Society, *Report of Spiritualism*, published by the Committee.
3 *G of D.D.H.*, pp. 354, 355.
4 F. W. H. Myers, Journal of S.P.R. 1893–94, pp. 310, 311.
5 Brian Inglis, op. cit., pp. 257, 258.
6 Ibid.
7 E. E. Fournier d'Albe, Life of Sir William Crookes, T. Fisher Unwin, 1923, p. 196.

## Chapter XXX. 'DISCERNING OF SPIRITS'

1 Journal of S.P.R., 6, 1893–94, pp. 176–179.
2 Frank Podmore, op. cit., Vol. II, p. 241.
3 Brian Inglis, op. cit., pp. 444–445.
4 Princess Caroline Murat, *My Memoirs*, Eveleigh Nash, London, 1910.
5 *L & M*, p. 367.
6 Ibid., p. 374.
7 Ibid., p. 387.
8 D. D. Home, *Lights and Shadows of Spiritualism*, Virtue & Co., London 1877.
9 Louise Kennedy, op. cit.
10 *L & M*, p. 396.
11 D. D. Home, *Lights and Shadows of Spiritualism*,
12 *G of D.D.H.*, p. 291.
13 Ibid., p. 363, Letter to the S. C. Halls.
14 *Malvern News*, 7 April, 1833.

# INDEX